Certified Professional Secretary® Examination Review Series

Betty L. Schroeder, *Series Editor*

Schroeder, Lauer, and Stricklin *Certified Professional Secretary® Review for Behavioral Science in Business, Module I, Second Edition*

Cherry *Self-Study Guide to CPS® Review for Behavioral Science, Module I*

Schroeder, Clark, and DiMarzio *Certified Professional Secretary® Review for Business Law, Module II, Second Edition*

Cherry *Self-Study Guide to CPS® Review for Business Law, Module II*

Schroeder, Lewis, and Stricklin *Certified Professional Secretary® Review for Economics and Management, Module III, Second Edition*

Cherry *Self-Study Guide to CPS® Review for Economics and Management, Module III, Second Edition*

Schroeder and Webber *Certified Professional Secretary® Review for Accounting, Module IV, Second Edition*

Cherry *Self-Study Guide to CPS® Review for Accounting, Module IV*

Schroeder and Graf *Certified Professional Secretary® Review for Office Administration and Communication, Module V, Second Edition*

Cherry *Self-Study Guide to CPS® Review for Office Administration and Communication, Module V*

Schroeder and Graf *Certified Professional Secretary® Review for Office Technology, Module VI, Second Edition*

Cherry *Self-Study Guide to CPS® Review for Office Technology, Module VI*

Certified Professional Secretary®
Examination Review Series

Business Law, Module II
Second Edition

Betty L. Schroeder, Ph.D., Editor
Northern Illinois University

Lawrence S. Clark, J.D., LL.M.
Louisiana State University

Philip DiMarzio, J.D., LL.M.
Sycamore, Illinois

A joint publication of
PSI® Professional Secretary International and

Regents / Prentice Hall
Englewood Cliffs, New Jersey 07632

Library of Congress Cataloging-in-Publication Data
(Revised for volumes 3 and 4)

Certified professional secretary examination review series

    Contents: module 1. Behavioral science in business / Wilma D. Stricklin, Deborah Lauer— — module 3. Review for Economics and management — module 4. Review for accounting
    1. Office practice—Problems, exercises, etc.
I. Stricklin, Wilma D. II. Lauer, Deborah.
III. Professional Secretaries International.
HF5547.5.C44 1986   651.3'74'076   87-100577
ISBN 0-13-188517-0

Acquisition editor: *Elizabeth Kendall*
Production editor: *Jacqueline A. Martin*
Copy editor: *Patty Boyd*
Cover designer: *Marianne Frasco*
Prepress buyer: *Ilene Levy*
Manufacturing buyer: *Ed O'Dougherty*
Supplements editor: *Lisamarie Brassini*
Editorial assistant: *Jane Baumann*

 © 1992, 1984 by Prentice-Hall, Inc.
A Simon & Schuster Company
Englewood Cliffs, New Jersey 07632

The following are registered marks owned by Professional Secretaries International:

Trademarks and Registered Service Marks

PSI®
Professional Secretaries International®
Since 1942 known as The National Secretaries Association (International)
10502 N.W. Ambassador Drive, Kansas City, MO 64153, 816-891-6600

A.I.S.P. (French equivalent of PSI®)
l'Association Internationale des Secretaries Professionalles

CPS®
Certified Professional Secretary®
Professional Secretaries Week®
Professional Secretaries Day
The Secretary®

FSA®
Future Secretaries Association®
International Secretary of the Year®
All rights reserved. No part of this book may be
reproduced, in any form or by any means,
without permission in writing from the publisher.

Printed in the United States of America
10 9 8 7 6 5 4 3 2

ISBN 0-13-188517-0

Prentice-Hall International (UK) Limited, *London*
Prentice-Hall of Australia Pty. Limited, *Sydney*
Prentice-Hall Canada Inc., *Toronto*
Prentice-Hall Hispanoamericana, S.A., *Mexico*
Prentice-Hall of India Private Limited, *New Delhi*
Prentice-Hall of Japan, Inc., *Tokyo*
Simon & Schuster Asia Pte. Ltd., *Singapore*
Editora Prentice-Hall do Brasil, Ltda., *Rio de Janeiro*

Contents

Preface xiii

Acknowledgments xv

CHAPTER 1 Introduction To Business Law 1

   Overview 1

   Definition of Terms 1

   A. Origin of Law 2
       1. Common Law 2
       2. Constitutional Law 3
       3. Statutory Law 3
       4. Regulations 3
       5. Executive Orders 4
   B. Classifications of Law 4
       1. Civil Law 4
       2. Tort Law 4
       3. Criminal Law 5
       4. Procedural Law 5
       5. Substantive Law 5

   Review Questions 7

   Solutions 11

CHAPTER 2 Court Procedures 13

   Overview 13

   Definition of Terms 14

   A. The Tort Suit 16
       1. Tort 16
       2. Parties 17
       3. Pleadings 17
       4. Service 18
       5. Motions 19
       6. Discovery 19
       7. Pretrial Conference 21
       8. Trial 21
   B. Court Orders 23
       1. Injunction 23
       2. Mandamus 24

   Review Questions 25

   Solutions 33

CHAPTER 3 Contracts   37

Overview 37

Definition of Terms 37

- A. Elements of a Contract 39
  1. Legality 39
  2. Mutuality of Agreement 41
  3. Consideration 44
  4. Capacity of Parties 45
  5. Form Required by Law 47
- B. Formation 48
  1. Offer 48
  2. Termination 48
  3. Acceptance 50
- C. Types of Contracts 52
  1. Quasi Contract 52
  2. Unilateral Contract 53
  3. Bilateral Contract 53
  4. Express Contract 53
  5. Implied Contract 53
  6. Formal Contract 53
  7. Simple Contract 53
- D. Statute of Limitations 54
- E. Statute of Frauds 54
  1. Sale of Land 54
  2. Sale of Goods 54
  3. Promise in Consideration of Marriage 54
  4. Promise to Perform for Another Party 54
  5. Contracts That Cannot Be Performed within One Year 54
  6. Promise of Responsibility for Obligation of Estate 55
- F. Assignment of Rights and Delegation of Duties 55
  1. Assignment 55
  2. Delegation 57
- G. Breach of Contracts—Remedies 58
  1. Money Damages 58
  2. Specific Performance 59
  3. Restitution 59

Review Questions 61

Solutions 73

CHAPTER 4 Sales   79

Overview 79

Definition of Terms 80

- A. Sale of Goods 81
  1. Goods 81
  2. Elements of Contract for Sale of Goods 81
  3. Good Faith 82
  4. Contract for Sale Other Than Goods 82
  5. Modifications to Sales Contracts 82
- B. Creation of the Sales Contract 82
  1. The Offer 82
  2. Firm Offer 82
  3. The Acceptance 82
  4. The Sales Contract 84
  5. Identification 86
- C. Transfer of Title/Risk of Loss 86
  1. Passage of Title (Legal Ownership) 86
  2. Risk of Loss 87

Contents

D. Warranties **89**
  1. Warranty of Title **89**
  2. Express Warranty **90**
  3. Implied Warranty of Merchantability **90**
  4. Implied Warranty of Fitness for a Particular Purpose **90**
  5. Appropriate Plaintiffs **91**
  6. UCC Disclaimers **91**
  7. Magnuson-Moss Warranty Act **92**

E. Remedies **93**
  1. Right to Cure **93**
  2. Seller's Remedies, Buyer at Fault **93**
  3. Buyer's Remedies for Seller's Breach **93**

F. Products Liability **94**
  1. Negligence **94**
  2. Strict Liability **95**
  3. Warranty Liability **95**
  4. Multiple Theories of Recovery **96**

Review Questions **97**

Solutions **103**

CHAPTER 5 Negotiable Instruments   107

Overview **107**

Definition of Terms **107**

A. The Significance of Negotiability **108**
  1. Legal Requirements **108**
  2. Effect of Negotiability **109**

B. Elements of a Negotiable Instrument **109**
  1. Writing **110**
  2. Signature **110**
  3. Unconditional Promise **110**
  4. Specific Sum of Money **112**
  5. Payable at Specific Time or Upon Demand **112**
  6. Payable to Order or Bearer **113**

C. Types of Negotiable Instruments **114**
  1. Checks **114**
  2. Drafts **114**
  3. Promissory Notes **115**
  4. Certificates of Deposit **115**

D. Transfer of Negotiable Instruments **115**
  1. Assignment **115**
  2. Negotiation **115**

E. Defenses **117**
  1. Personal Defenses **117**
  2. Real Defenses **118**

Review Questions **121**

Solutions **129**

CHAPTER 6 Personal and Intellectual Property   133

Overview **133**

Definition of Terms **134**

A. Classification of Property **134**
  1. Types of Personal Property **134**
  2. Acquisition of Ownership **135**
  3. Chattel Mortgages on Personal Property **135**

B. Copyrights **137**

1. Protection of Rights in Literary Works 137
2. Protection is Not Automatic 137
3. Duration of Copyright Protection 137
4. Nature of Copyright Protection 138
5. Enforcement of Copyrights 138
C. Patents 139
1. Protection of Rights of Inventors 139
2. New and Useful Requirement 139
3. Obtaining a Patent 140
4. Duration of Patent Protection 140
5. Nature of Patent Protection 140
6. Enforcement of Patent Rights 140
D. Trademarks 141
1. Qualification as a Trademark 141
2. Registration Not Required 141
3. Infringement 141

Review Questions 143

Solutions 149

CHAPTER 7 Real Property 151

Overview 151

Definition of Terms 152

A. Classification of Property 153
1. Real Property 153
2. Personal Property 154
B. Acquisition of Real Property 154
1. Purchase 154
2. Gift 154
3. Adverse Possession 155
C. Types of Deeds 155
1. Quitclaim Deed 156
2. Warranty Deed 156
3. Special Warranty Deeds 157
D. Types of Ownership 157
1. Joint Tenancy 157
2. Tenancy in Common 158
3. Tenancy by the Entirety 158
4. Community Property 158
5. Tenancy in Partnership 159
E. Mortgages 159
F. Easements 159
1. Characteristics of an Easement 160
2. Types of Easements 160
G. The Landlord-Tenant Relationship 162
1. The Nature of the Lease 162
2. Types of Leasehold Estates 163
3. Rights of Landlord 163
4. Duties of Landlord to Tenant 163
5. Tenant's Transfer of Interest 164

Review Questions 165

Solutions 171

CHAPTER 8 Credit, Security, and Bankruptcy 173

Overview 173

Definition of Terms 174

Contents

        A. Credit **175**
            1. Credit Regulations **175**
            2. Truth in Lending Act **175**
            3. Equal Credit Opportunity Act **176**
            4. Fair Credit Reporting Act **177**
            5. Fair Debt Collection Practices Act **178**
        B. Security **178**
            1. Types of Security **178**
            2. Suretyship **179**
            3. Security Interest in Personal Property **179**
            4. Real Property as Collateral **181**
        C. Bankruptcy **183**
            1. Purposes of Bankruptcy **183**
            2. Types of Bankruptcy **183**

Review Questions **187**

Solutions **193**

CHAPTER 9 Insurable Interest   195

Overview **195**

Definition of Terms **195**

        A. Purpose of the Insurable Interest Requirement **196**
            1. Limitations on Purchase of Insurance **196**
            2. Prevention of Gambling **196**
            3. Reduction of Incentive for Wrongdoing **196**
        B. Insurable Interest in the Life of Another Person **196**
            1. Financial Dependence or Close Relationship Required **196**
            2. Relationship Requirement **197**
            3. Business Associates' Insurable Interest **197**
            4. Employer's Insurable Interest **197**
            5. Creditor's Insurable Interest **197**
            6. When Insurable Interest Must Exist **198**
            7. Beneficiary Need Not Have Insurable Interest **198**
        C. Insurable Interest in Property **198**
            1. Financial Interest **198**
            2. When Insurable Interest Must Exist **199**
            3. Assignability **199**

Review Questions **200**

Solutions **205**

CHAPTER 10 Agency   207

Overview **207**

Definition of Terms **207**

        A. Creation **209**
            1. Consideration Not Required **209**
            2. No General Requirement for Writing **209**
            3. Capacity of Principal **210**
            4. Capacity of Agent **210**
        B. Types of Agencies **211**
            1. Disclosed Principal **211**
            2. Partially Disclosed Principal **211**
            3. Undisclosed Principal **211**
        C. Types of Agents **212**
            1. Gratuitous Agent **212**
            2. General Agent **212**
            3. Special Agent **212**

          4. Independent Contractor 212
          5. Employee 212
     D. Types of Authority 213
          1. Express Authority 213
          2. Implied Authority 213
          3. Emergency Authority 213
          4. Apparent Authority 213
     E. Obligations of Agent to Principal 214
          1. Duty to Act within Authority 214
          2. Duty to Perform 214
          3. Duty to Exercise Care and Skill 215
          4. Duty to Account to Principal 215
          5. Duty Not to Commingle Property 215
          6. Duty to Inform Principal 216
          7. Duty to Avoid Conflicts of Interest 216
          8. Duty to Make No Secret Profit 216
          9. Duty Not to Use Agency-Related Information for Personal Gain 216
     F. Obligations of Agent to Third Party 217
          1. Contract on Behalf of Disclosed Principal 218
          2. Contract on Behalf of Partially Disclosed Principal 218
          3. Contract on Behalf of Undisclosed Principal 218
          4. Recovery of Losses Resulting from Fraud 218
          5. Liability for Injury Resulting from Negligence 219
     G. Obligations of Principal to Agent 219
          1. Duty to Compensate 219
          2. Duty to Honor Contract Terms 219
          3. Duty to Reimburse Expenses 220
          4. Duty to Indemnify 220
          5. Duty to Compensate Injured Employees 220
     H. Obligations of Principal to Third Parties 221
          1. Principal's Duty to Perform Contract 221
          2. Principal's Liability for Injuries to Third Parties 222
     I. Obligations of Third Parties to Principals and Agents 223
          1. Contract with Agent for Disclosed Principal 223
          2. Contract with Agent for Partially Disclosed Principal 223
          3. Contract with Agent for Undisclosed Principal 223
          4. Third-Party Performance on Contract 223
     J. Termination of Agency Relationship 224
          1. Mutual Agreement 224
          2. Agency Agreement 224
          3. Notification of Intent to Terminate Agency 224
          4. Death 224
          5. Insanity 224
          6. Impossibility of Performance 224
          7. Illegality of Agency Agreement 224
          8. Change in Circumstances 225
     K. Notification of Termination of Agency Relationship 225
          1. Oral or Written Notice 225
          2. Notice Published in Newspaper 225
          3. No Formal Notification Needed 225

Review Questions 227

Solutions 239

CHAPTER 11 Business Entities 243

Overview 243

Definition of Terms 243

     A. Sole Entrepreneurship 245
          1. Formation of Sole Entrepreneurship 245

        2.   Creation of Sole Entrepreneurship **245**
        3.   Operation **245**
    B. Partnership **246**
        1.   Formation of Partnerships **246**
        2.   Creation of Partnerships **246**
        3.   Theories of Partnerships **248**
        4.   Types of Partnerships **249**
        5.   Partnership Operations **250**
        6.   Relationship of Partners to Third Persons **253**
        7.   Partnership Dissolution **255**
        8.   Settlement of Partnership Accounts at Termination **258**
    C. Corporation **258**
        1.   Organization of a Corporation **258**
        2.   Formation of a Corporation **262**
        3.   The Role of the Shareholder **264**
        4.   The Role of Corporate Directors **265**
        5.   The Role of Officers **266**
        6.   Corporate Finances—Stock **266**

Review Questions **269**

Solutions **276**

CHAPTER 12 Regulatory Law **279**

Overview **279**

Definition of Terms **280**

    A. Administrative Agencies **281**
        1.   Relationship to Other Branches of Government **281**
        2.   Administrative Agency Functions **281**
        3.   Administrative Agency Configuration **282**
    B. Antitrust Laws **283**
        1.   Applicable Statutes **283**
        2.   Major Objectives of Antitrust Laws **283**
        3.   Types of Offenses **283**
        4.   Possible Sanctions (Punishments) and/or Remedies **284**
        5.   Violations Under the Sherman Act **284**
        6.   Clayton Act Violations **285**
        7.   Robinson-Patman Act (price discrimination/rule
              of reason defense) **286**
    C. Government Regulatory Agencies **287**
        1.   Interstate Commerce Commission (ICC) **287**
        2.   Federal Energy Regulatory Commission (FERC) **288**
        3.   Federal Communications Commission (FCC) **289**
        4.   Environmental Protection Agency (EPA) **291**
        5.   Consumer Product Safety Commission (CPSC) **292**
        6.   The Federal Trade Commission (FTC) **293**
        7.   Food and Drug Administration (FDA) **295**
        8.   Securities and Exchange Commission (SEC) **295**
    D. The Freedom of Information Act (FOIA) **301**
        1.   Objectives of the FOIA **301**
        2.   Procedures for Requesting Government Information **301**
        3.   Exemptions **302**
        4.   Reverse FOIA Request **302**
    E. State Public Utility Commissions **303**
        1.   Purposes of State Utility Regulation **303**
        2.   State Delegation of Utility Regulation **303**
        3.   Tariffs **304**

Review Questions **305**

Solutions **311**

CHAPTER 13 Employment Laws 315

Overview 315

Definition of Terms 316

- A. Federal Laws Regulating Employment 317
  1. Fair Labor Standards Act 317
  2. Unemployment Insurance (Part of the Social Security Act) 318
  3. Social Security (FICA) 319
  4. Employee Retirement Income Security Act (ERISA) 320
  5. Occupational Safety and Health Act 321
- B. State Legislation—Workers' Compensation 322
  1. Purpose of Legislation 322
  2. Employer Requirements 322
  3. Employee Eligibility for Benefits 322
- C. Employment Discrimination 323
  1. Title VII 323
  2. Equal Pay for Equal Work Act 325
  3. Age Discrimination in Employment Act (ADEA) 326
  4. Rehabilitation Act of 1973 327
  5. The Americans with Disabilities Act (ADA) 328
- D. Labor-Management Relations (Private Employers) 329
  1. The National Labor Relations Act (NLRA) 329
  2. The Wagner Act (1935) 330
  3. Taft-Hartley Act (1947) 330
  4. Landrum-Griffin Act (1959) 330
  5. Means and Effect of Union Recognition 331
  6. The Election Process 331
  7. Unfair Labor Practices by Employer 332
  8. Unfair Labor Practices by Union 332
  9. The Role of the Arbitrator 333
  10. Potential NLRB Remedies 333
- E. Emerging Employment Issues 333
  1. Decline of the Employment At-Will Doctrine 333
  2. Employee Privacy Issues 334

Review Questions 337

Solutions 343

GLOSSARY 345

Preface

The PRENTICE HALL CERTIFIED PROFESSIONAL SECRETARY® EXAMINATION REVIEW SERIES consists of six review manuals, jointly published by Prentice Hall and Professional Secretaries International® (PSI®), designed as review materials for the Certified Professional Secretary® (CPS®) Examination. The content of each module is based on the current CPS® Study Outline published in *CAPSTONE,* the publication of the Institute for Certifying Secretaries publicizing application and requirements for the CPS® Examination.

Module II—Business Law is meant to be a *review* for those secretaries who already have completed one or more courses in business law or an *introduction* to business law for those secretaries who have never before enrolled in a business law course. A thorough study of this module, of course, does not guarantee passage of Part II of the CPS® Examination. Using this review manual, however, should provide valuable assistance for individual study or group review sessions. In addition to using this review manual for study, it will probably be necessary for secretaries to enroll in at least one business law course for a more thorough review.

The format used for each of the six modules in the series is identical. The current CPS® Study Outline and Bibliography were used initially to define exactly what the content of the module should be and the types of references that the Institute was recommending for study. Then, this outline was expanded so that more comprehensive coverage of the topics could be planned and included in the manual. Each chapter includes:

- an **Overview** introducing the reader to the chapter and its content.
- the **Definition of Terms** to be found within the chapter.
- a complete **sentence/paragraph outline**, with examples highlighted in italic type to enhance the sentence outline.
- **Review Questions** at the end of the chapter, developed in similar format to those found on the CPS® Examination.
- **Solutions** to the review questions, with the identification of the correct answer, reference to the sentence/paragraph outline, and any necessary explanation of that answer.

Module II—Business Law emphasizes basic content in business law, as outlined in the current CPS® Study Outline. The question formats used for the review questions at the end of each chapter include multiple-choice questions, matching sets, and problem situations with multiple-choice questions pertaining to them. The current CPS® Examination presents questions primarily as multiple-choice questions, alone or in problem situations. For review of technical terms as well as developing an understanding of basic concepts and principles, the authors believe that other question formats can also be helpful tools. Therefore, some matching sets are included with each set of review questions to provide adequate practice in studying terms, definitions, and other basic principles included in the chapter. Past CPS® Examinations have sometimes included questions in this format as well.

The solutions to the review questions are presented in a format that should be particularly helpful for review. These solutions include the correct answer, a reference to the section of the chapter content that has a more complete explanation, and any additional explanation that the authors believe may be necessary in understanding the correct response to the question. Here is an example:

Answer   **Refer to Chapter Section**

4. (d)   [B-3-d]   Under the UCC, an offer requesting prompt shipment can be accepted . . .

The content reference [B-3-d] refers to:

Section B, Point 3, Subpoint d of the chapter.

When a solution seems unclear, it is an excellent idea to return to the sentence/paragraph outline and review the material included under that topic. Review questions have been included to give candidates further review and practice with questions similar to those found on the exam before going on to the next chapter.

At the end of this module, a complete Glossary of terms and definitions included in each chapter of *Module II—Business Law* is presented as a quick guide to terms. A reference is included to the chapter where the term may be found in context.

The question arises as to why this review manual and the other review manuals in the series are formatted in this particular way. The response is simple: we want you to have a thorough, but rather quick, review of the content that may appear on the CPS® Examination this year. You should still refer to other business law references, especially those referred to in the CPS® Study Outline and Bibliography, for more detailed explanations and/or a variety of learning materials to test your knowledge and competence in these topical areas.

The INSTRUCTOR'S MANUAL is a separate publication, correlated to accompany MODULE II—BUSINESS LAW. This manual is available to instructors of CPS review courses in business law and includes the following helpful materials:

- **Teaching Suggestions**: Suggested teaching ideas for business law review sessions; learning activities to incorporate into classroom or seminar instruction.
- **Test Bank**: A sample test for business law; solutions for the test, with outline references correlated with the review manual.
- **Reading References**: Bibliography of books, periodicals, and special references that may be helpful to secretaries as well as instructors.

We hope that the contents of this INSTRUCTOR'S MANUAL will help instructors provide a successful CPS® review program in business law.

Betty L. Schroeder, Ph.D.
Series Editor

Acknowledgments

The development of the second edition of *Module II—Business Law* of the PRENTICE HALL CERTIFIED PROFESSIONAL SECRETARY® EXAMINATION REVIEW SERIES was possible only because of the sincere and dedicated efforts of a number of individuals who are committed to helping secretaries, office administration students, and business educators become Certified Professional Secretaries. Like the other review manuals in the series, *Module II—Business Law* has become a successful review tool because of the contributions of a number of people who have given of their time and expertise to assist in the review process to be sure that the content of the review manuals is appropriate for this particular examination.

We gratefully acknowledge the contributions of Dr. Susan Fenner, Ms. Janet Head, Ms. Adella C. La Rue, CPS, Ms. Shelley J. Stoeckl, CPS, and Ms. Susan Wilbanks, CPS, for their extremely helpful reviews and critiques of the manuscript.

Professional Secretaries International, through the Institute for Certifying Secretaries, has provided not only the incentive for the development of the Second Edition of this review manual but also valuable input during the review process. We sincerely thank the following individuals for their continued interest in and enthusiasm for the development and revision of the series:

Mrs. Jean Mills, Dean, Institute for Certifying Secretaries

Jerome Heitman, Executive Director, Professional Secretaries International

Dr. Susan Fenner, Education/Professional Development Manager, Professional Secretaries International

Mrs. Janet Head, Operations/CPS/Membership, Professional Secretaries International

A very special thank you is given to the members of the Illinois Division of Professional Secretaries International and, in particular, those members of Kishwaukee Chapter, DeKalb, Illinois, who have pursued or have received their professional certification over the past several years. They have continued to be extremely supportive and positive about the use of these review manuals, and their friendship is very much appreciated.

Lastly, we are most appreciative of the leadership and assistance given by Harry Moon and Liz Kendall of Prentice Hall, for their continued strong support of this series. It is a joy to work with individuals so professional in their judgment of what secretaries need in preparation for the CPS Examination.

And, of course, thank you to anyone else who helped along the way!

We hope that all of the input provided by professionals throughout the revision process will continue to make this review manual (and the other five in the series) the "leaders" in providing an excellent review for the CPS® Examination in the future.

> Betty L. Schroeder, Ph.D.
> Lawrence S. Clark, J.D., LL.M.
> Philip DiMarzio, J.D., LL.M.

CHAPTER 1

Introduction to Business Law

OVERVIEW

Law provides a consistent means of defining rights and resolving disputes. Since the business community desires an atmosphere of stability, business law in particular must be sound and predictable. In order to gain an adequate understanding of law, one should be familiar with the sources of law, including their hierarchy. Basic legal terminology needs to be mastered and an awareness developed of the major areas of law.

This chapter serves as a basic introduction to law. The chapters that follow will explore specific areas of law in greater detail.

DEFINITION OF TERMS

CIVIL LAW. Law pertaining to private as opposed to public rights.

COMMON LAW. A vast body of law, consisting of decided case law, which includes the case law and custom of England prior to the American Revolution to the extent that it has not been expressly superseded or overruled by cases or laws of the United States. Common law includes all published opinions of courts in the United States.

CONSTITUTIONAL LAW. Law derived from the United States Constitution and the Bill of Rights.

CRIMINAL LAW. Law which defines offenses against the government (representing all of society) and provides penal sanctions.

EXECUTIVE ORDER. A law issued by the President of the United States.

FELONY. A crime punishable by one year or more of incarceration.

MISDEMEANOR. A crime punishable by up to one year of incarceration.

PRECEDENT. A previously decided case.

PROCEDURAL LAW. Law which specifies rules governing how rights are to be enforced.

PROMULGATE. A term describing the act of an administrative agency in creating a regulation.

REGULATION. A law promulgated by an administrative agency.

STARE DECISIS. The doctrine that precedent should be followed.

STATUTORY LAW. Law enacted by legislative bodies.

STRICT LIABILITY. A legal doctrine that requires one engaged in a highly dangerous activity to compensate those injured as a result of the activity even in the absence of any negligence. One who sells a product in a defective, unreasonably dangerous condition is liable for physical harm caused to the consumer or user of the product if the seller is in the business of selling such a product and the product is expected to and does reach the consumer or user without substantial change in the condition in which it is sold.

SUBSTANTIVE LAW. Law which defines rights and duties.

TORT LAW. The law of civil wrongs including intentional acts, negligence, and strict liability.

A. Origin of Law

The origin of our legal system is the English common law. With the signing of the Magna Charta in 1215, King John formally recognized certain rights of landowners and provided a means of adjudicating those rights. Over time, a court system evolved and judicial opinions were recorded. These opinions became precedent for future cases involving similar facts. The vast body of case law that has developed is known as *common law*.

1. *Common Law:* Common law is case law. Our common law actually includes the case law and custom of England prior to the American Revolution insofar as it has not been expressly superseded or overruled by cases or laws of the United States. Our common law also includes all published opinions of courts in the United States. Needless to say, the common law is an immense body of case law that is the subject of much legal research by attorneys and legal scholars.

    a. *Basis for common law:* Common law is based upon the concept of precedent. A goal of the common law is consistency. Once a legal principle is established, it should be followed. Thus, once a case is decided, it becomes a precedent to be considered by future courts in adjudicating similar issues.

Introduction to Business Law

    b. *The doctrine of stare decisis:* The doctrine that precedent should be followed is known as *stare decisis* (the decision stands). In applying stare decisis, a court would follow precedent and decide the same legal issue consistent with the earlier court's ruling.

2. *Constitutional Law:* Constitutional law is derived from the United States Constitution. The Constitution and the accompanying Bill of Rights are the highest law of the land. The Constitution prevails over any other law.

    a. *Supreme Court opinions:* The Constitution has been interpreted in numerous cases decided by the Supreme Court. These Supreme Court opinions are part of what is commonly known as Constitutional law.

    b. *Final authority:* The Supreme Court of the United States is the final authority on what the Constitution means.

3. *Statutory Law:* Statutory law is enacted by legislative bodies.

    a. *Congressional acts:* The Congress of the United States enacts federal statutes that apply throughout the United States.

    b. *State legislative statutes:* The legislature of each state enacts statutes that apply within the boundaries of that state.

    c. *Federal law:* Federal law governs over any inconsistent state law.

    d. *An unconstitutional statute:* A statute, state or federal, may be declared unconstitutional by the Supreme Court.

4. *Regulations:* Regulations are promulgated by administrative agencies (see Chapter 10).

    a. *Regulatory agencies:* Congress has created regulatory agencies and has granted rule-making authority to some of them.

        (1) Agency employees are capable of acquiring a high level of expertise in a given field.

        (2) Agencies can only promulgate regulations within the scope of the authority granted by Congress.

        (3) Specific procedures exist for rule making by agencies. These are addressed in Chapter 10.

    b. *Prevailing statute:* A statute prevails over a conflicting regulation.

5. *Executive Orders:* Executive orders are laws issued by the President of the United States.

   a. *Authority:* The President's authority to issue executive orders is limited. Such authority must be traceable to an Act of Congress or to the Constitution.

   b. *Prevailing statute:* A federal statute prevails over a conflicting executive order.

B. **Classifications of Law**

Although there are many subdivisions of law, this chapter will address only several broad classifications.

1. *Civil Law:* Civil law pertains to private, as opposed to public, rights.

   EXAMPLES OF CIVIL LAW: Contract law (Chapter 3) and property law (Chapters 6 and 7).

2. *Tort Law:* Tort law is a broad area of civil law. Tort law is the law of civil wrongs which include intentional wrongs and negligence.

   a. *Negligence:* Negligence is the breach of a duty of care owed to another person.

      EXAMPLE: One who drives an automobile owes a duty of care to other motorists and to pedestrians. A breach of that duty of care may consist of driving too fast and not maintaining a proper lookout.

      If such negligent conduct results in injury, the injured party may sue and recover for his/her losses. (See Chapter 2: Court Procedures.)

   b. *Strict liability:* Strict liability provides a basis for an injured party to sue for and recover damages without having to prove negligence.

      (1) *Dangerous activities:* Strict liability is limited to highly dangerous activities.

         EXAMPLE: Al decides to use dynamite to clear his property of old tree stumps. Blasting dynamite is a highly dangerous activity. Al is legally responsible for any damage caused by the blasting even if he employs all reasonable precautions.

(2) *No real defense:* When strict liability exists, there is no real defense. The trial would focus on the extent of damage to be compensated.

3. *Criminal Law:* Criminal law defines offenses against the government and provides penal sanctions for such violations.

   a. *Criminal suit:* A criminal case is brought in the name of and on behalf of the state or federal government against the alleged violator.

   b. *Protection of individual rights:* Because the liberty of one charged with a crime is at stake, the individual's rights are carefully protected. A person charged with a crime has a right to remain silent and, if jail is a possibility, a right to free legal representation if he or she cannot afford to hire a lawyer.

   c. *Presumption of innocence:* The prosecution is required to prove guilt beyond a reasonable doubt before there can be a conviction. The person charged with a crime is presumed innocent until proven guilty.

   d. *Felony:* A felony is a crime punishable by one year or more in prison.

   e. *Misdemeanor:* A misdemeanor is a crime punishable by up to one year of incarceration.

   f. *Tort or crime:* The same act may be both a tort and a crime [see Chapter 2, Section A-1-a(4)].

4. *Procedural Law:* Procedural law consists of rules governing the enforcement of laws and rights. Lawsuits are governed by these procedural rules.

   EXAMPLE: *A statute may set forth the exact method of jury selection to be used in that state. This is a procedural law.*

5. *Substantive Law:* Substantive law defines rights and duties.

   EXAMPLE: *A statute may bestow a right to sue for damages in certain types of cases where no such right is specifically guaranteed by the Constitution and where no such right is recognized as common law. Such a statute is substantive law.*

   Thus, while substantive law defines rights, procedural law provides the means or rules whereby these rights are enforceable.

Introduction to Business Law

Chapter 1: Review Questions

PART A: Multiple-Choice Questions

DIRECTIONS: Select the best answer from the four alternatives. Write your answer in the blank to the left of the number.

____c____ 1. A lawyer arguing a case in a state court cites an earlier case decided by that court and asks the court to follow the earlier decision. The lawyer is relying upon the principle of

   a. strict liability.
   b. constitutional supremacy.
   c. stare decisis.
   d. tort law.

____b____ 2. The final authority in interpreting the United States Constitution is the

   a. Congress.
   b. Supreme Court.
   c. President.
   d. Senate Judiciary Committee.

____d____ 3. A federal statute prevails over any of the following except

   a. a state statute.
   b. an executive order.
   c. a regulation promulgated by a federal agency.
   d. a provision in the Constitution.

____a____ 4. Which of the following is <u>not</u> considered to be in the area of civil law?

   a. A prosecution for bank robbery.
   b. A tort suit.
   c. A contract dispute.
   d. A suit between two citizens over ownership of a plot of real estate.

___c___ 5. In a suit based upon strict liability, the injured party would need prove *only*

   a. negligence.
   b. breach of a duty of care.
   c. damages.
   d. his/her own exercise of due care.

___d___ 6. The burden of proof in a criminal case is

   a. proof by a preponderance of the evidence.
   b. proof beyond a doubt.
   c. proof by clear and convincing evidence.
   d. proof beyond a reasonable doubt.

___a___ 7. William is charged with striking James and breaking his nose. The charge is brought under a state statute that provides for punishment, upon conviction, of up to three years in prison. Which of the following statements is <u>not</u> true?

   a. William is charged with a misdemeanor.
   b. William has the right to free legal representation if he cannot afford the services of a lawyer.
   c. William is presumed innocent.
   d. William may be sued by James for committing a tort even though there is a criminal prosecution.

___d___ 8. Which of the following is a substantive *rights*, as opposed to a procedural, law?

   a. A law requiring all legal documents to be filed on 8 1/2" x 11" paper.
   b. A law providing that only the judge may question prospective jurors.
   c. A law requiring the parties to a suit to hold a pretrial conference with the judge.
   d. A law permitting a handicapped person a right to recover damages from a municipality for not providing the required number of handicapped parking places.

Introduction to Business Law

PART B: Matching Sets

Matching Set 1

Match each of the sources of law (A-D) with the correct descriptive phrase (9-12). Write the letter of your response in the blank to the left of the number.

SOURCES OF LAW

A. Common Law
B. Statutory Law
C. Constitutional Law
D. Executive Order

DESCRIPTIVE PHRASES

____C____ **9.** Bill of Rights

____D____ **10.** Issued by President

____A____ **11.** Case Law

____B____ **12.** Legislative Action

Matching Set 2

Match each legal term (A-C) with the appropriate descriptive phrase (13-15). Write the letter of your response in the blank to the left of the number.

LEGAL TERMS

A. Felony
B. Misdemeanor
C. Strict Liability

DESCRIPTIVE PHRASES

____B____ **13.** Punishable by up to one year of incarceration.

____C____ **14.** Does not require proof of negligence for recovery of damages.

____A____ **15.** Punishable by one year or more incarceration.

10 Introduction to Business Law

PART C: Case Problems

DIRECTIONS: For each of the following case situations, select the best answer from the four alternatives. Write the letter of your response in the blank to the left of the question.

Case 1

Frank did not remove any snow or ice from the sidewalk leading to his house. Jake slipped while walking to Frank's house to visit him. Jake sued Frank to recover damages for his broken hip. At common law, one who leaves his walk in its natural state, without attempting to remove snow or ice, is not liable for injuries suffered.

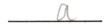 16. Frank's lawyer will rely upon

    a. stare decisis.
    b. statutory law.
    c. regulatory law.
    d. strict liability.

Case 2

Shirley called the police when she discovered Sandy had stolen her jewelry. Sandy was charged with the offense of theft under $300 which was punishable in that state by fine or jail sentence of up to one year. Before the case came to trial, Shirley decided she did not want to see Sandy prosecuted.

 17. Which of the following statements is true in regard to the dismissal of the case?

    a. Shirley has authority to dismiss the case because it is civil in nature.
    b. Shirley could dismiss the case if it were a felony but cannot dismiss a misdemeanor.
    c. Shirley cannot dismiss a criminal case because it is brought on behalf of the government.
    d. Shirley can dismiss the case because it is a misdemeanor but could not dismiss it if it were a felony.

Introduction to Business Law

Chapter 1: Solutions

PART A: Multiple-Choice Questions

	Answer	**Refer to Chapter Section**
1.	(c)	[A-1-b] The doctrine that legal precedent should be followed is stare decisis.
2.	(b)	[A-2-b] The Supreme Court's interpretation of the Constitution governs over any other interpretation.
3.	(d)	[A-2] The Constitution is the highest law of the land.
4.	(a)	[B-3] A criminal prosecution is brought in the name of and on behalf of the government.
5.	(c)	[B-2-b] Strict liability does not require proof of negligence. The law recognizes that certain activities are so inherently dangerous that one who engages in them should be held strictly liable for any injuries caused, even if due care was exercised.
6.	(d)	[B-3-c] Because criminal cases involve the possible loss of one's freedom, the highest burden of proof, proof beyond a reasonable doubt, is required for a conviction.
7.	(a)	[B-3-d] A crime punishable by one year or more of incarceration is a felony.
8.	(d)	[B-5] A substantive law defines rights whereas procedural law sets forth rules governing enforcement of rights.

PART B: Matching Sets

Matching Set 1

9.	(C)	[A-2]
10.	(D)	[A-5]
11.	(A)	[A-1]
12.	(B)	[A-3]

Matching Set 2

13.	(B)	[B-3-e]
14.	(C)	[B-2-b]
15.	(A)	[B-3-d]

PART C: Case Problems

16. (a)   [A-1-b] Stare decisis, the doctrine of following precedent, is an integral part of the common law. Since the common law supports Frank's position, his lawyer will rely upon it.

17. (c)   [B-3-a] A criminal case is brought on behalf of the government. While Shirley is a witness, she does not have authority to dismiss the case. Only the appropriate government representative may move to dismiss the case.

CHAPTER 2
Court Procedures

OVERVIEW

The number of law suits filed grows each year as society looks increasingly to the court system as a means of resolving disputes. Parties may become involved in a law suit in various ways. They may resort to litigation to protect legal rights. They may be sued by others who claim that their rights have been violated. Individuals may be called as witnesses in law suits because they possess relevant information. Even to those who are not directly involved in the suit, the result may be of importance because a precedent may be established. Moreover, the outcome of a suit may have long-term effects on the business community.

A large corporation may be ordered to sell its subsidiaries or to refrain from certain business practices which have been damaging to its competitors. A company may be ordered to pay millions of dollars in damages as a result of a product liability suit or an antitrust judgment. The value of that company's stock will decline. A company may file for bankruptcy and thus affect the interests of its creditors.

A familiarity with court procedures is an advantage in such a suit-conscious society. This chapter presents a look at some of the basic court procedures and legal terminology. While the candidate is not expected to fully understand legal procedure, knowledge of the fundamentals presented in this chapter is an attainable goal.

DEFINITION OF TERMS

AFFIDAVIT OF SERVICE. A sworn statement by one who has served a legal notice specifying how and when the service was accomplished.

AFFIRMATION. A ruling by an appellate court upholding the lower court's judgment.

ANSWER. A document filed in court by the defendant in response to the complaint.

APPELLANT. One who brings an appeal.

APPELLEE. One who defends the lower court's judgment against an appeal (the winning party at the trial).

ASSAULT. An act or threat that causes another person to reasonably believe that he/she is in immediate danger of suffering a battery.

BANKRUPTCY. A procedure governed by federal law which provides a means of obtaining relief for debtors and for the uniform and fair treatment of creditors.

BANKRUPTCY PETITION. A document filed in the bankruptcy court to commence a bankruptcy proceeding.

BATTERY. An intentional and unjustified contact with another person which is either harmful or offensive.

BENCH TRIAL. A trial before a judge without a jury.

CLOSING ARGUMENT. An address delivered to the judge or jury by a lawyer representing a party to the suit. It is delivered after all evidence has been presented.

COMPENSATORY DAMAGES. Damages which consist of the amount of money required to compensate the plaintiff for his/her loss.

COMPLAINT. A document filed in court by the plaintiff in which the plaintiff sets forth an account of the facts and requests a certain remedy. (In some contexts, such a document may be designated as a petition.)

CONTEMPT OF COURT. A willful disobeyance of a court order.

CROSS EXAMINATION. Questioning of a witness who was called to testify by the opposing party to the suit.

COUNTERCLAIM. A document filed by a defendant asserting a claim and seeking a remedy from the plaintiff. A defendant who files a counterclaim is known also as a counterplaintiff, and the plaintiff is known also as a counterdefendant.

DEFENDANT. One against whom a complaint is filed.

DEPONENT. One who is questioned at a deposition.

DEPOSITION. A discovery device which consists of the taking of sworn testimony outside of court prior to the trial.

DIRECT EXAMINATION. Questioning of a witness who was called to testify by the party doing the questioning.

DISCOVERY. A process through which parties to a suit gather information from each other.

EXEMPT PROPERTY. Property that may be kept by a debtor when property is taken away from a debtor by a court order such as in judgment debt or bankruptcy.

GARNISHMENT. A legal means whereby a creditor may obtain a debtor's property which is held by a third party (such as an employer).

INJUNCTION. A court order directing a party to do or to refrain from doing a particular act.

INSTRUCTIONS. An explanation by the judge to the jury directing the jury as to the law which must be applied in deciding the case.

INTERROGATORIES. A discovery device which consists of written questions which must be answered in writing and under oath.

JUDGMENT. The official decision of a court.

JURISDICTION. The power of a particular court to decide a case.

LIBEL. A written statement which is false and which injures another party's reputation.

LIQUIDATE. To settle debts by distributing the debtor's assets. Liquidation usually involves selling property to obtain cash for the purpose of paying creditors.

MOTION. A formal request for a court order.

NEGLIGENCE. The failure to exercise reasonable care in a situation where a law recognizes a duty of care.

NOMINAL DAMAGES. Damages awarded when the plaintiff has established that his/her rights were violated but has failed to prove any loss. Nominal damages typically consist of one dollar.

PLAINTIFF. One who files a complaint.

PRETRIAL CONFERENCE. A meeting held before the trial between a judge and the lawyers who represent the parties to the suit.

PUNITIVE DAMAGES. Damages which are designed to punish the defendant for wrongful conduct that was willful or outrageous.

REAFFIRMATION AGREEMENT. An agreement whereby a debtor may agree to pay debts which would otherwise be discharged.

REVERSE. A ruling by a court to which an appeal was taken, setting aside the lower court's judgment.

SECURED CREDITOR. One who extended credit to the debtor in return for a legally recognized interest in certain property of the debtor.

SECURITY INTEREST. A legally recognized interest of a creditor in certain property of the debtor.

SERVICE BY PUBLICATION. A type of service which is accomplished by publishing a notice in a newspaper of general circulation in the area of the defendant's residence. This type of service is permitted only in certain types of cases when the defendant cannot be located.

SLANDER. An oral statement which is false and which injures another party's reputation.

STAY. A court order suspending all other court actions from proceeding any further.

STIPULATION. An agreement between the parties that certain facts exist and should be presented as evidence in the case (usually in the form of a written statement).

SUBPOENA. A court order directing a person to appear at a certain time and place.

SUBPOENA DUCES TECUM. A subpoena which requires the person to whom it is directed to produce certain documents at the required time and place.

SUMMONS. A document which notifies the defendant that a complaint has been filed against him/her and that there is a certain time period within which to respond to the complaint.

TORT. A wrongful act committed against another person or that person's property. A tort is civil in nature rather than criminal. A breach of contract is not a tort.

TRESPASS. An act of wrongfully entering another person's property, real or personal.

TRUSTEE. A person appointed by the court in a bankruptcy case who has the duty of managing the bankrupt party's property.

VERDICT. The decision of a jury.

VOIR DIRE. The process by which impartial jurors are selected from among those gathered for jury duty.

WRIT OF MANDAMUS. A court order directed to a public official commanding that official to perform a certain act.

A. The Tort Suit

A common type of law suit is one based upon the alleged commission of a tort.

1. *Tort:* A tort is a civil wrong. Assault, battery, trespass, libel, slander, and negligence are examples of torts.

    a. *Characteristics of tort suit:* A tort suit may be distinguished from a criminal case by the following:

    (1) In a criminal case, the government (state or federal) files charges against a party. In a tort suit, one private party (an individual, partnership, or corporation) sues another party.

    (2) A crime is punishable by a fine or by incarceration, or both. The purpose of a tort suit is to gain compensation for damages caused by the tort.

    (3) The procedures required in a criminal case differ greatly from those in a tort suit.

    (4) The burden of proof in a criminal case (proof beyond a reasonable doubt) is greater than that required in a civil case (proof by a preponderance of the evidence).

    (5) Although the same act may be both a tort and a crime, the criminal case and the tort case resulting from the act will progress through the court system independent of one another. (Protection against double jeopardy does not apply because a tort case is not criminal in nature.)

EXAMPLE: Gary struck Tom in the face without justification. Gary has committed both a tort and a crime. Both are known as battery. Tom may sue Gary for money damages to compensate him for medical expenses and the pain he suffered. A prosecutor representing the state may file a criminal charge against Gary. The two cases are treated in the law as being separate and distinct.

b. *Breach of contract:* Breach of contract is not a tort. A party who breaches a contract is liable for any damages caused by the breach, but a tort has not necessarily been committed.

EXAMPLE: The Acme Tire Company contracted to deliver 20,000 tires to American Car Rental by November 1 at a price of $35 per tire. Acme, due to other commitments, failed to deliver the tires. American was forced to pay $45 for comparable tires elsewhere. Acme is liable for damages but has not committed a tort.

c. *Breach of duty:* For there to be a tort, one party must have breached a duty owed to another party.

EXAMPLE: Merle drove his car through a busy intersection without stopping at the stop sign. His car struck one driven by Mona causing her to suffer damages. Merle owed a duty to exercise reasonable care toward Mona and any others who were in the vicinity. His failure to live up to that duty caused Mona's loss. Merle committed the tort of negligence.

EXAMPLE: Todd says to a group of his friends, "Bart has been convicted of theft." The statement is false. Todd has committed the tort of slander. Todd owes a duty to Bart not to damage Bart's reputation with false statements made to others. Todd's failure to meet that duty caused Bart to suffer damage to his reputation.

2. *Parties:* The parties in a tort suit are known as the *plaintiff* and the *defendant.*

   a. *Plaintiff:* The party who files the suit.

   b. *Defendant:* The party against whom the suit is filed.

   c. *Parties to law suit:* Any person or corporation may sue or be sued. In most states, partnerships may also be parties in law suits.

3. *Pleadings:* The basic pleadings consist of the *complaint* and the *answer.*

   a. *The complaint:* A complaint is a document filed in court by the plaintiff, setting forth an account of the relevant facts and asking the court for a certain remedy. The remedy most commonly sought in a tort suit is money damages. (In some contexts, a document meeting the description of a complaint may be referred to as a *petition*.)

    (1)   The complaint must specifically state the alleged acts or omissions of the defendant which the plaintiff claims were wrongful.

    (2)   The complaint must be filed in a court which has *jurisdiction*.

        (a)   Jurisdiction is the power of a court to decide a case.

        (b)   State trial courts have jurisdiction to hear tort cases.

        (c)   Federal courts have jurisdiction over tort cases in which the parties reside in different states and the amount being sued for exceeds $50,000.

b.   *The answer:* A document filed in court by the defendant in response to the complaint is the *answer*.

    (1)   The answer must specifically admit or deny each allegation in the complaint.

    (2)   If the defendant lacks sufficient knowledge to admit or deny a particular allegation, he/she may, upon stating that to be the case, decline to admit or deny that allegation.

4.   *Service:* Pleadings and other notices pertaining to the suit must be served on the opposing party.

    a.   *Summons:* The complaint must be served on the defendant with a summons.

        (1)   The summons is a document which notifies the defendant that a suit has been filed against him/her.

        (2)   The summons informs the defendant that he/she must respond to the complaint within a certain time period. (Some summons require the defendant to appear in court on a certain date.)

        (3)   The law in most states requires that the summons be personally delivered to the defendant by a deputy or other process server. It is permissible in most states for the process server to leave the summons at the defendant's home with an adult who resides there.

Court Procedures 19

(4) If the defendant cannot be located, the law in most states permits *service by publication* in certain types of cases. Service by publication consists of publishing a notice to the defendant in a newspaper of general circulation in the area of the defendant's last known address.

b. *Personal or mail service:* The answer and other notices pertaining to the suit may be served personally or by mail.

  (1) Service of these documents need not be made by a deputy or process server.

  (2) Proof of service should be made in the form of an *affidavit of service*. This is a sworn statement by the server specifying how and when service was accomplished.

5. *Motions:* It is common in a tort suit for the parties to file motions. A motion is a formal request for a court order. A motion may be oral, although most are in writing.

  a. *Types of motions:* There are many types of motions. Motions to dismiss the complaint, motions to amend pleadings, and motions for a continuance are commonly filed motions.

  b. *Notice of hearing on motions:* The opposing party is entitled to notice prior to a hearing on the motion.

  c. *Decision on motions:* The judge will either grant the motion or deny it.

6. *Discovery:* Discovery is a process through which the parties gather information from each other. Paralegals and secretaries may become involved in the discovery process, especially in terms of taking dictation for and transcribing interrogatories and answers for them. In addition, they may be involved in gathering or assembling documents and files to be produced for examination by the opposing party. Several tools of discovery are commonly used.

  a. *Deposition:* A deposition is a discovery device which consists of the taking of sworn testimony outside of court prior to the trial.

   (1) The person who answers the questions under oath at a deposition is known as the *deponent*.

   (2) The questions at a deposition are asked by a lawyer who represents one of the parties. The opposing lawyer has a right to be present.

(3) The questions and answers are recorded. This is usually done by a court reporter.

(4) A deposition serves two main purposes:

(a) It allows a party to gather information from a witness.

(b) It provides a record of the witness's statements. If the witness testifies at trial in a manner that is inconsistent with the deposition, the deposition may be used to demonstrate the witness's inconsistency.

b. *Interrogatories:* An interrogatory is a useful discovery device which is usually less expensive than a deposition. Interrogatories are limited to parties to the suit.

(1) Interrogatories are written questions which must be answered in writing under oath.

(2) Interrogatories differ from depositions in that the party answering the interrogatories is given a certain time period within which to furnish the *written* answers. A deponent must respond *orally* to the questions asked.

c. *Request for production of documents and records:* This procedure requires the opposing party to produce specifically requested documents on which it relies to prove or disprove claims or defenses.

d. *Subpoena:* A subpoena, used as a discovery device, is a court order directing a person to appear at a certain time and place.

(1) A subpoena may be used to obtain the presence of a person at a deposition or at a court hearing.

(2) One who has been served with a subpoena and who fails to obey its command may be found to be in *contempt of court.* One who is in contempt may be fined or jailed or both.

(3) A *subpoena duces tecum* is a subpoena which requires the named person to produce certain specified documents at the required time and place.

e. *Motions:* Motions are commonly used to obtain information from the other party to the suit.

(1) A motion requesting that the judge order the opposing party to produce a list of witnesses is commonly granted.

Court Procedures

(2) A motion requesting an order allowing a party to inspect the opposing party's physical evidence is nearly always granted.

7. *Pretrial Conference:* A pretrial conference is a meeting between a judge and the lawyers who represent the parties to a suit. It serves two main purposes:

   a. *Settlement of case:* The pretrial conference usually involves a last effort on the part of the judge and the lawyers to arrive at an acceptable settlement of the case.

   b. *Planning the trial:* The pretrial conference is used to plan for the trial so that it will run as efficiently as possible.

8. *Trial:* The trial of a tort suit may be a bench trial or a jury trial.

   a. *Bench trial:* A trial before the judge without a jury is called a bench trial.

   b. *Jury trial:* A trial before a number of impartial citizens selected from a group of individuals randomly drawn from the relevant area is called a jury trial.

      (1) Traditionally, a jury consists of 12 persons, but many states now permit six-member juries.

      (2) The process by which impartial jurors are selected from among those gathered for jury duty is known as the *voir dire*.

      (3) Even in a jury trial, a judge presides over the trial and decides law. The jury, however, decides the factual disputes and renders the verdict. The judge may set aside the jury's verdict and enter a judgment notwithstanding the verdict. (This is done when the judge finds that no reasonable person could have arrived at the verdict rendered by the jury. A judgment notwithstanding the verdict is not common.)

   c. *Opening statements:* The trial begins with opening statements by the lawyers.

      (1) The plaintiff's lawyer has the right to deliver the opening statement first. The defendant's attorney then has the right to deliver his or her opening statement.

      (2) The opening statement introduces the judge or jury to the case, but it does not constitute evidence in the case.

   d. *Presentation of evidence by plaintiff:* The plaintiff presents evidence after the opening statements. Evidence is presented in a number of different ways.

(1) *Direct examination:* The questioning of a witness by the lawyer who called that witness to testify is called direct examination.

(2) *Cross examination:* Questioning of witnesses by the opposing lawyer is called cross examination. Cross examination follows direct examination.

(3) *Introduction of physical evidence:* Physical evidence may be introduced with the permission of the judge after certain legal requirements have been met. Evidence may consist of documents, photographs, charts, or other relevant material.

(4) *Stipulations:* A stipulation is an agreement between the parties that certain facts exist and should be presented as evidence (usually in the form of a written statement).

e. *Presentation of evidence by defendant:* Following the conclusion of the plaintiff's case, the defendant has the opportunity to present evidence.

f. *Closing arguments:* Following the presentation of the evidence, the lawyers have the opportunity to make closing arguments to the judge and jury. In their closing arguments, the lawyers attempt to summarize their case and emphasize its strength.

g. *Jury instructions:* In a jury trial, the judge gives the jury instructions as to the law it is required to apply.

h. *Judgment:* At the end of the trial, the judge enters a judgment which states the court's ruling.

(1) *Judgment for defendant:* In a tort suit, the judgment may be for the defendant. If the judgment is for the defendant, the plaintiff is entitled to no relief.

(2) *Judgment for plaintiff:* If the judgment in a tort suit is for the plaintiff, the plaintiff is entitled to damages. Several kinds of damages may be awarded to the plaintiff.

(a) *Compensatory damages:* Compensatory damages are the amount of money required to compensate the plaintiff for the loss.

(b) *Punitive damages:* Punitive damages may be awarded

Court Procedures   23

>   to the plaintiff in addition to compensatory damages. The purpose of punitive damages is to punish the defendant for wrongful conduct that was willful or outrageous and to deter others from similar misconduct.
>
>   (c) *Nominal damages:* Nominal damages will be awarded if the plaintiff has proven that the defendant committed a tort but has failed to prove any loss as a result of the tort. Nominal damages may consist of one dollar.

   i. *Appeal of case:* The party who loses at the trial may elect to appeal the case to a higher court. (An exception is that the prosecution in a criminal case that ends in a verdict of *not guilty* is not permitted to appeal.)

   (1) *Appellant:* The party making the appeal is the appellant.

   (2) *Appellee:* The party who defends the trial court's judgment against the appeal is the appellee.

   (3) *Affirmation of judgment:* If the higher court approves the trial court's judgment, it *affirms* the judgment.

   (4) *Reversal of judgment:* If the higher court finds that errors which occurred at the trial affected the outcome, it will *reverse* the judgment and usually will order a new trial.

B. **Court Orders**

Among the various types of orders which a court is empowered to issue are *injunctions* and *writs of mandamus*.

1. *Injunction:* An injunction is a court order directing a party to do or to refrain from doing a particular act.

   a. *Temporary injunction:* An injunction may be temporary or preliminary. Such an injunction is subject to being terminated by the court at a later time.

   b. *Permanent injunction:* An injunction which is permanent will not be terminated by the court which issued it but may be appealed to a higher court.

   c. *Restraining order:* This term is sometimes used to describe a court order directing a party to refrain from doing a particular act.

   d. *Violation of injunction or restraining order:* One who violates an injunction or a restraining order may be found to be in contempt of court.

2. *Mandamus:* A writ of mandamus is a court order directed to a public official commanding that official to perform a certain act.

   EXAMPLE: Lucy went to the county clerk's office to obtain a death certificate for her deceased husband. The clerk refused to issue the certificate despite the fact that state law required him to do so. Lucy may sue for a writ of mandamus directing the county clerk to issue the death certificate.

Chapter 2: Review Questions

PART A: Multiple-Choice Questions

DIRECTIONS: Select the best answer from the four alternatives. Write your answer in the blank to the left of the number.

_c_ 1. Daron intentionally struck Tim on the head with a baseball bat. Which of the following is true?

    a. Daron has committed a tort.
    b. Daron has committed a crime.
    c. Daron has committed a tort and a crime.
    d. None of the above.

_c_ 2. Which of the following statements is *not* true regarding a law suit?

    a. The complaint is filed by the plaintiff.
    b. The answer is filed by the defendant.
    c. A summons is a formal request for a court order.
    d. Jurisdiction is the power of a court to decide a case.

_a_ 3. Each of the following terms relates to discovery except

    a. service by publication.
    b. deposition.
    c. interrogatories.
    d. subpoena.

_c_ 4. A deposition differs from an interrogatory in that

    a. a deposition requires that answer be under oath, but answers to interrogatories need not be under oath.
    b. a deposition allows a party to obtain new information, but interrogatories are limited to facts which have already been admitted.
    c. a deposition involves oral or written questions and answers, but interrogatories involve only written questions and answers.
    d. a deposition results in a record of the deponent's testimony, but an interrogatory does not establish a record of the questions and answers.

___a___ 5. Which of the following terms describes the jury selection process?

   a. Voir dire
   b. Bench trial
   c. Instructions
   d. Pretrial conference

___d___ 6. If the judgment in a tort suit is for the plaintiff, the court may award any of the following except

   a. compensatory damages.
   b. punitive damages.
   c. nominal damages.
   d. specific performance.

___a___ 7. If the appellee prevails in a case which has been appealed, the appellate court will

   a. affirm the lower court's judgment.
   b. reverse the lower court's judgment.
   c. award compensatory damages.
   d. none of the above.

___b___ 8. A court order directing a party to do or to refrain from doing a certain act is known as a/an

   a. writ of mandamus.
   b. injunction.
   c. interrogatory.
   d. appeal.

___a___ 9. Jack was served with a subpoena duces tecum directing him to appear in court on May 15 and to bring a copy of a certain contract. If Jack fails to comply

   a. he may be found to be in contempt of court.
   b. he may be served with a writ of mandamus.
   c. he may not be punished because a subpoena duces tecum does not require a party to produce documents.
   d. none of the above.

Court Procedures

PART B: Matching Sets

Matching Set 1

Match each fact statement (10-14) with the appropriate type of trial (A-B). Write the letter of your answer in the blank to the left of the number.

TYPES OF TRIALS

A. Jury Trial
B. Bench Trial

FACT STATEMENTS

___A___ 10. Requires voir dire.

___B___ 11. Does not require formal instructions of law.

___A___ 12. May result in judgment notwithstanding the verdict.

___A___ 13. Judge does not initially decide factual disputes or render verdict.

___A___ 14. Traditionally involves 12 persons, but may, in some states, involve fewer.

Matching Set 2

Match each fact statement (15-19) with the appropriate method of presenting evidence (A-D). Write the letter of your answer in the blank to the left of the number.

METHODS OF PRESENTING EVIDENCE

A. Direct Examination
B. Cross Examination
C. Stipulation
D. Physical Evidence

FACT STATEMENTS

__A__ 15. Conducted by the attorney representing the party who called the witness to testify.

__C__ 16. Agreed-upon statement of certain facts.

__D__ 17. Items that may be introduced into evidence with permission of the judge after certain legal requirements have been met.

__B__ 18. Questioning by the lawyer who did not call the witness to testify.

__C__ 19. Usually in the form of a written statement.

Court Procedures

Matching Set 3

Match each fact statement (20-24) with the appropriate type of damages (A-C). Write the letter of your answer in the blank to the left of the number.

TYPE OF DAMAGES

A. Compensatory Damages
B. Punitive Damages
C. Nominal Damages

FACT STATEMENTS

___B___ 20. May be awarded in addition to other damages.

___C___ 21. Awarded when the plaintiff fails to prove any loss.

___B___ 22. May be awarded when defendant's wrongful conduct was willful.

___A___ 23. Awarded to compensate plaintiff for actual loss.

___B___ 24. Designed to punish the defendant.

Matching Set 4

Match each fact statement (25-29) with the correct type of document (A-B). Write the letter of your answer in the blank to the left of the number.

DOCUMENTS

A. Summons
B. Subpoena

FACT STATEMENTS

~~A~~ B   25. Enforceable through contempt proceedings.

A   26. Notifies defendant that suit has been filed against him/her.

B   27. May be used to obtain presence of person at a deposition.

~~B~~ A   28. Is served with a copy of the complaint.

A   29. May be served by publication under certain circumstances.

Court Procedures

PART C: Case Problems

DIRECTIONS: For each of the questions relating to the case problems, select the best answer from the four alternatives. Write the letter of your answer in the blank to the left of the number.

Case 1
Sam decides to sue Ron for the tort of negligence after Ron's lawnmower threw a rock into the eye of Sam's dog, injuring the animal and requiring medical treatment.

___c___ 30. The most likely sequence of procedure is

    a. complaint, answer, summons, discovery.
    b. complaint, summons, discovery, answer.
    c. complaint, summons, answer, discovery.
    d. complaint, summons, pretrial, conference, answer.

___a___ 31. If Sam establishes Ron's liability, he will collect

    a. compensatory damages only.
    b. punitive damages only.
    c. nominal damages only.
    d. compensatory and punitive damages.

Case 2
During the course of an argument, Al struck Bob with a golf club, causing a severe gash in Bob's head.

___d___ 32. Al has committed

    a. a tort, but not a crime.
    b. a crime, but not a tort.
    c. neither a crime nor a tort.
    d. both a tort and a crime.

___d___ 33. Al will likely be ordered to pay

    a. compensatory, punitive, and nominal damages.
    b. compensatory and nominal damages.
    c. punitive damages, but not compensatory damages.
    d. compensatory damages and possibly punitive damages.

Chapter 2: Solutions

PART A: Multiple-Choice Questions

	Answers	Refer to Chapter Section
1.	(c)	[A-1-a(5)] Daron committed the tort of battery. He also committed the crime of battery. He may be sued for the tort. He may also be prosecuted for the crime. The two cases would progress through the court system independent of each other.
2.	(c)	[A-4-a(1) and (2)] A summons notifies the defendant that a suit has been filed against him or her. A motion is a request for a court order. Answers (a), (b), and (d) are correct statements.
3.	(a)	[A-4-a(4)] Service by publication is a means of serving a party who cannot be located. It consists of publishing a notice to the defendant in a newspaper of general circulation in the area of the defendant's last known address. Depositions, interrogatories, and subpoenas are discovery devices.
4.	(c)	[A-6-a and A-6-b] Depositions involve oral questions and answers whereas interrogatories are in writing.
5.	(a)	[A-8-b(2)] The jury-selection process is known as voir dire.
6.	(d)	[A-8-h(2)] Specific performance is a remedy that may be awarded in a breach of contract suit under limited circumstances. Answers (a), (b), and (c) each refer to a type of damages that could be awarded in a tort suit.
7.	(a)	[A-8-i(2) and (3)] The appellee is the party who is defending the appeal. The appellant is the party who seeks to have the appellate court reverse the trial court's judgment. Therefore, when the appellee prevails, the appellate court will affirm the trial court's ruling.
8.	(b)	[B-1] An injunction is a court order directing a party to do or to refrain from doing a certain act.
9.	(a)	[A-6-d(2) and A-6-d(3)] A party who willfully disobeys a subpoena may be found to be in contempt of court.

PART B: Matching Sets

Matching Set 1

10.	(A)	[A-8-b(2)]
11.	(B)	[A-8-g]
12.	(A)	[A-8-b(3)]
13.	(A)	[A-8-b(3)]
14.	(A)	[A-8-b(1)]

Matching Set 2

15.	(A)	[A-8-d(1)]
16.	(C)	[A-8-d(4)]
17.	(D)	[A-8-d(3)]
18.	(B)	[A-8-d(2)]
19.	(C)	[A-8-d(4)]

Matching Set 3

20.	(B)	[A-8-h(2)]
21.	(C)	[A-8-h(2)]
22.	(B)	[A-8-h(2)]
23.	(A)	[A-8-h(2)]
24.	(B)	[A-8-h(2)]

Matching Set 4

25.	(B)	[A-6-d(2)]
26.	(A)	[A-4-a(1)]
27.	(B)	[A-6-d(1)]
28.	(A)	[A-4-a]
29.	(A)	[A-4-a(4)]

Court Procedures

PART C: Case Problems

30. (c)   [A] The filing of the complaint begins the suit. The summons notifies the defendant of the suit and requires him/her to respond. The answer is the defendant's formal response. Discovery generally occurs after the answer has been filed.

31. (a)   [A-8-h(2)] Because Ron's conduct was not willful or outrageous, punitive damages will not be awarded. Nominal damages are awarded only when the plaintiff incurred no loss. In this case, Sam is entitled to compensatory damages to reimburse him for the medical bills.

32. (d)   [A-1] Al's act is both a tort (battery) and a crime. It may be the subject of two entirely different legal proceedings, a tort suit and a criminal prosecution.

33. (d)   [A-8-h(2)] Because Al's act was willful, he will likely be ordered to pay punitive as well as compensatory damages. Nominal damages are only awarded when there is no measurable loss by the plaintiff.

CHAPTER 3
Contracts

OVERVIEW

Modern business transactions involve numerous agreements--employment agreements; agreements to buy or sell goods; agreements to buy, sell, or lease land; and agreements to lend or borrow money, to name just a few. Not all agreements, however, are legally enforceable. The legal principles used to determine which agreements are enforceable are embodied in the law of contracts. This chapter presents a look at the major principles of contract law.

Although knowledge of the terms and principles presented in this chapter is essential to an understanding of contract law, mere knowledge is not enough for success on the examination. The candidate must be able to apply the principles of contract law to fact situations and determine whether a contract exists. In some cases it will also be necessary to determine what type of contract is involved and what remedies are available in the event the contract is breached.

DEFINITION OF TERMS

ACCEPTANCE. A clear expression by the offeree of agreement to the terms of the offer.

ASSIGNEE. One to whom an assignment is made.

ASSIGNMENT. A transfer of a contractual right to one who is not a party to the original contract.

ASSIGNOR. One who makes an assignment.

BILATERAL CONTRACT. A contract in which the parties make a bargained-for exchange of promises.

BREACH OF CONTRACT. A failure by a party to a contract to perform the duties imposed by the terms of the agreement.

COMMON LAW. A vast body of recorded cases that have been decided by courts (past decisions).

CONSIDERATION. The bargained-for exchange of something of value; an essential element of an enforceable contract.

CONTRACT. A legally enforceable agreement.

CONTRACTUAL CAPACITY. The ability to understand the subject matter and consequences of an agreement; only adults may possess this kind of capacity.

DELEGATION. A transfer of one's contractual duties to another party.

DISAFFIRMANCE. An expression by a person lacking contractual capacity of an intent not to be bound by the terms of an agreement.

DURESS. The use of a wrongful threat that causes a person to enter into an agreement which the person would otherwise have rejected.

EXPRESS CONTRACT. A contract in which the agreement is put into words, either written or oral.

FORMAL CONTRACT. One that complies with a specific form required by law for contracts of that particular type.

GRATUITOUS [...] consideration.

ILLUSORY PR[...] lly enforceable obligation upon [...]

IMPLIED CON[...] pressed by their conduct rather th[...]

NOVATION. A[...] other party from its contractual o[...] perform those duties.

OFFER. A com[...] ns of a specific proposed contra[...] the part of the intended recipie[...]

OFFEREE. On[...]

OFFEROR. On[...]

QUASI-CONT[...] not stem from the agreement betw[...] est in preventing an injustice.

RATIFICATION. An expression of an intent to be bound by the terms of an agreement that was entered into at a time when the party was lacking in contractual capacity. Ratification can only occur after capacity is attained.

RESTITUTION. A remedy for a breach of contract that involves the return of things received under the contract in an effort to put the parties in the position they were in before the contract.

REVOCATION. The withdrawal of an offer by the offeror.

SIMPLE CONTRACT. A contract that does not come within the narrow category

Contracts

of formal contracts.

STATUTE. A law passed by a legislative body.

UNIFORM COMMERCIAL CODE (UCC). A body of law that governs many commercial transactions; it has been adopted in every state. (Louisiana has adopted major parts of the UCC, but not all of it.)

UNILATERAL CONTRACT. A contract in which the offer is accepted by performance of the requested act. Only one promise is involved.

VOID CONTRACT. An attempt at forming a contract which failed due to the absence of an essential element.

VOIDABLE CONTRACT. A contract that may be set aside at the option of one of the parties.

A. Elements of a Contract

In order for an agreement to be a legally enforceable contract, five elements must be present. First, the agreement must be legal as to both subject matter and purpose. Second, there must be mutuality of agreement. Third, there must be legal consideration. Fourth, the parties to the agreement must have contractual capacity. Fifth, the agreement must conform to any specific, additional requirements imposed by statute.

1. *Legality:* Courts will not enforce illegal agreements. If the law were otherwise, the courts would actually be facilitating the breaking of the law. Consider the absurdity of a court enforcing the following agreement:

    EXAMPLE: Al agrees to pay Bob $50 in return for Bob's promise to break Chad's arm. Al cannot enforce this agreement by obtaining a court order directing Bob to perform as promised. Likewise, Bob, if he had actually broken Chad's arm, could not obtain a judgment against Al for the promised $50.

    a. *Subject matter:* Agreements may be found to be illegal for various reasons. The subject matter may be illegal.

       EXAMPLE: Alice agrees to sell a gram of cocaine to Barb for $200.

    b. *Purpose:* The purpose of the agreement may be illegal.

       EXAMPLE: Sam promises to pay Wally $100 in return for Wally's promise to testify falsely at Sam's criminal trial that Sam was visiting Wally in another city at the time the crime was committed. The purpose of this agreement is for Wally to commit perjury to assist Sam in defending himself against the charge.

    c. *Violation of statute:* The agreement may violate a statute.

EXAMPLE: Sally and Pam bet $100 on the outcome of a football game. Gambling is outlawed by a state statute. (Some states permit certain types of regulated gambling.)

EXAMPLE: Peter agrees to loan Paul $300 in return for Paul's promise to repay the $300 with 50 percent interest at the end of one year. Most states have usury statutes regulating the maximum amount of interest that may be charged. An agreement that requires the payment of interest in excess of the statutory maximum is illegal. (Such excess interest is called usury *or is said to be* usurious.*)*

EXAMPLE: Don hires Ed to remove a tumor surgically from Don's arm. Ed is not licensed to practice medicine. Each state has laws requiring that persons practicing trades or professions such as medicine, law, dentistry, architecture, building, and plumbing be licensed by the state. An agreement that requires an unlicensed party to perform such work is illegal.

d. *Public policy:* The agreement may be against public policy.

EXAMPLE: The Acme Catering Company, which provides food for wedding receptions and banquets, requires its customers to sign an agreement that relieves Acme of any liability resulting from its negligence in preparing or serving food. Such an exculpatory clause is illegal because it violates public policy. The public has an interest in ensuring that the food served at such functions is safe to eat. Removing liability from the preparer and server of the food takes away a major incentive for the exercise of due care and is likely to leave the injured parties without an effective legal remedy.

e. *Partial legality:* Some agreements are only partially illegal.

EXAMPLE: The Atlas Pharmaceutical Company agrees to sell 300 units of drug A and 300 units of drug B to the Hamilton Drug Stores, Inc. The federal Food and Drug Administration has banned the sale of drug A.

(1) If the legal portion of a partially illegal agreement can be severed from the illegal part, the court will probably enforce the legal portion.

EXAMPLE: The Atlas Pharmaceutical Company agrees to sell 300 units of drug A (illegal) for $600 and 300 units of drug B (legal) for $300 to Hamilton Drug Stores, Inc. The court will probably enforce the part of the agreement pertaining to the legal drug B. Because that part carried a separate price term, the contract is severable.

(2) If the agreement cannot be severed, no part of it will be enforced.

EXAMPLE: The Atlas Pharmaceutical Company agrees to sell 300 units of drug A (illegal) and 300 units of drug B (legal) to Hamilton Drug Stores, Inc. for $900. The court will not enforce any part of this agreement because the legal part cannot be severed from the illegal part since there is only one price for both drugs.

2. *Mutuality of Agreement:* In order for there to be a contract, the words or conduct of the parties must indicate that there is an agreement between them.

   a. *Intent of parties:* The law does not ordinarily delve into the minds of the parties to find what they actually were thinking; instead, it judges their intent from their words and conduct.

   EXAMPLE: Eunice, an elderly widow, offers to give her diamond necklace to Agnes in return for Agnes's promise to move into Eunice's home and care for Eunice for the next six months. Even if, in fact, Eunice had no intention of ever delivering the necklace to Agnes, Eunice has nevertheless entered into a binding contract. Her intent is judged by her words.

   EXAMPLE: Robert offers to pay David $10 in return for David's promise to mow Robert's lawn. Without saying anything, David began to mow Robert's lawn as Robert watched. After mowing half of Robert's lawn, David stopped mowing when Philip offered him more money to mow Philip's lawn. David claims he had no contract with Robert because he never said that he accepted Robert's offer. David's conduct, however, indicated that he accepted Robert's offer. There was mutual assent between Robert and David.

   b. *Mutual assent:* In some situations, even though it *appears* that there is mutual assent, underlying facts make it clear that the agreement of a party was not voluntary.

      (1) *Duress:* The expression of assent may be the result of duress. Duress is present when a party uses an improper threat to obtain another party's assent.

      EXAMPLE: Ed threatens to break Jim's arm unless Jim signs a contract. As a result of the threat, Jim signs the contract. If Ed sues Jim to enforce the contract, duress provides a valid defense for Jim.

(2) *Undue influence:* The expression of assent may be the result of undue influence. Undue influence is present when a party takes unfair advantage of the high level of trust and confidence another person has placed in him in order to obtain that person's expression of assent. For undue influence to apply, the relationship between the parties must be a close one built on trust.

EXAMPLE: Joan is an 86-year-old invalid who relies on her sister Jane to care for her and handle her financial affairs. Jane tells Joan to invest all of her savings in stock of the Green Company. Trusting Jane, Joan agrees to make the investment. Joan does not know that Jane and her husband operate the Green Company, which is deeply in debt. Joan's assent was obtained through undue influence. Joan, therefore, has a valid defense if Jane attempts to enforce the agreement.

(3) *Fraud:* The expression of assent may be the result of fraud.

   (a) Fraud requires that there be a false representation.

   (b) The false statement must be one of a fact, not of an opinion.

   (c) The falsely stated fact must be likely to influence the decision of the person to whom it is made. (In other words, the falsely stated fact must be material to the agreement.)

   (d) The false statement must be made by one who has knowledge of its falsity and intent to deceive.

   (e) The false statement must be justifiably relied on by the party to whom it was made.

   EXAMPLE: George offers to sell his airplane to Mel. George says to Mel, "I think you will really enjoy owning this plane." In fact, George does not believe Mel will enjoy owning the plane. There is no fraud because George's statement was one of opinion, not of fact.

   EXAMPLE: George offers to sell his airplane to Mel. George tells Mel that the plane has never been in a crash. In fact, the plane was damaged in a crash. George had the plane repaired. There is no apparent evidence of the earlier damage. If Mel agrees to buy the

Contracts

plane based upon George's statement, fraud has occurred and Mel can succeed in having the agreement set aside and may collect any damage from George. The court may also assess punitive damages against George because Mel relied on George's statement which was an intentional misrepresentation of an important fact.

(4) *Misrepresentation:* The expression of assent may be the result of *innocent misrepresentation*.

    (a) The elements of innocent misrepresentation are the same as those of fraud, with one exception. There is no requirement that the party making the statement know of its falsity.

        EXAMPLE: George offers to sell his airplane to Mel. George tells Mel that the plane has never been in a crash. Unknown to George the plane was in a crash before he purchased it. George has made an innocent misrepresentation.

    (b) The victim of innocent misrepresentation may succeed in having the agreement set aside but cannot collect punitive damages from the party making the representation.

(5) *Mutual mistake:* The expression of assent may be the result of a mutual mistake.

    (a) If both parties agreed to enter into an agreement based on a fundamental mistake as to the subject of the agreement, the contract may be set aside.

        EXAMPLE: Angie agrees to sell her motorcycle to Sara. Unknown to either party, the motorcycle was totally destroyed by fire the day before their agreement. Both parties mistakenly believed that the motorcycle was still in existence. Their mistake was a mutual one that went to the very subject matter of the agreement.

    (b) If the mistake is not mutual, it does not affect the expression of assent.

        EXAMPLE: Angie agrees to sell her motorcycle to Sara for $600. Angie mistakenly believes that the motorcycle has a market value of $600. In fact, it has a market value of $800. Angie's mistake does not affect the agreement.

> *It is not mutual. Moreover, it does not involve the fundamental nature of the subject matter but relates only to its value.*

3. *Consideration:* In order for there to be a contract, there must be a bargained-for exchange of something of value. The legal term for this requirement is *consideration.*

   a. *Exchange of value:* Consideration may consist of a party giving up a legal right in return for something else of value.

      EXAMPLE: Sue agrees to refrain from smoking any cigarettes for six months in return for Gail's promise to pay Sue $100 at the end of that time. Sue has given up her right to smoke, and Gail has promised to give up $100. Consideration is present.

      EXAMPLE: Adam has sued Ryan for striking him in the face and breaking his nose. Adam agrees to dismiss the suit in return for Ryan's promise to pay for his medical expenses. Adam has given up his legal right to pursue the case. Consideration is present.

   b. *Bargained-for exchange:* Without a bargained-for exchange, there can be no consideration.

      EXAMPLE: Feeling guilty for having injured Adam, Ryan promises to pay for Adam's medical expenses. Adam, in a gesture of forgiveness, promises to dismiss the suit he had filed against Ryan. There is no consideration. The promises were not exchanged. Each was made without a return promise.

   c. *Exchange of equal value not required:* The bargained-for exchange need not involve things of equal value in order to constitute consideration.

      EXAMPLE: Paul agrees to pay Dan $50 for a fishing pole which Dan had recently purchased for $3. The courts are not concerned with the adequacy of what a party gets under the terms of the agreement. The courts are only concerned that there be an exchange of something of some value.

   d. *Promise to pay for services already rendered:* A promise to pay for work already performed does not involve consideration.

      EXAMPLE: Upon returning from vacation and finding that his neighbor has trimmed his hedges, Frank promises to pay his neighbor $20. There is no consideration. At the time of Frank's promise the work had already been completed. Frank's promise is unenforceable.

Contracts 45

      e. *Preexisting legal duty:* A promise to pay someone to do what that person is already legally bound to do does not involve consideration.

          EXAMPLE: Dick promises to pay John $35 in return for John's promise not to break any of Dick's windows during the month of May. Breaking Dick's windows is a violation of the law. John is obligated to obey the law. Therefore, Dick's promise is not legally enforceable. He has merely promised to pay John to obey the law—something John is already obligated to do.

          EXAMPLE: Wilson contracted to paint James' house for $400. Wilson stopped painting when he was only half finished. He refused to continue unless James promised to pay him an additional $100. James made the promise. Wilson then finished painting the house. James is not legally obligated to pay the additional $100. His promise to pay it was not part of a bargained-for exchange of something of value because Wilson did nothing more than promise to do what he was already legally obligated to do. Wilson gave up nothing in return for the additional promise.

      f. *Illusory promise:* An illusory promise does not provide a basis for consideration. An illusory promise is one that does not impose an enforceable obligation on the promisor.

          EXAMPLE: In return for receiving a 10 percent discount, Joe of Joe's Ice Cream Parlour promises to purchase all of the ice cream he *wants* from Jake's Wholesale Company. Joe may avoid any further obligation by stating he does not want any more ice cream from Jake's. The result would be the same if Joe had used the word "desire" instead of "want."

      g. *Promise to buy one's needs:* A promise to buy all of one's *needs* or *requirements* can serve as a basis for consideration. Courts regard such a promise as being enforceable. A good faith requirement is imposed on the promisor. Needs or requirements can be determined with reasonable definiteness. The same is true of a promise to sell all of one's output to a particular customer.

4. *Capacity of Parties:* Both parties to a contract must have *contractual capacity* if the agreement is to be fully enforceable.

      a. *Age of majority:* In order to have contractual capacity, a party must have attained the age of majority. Anyone who has not attained that age is a minor. The age of majority at common law was 21 years of age. Today in nearly all states the age of majority is 18 years of age.

          (1) *Minor's right to void contract:* A minor who enters into a

contract has the right to avoid (to make void) the contract if he/she elects to do so. When this happens, the minor is said to have *disaffirmed* the contract.

(2) *Minor's right to enforce contract:* A minor who has entered into a contract with an adult has the right to enforce the contract against the adult.

EXAMPLE: Dennis, who is 16 years old, contracts with Curt, who is an adult. Under the terms of the contract, Dennis is to pay Curt $20 per month for 14 months in return for Curt's jukebox. Dennis may elect to disaffirm the contract. In doing so, he will return the jukebox and be free of any contractual obligation. Instead, Dennis might elect to treat the contract as a binding one. If Curt failed to deliver the jukebox, for instance, Dennis could enforce the agreement. Only the minor has the option of disaffirming the contract.

(3) *Return of contract items:* Upon disaffirming a contract, a minor must return to the adult anything the minor received under the contract. If the minor no longer has what was received, however, most courts will nevertheless allow the minor to disaffirm.

(4) *Reasonable time for disaffirmance:* A minor may disaffirm anytime during minority and within a reasonable time after reaching majority.

(5) *Contract for necessary items:* Upon disaffirming a contract for necessary items such as food, clothing, or emergency medical care, the minor must pay the reasonable value of the necessities.

(6) *Ratification of contract by minor:* One who entered a contract while a minor may *ratify* the contract upon reaching majority. Once the contract is ratified, it may no longer be disaffirmed.

   (a) *Words or actions:* Ratification may result from words or actions of the minor that indicate an intent to recognize the contract as an enforceable obligation.

   (b) *Majority:* Ratification can occur after the age of majority has been attained.

   EXAMPLE: Shirley, while 17 years old, entered into a contract to purchase a camera. Under the terms of the contract, she was to pay $15 per month for three years.

Contracts 47

> *Shirley made six monthly payments after her 18th birthday. Shirley will be deemed to have ratified the contract or, in the alternative, the court will find that more than a reasonable time has passed since she reached majority. Under either interpretation, Shirley can no longer disaffirm.*

    b. *Contractual capacity:* A party who has attained the age of majority is presumed to have contractual capacity. Not all adults, however, have contractual capacity. There are two types of situations in which an adult will be found to lack capacity.

        (1) *Mental deficiency:* A person who is unable to understand the nature of the contract because of mental deficiency lacks contractual capacity.

            (a) The mental deficiency must have existed at the time the contract was formed.

            (b) The mental deficiency must be more severe than a mere lacking of normal intelligence. It must deprive the person of the ability to understand the subject matter of the agreement and its consequences.

            (c) The lack of capacity need not be permanent.

        (2) *Intoxication:* A person who is so intoxicated by alcohol or drugs that he/she is incapable of understanding the nature of the contract lacks contractual capacity.

    c. *Disaffirmance of contract:* Adults who lack capacity because of mental deficiency or intoxication may disaffirm a contract if they are able to substantially restore the other party to the precontractual position. The contract is said to be voidable.

    d. *Ratification of contract:* One who entered a contract while suffering from incapacity because of mental deficiency or intoxication may ratify the contract after capacity is regained.

5. *Form Required by Law:* Specific statutes require that certain types of agreements be in writing or meet other special requirements as to form. The Statute of Frauds is discussed in Section E of this chapter. Other statutes vary from state to state and have narrow application in their coverage. Negotiable instruments are discussed in Chapter 5, Negotiable Instruments.

B. **Formation**

An agreement is usually formed with an offer and an acceptance.

1. *Offer:* An offer is a communication of an intent to be bound to the terms of a specific proposed contract. The communication invites acceptance on the part of the intended recipient. There are three basic requirements for a valid offer:

    a. *Intent:* An offer must express an intent to enter into a contract.

    EXAMPLE: Tom, whose new car has stalled at a busy intersection, says to Bill, "I will sell you this heap of junk for $10." There is no offer because Tom's words are uttered in anger and do not actually express an intent on his part to enter into such a contract.

    b. *Definite terms:* An offer must be sufficiently definite in its terms.

    EXAMPLE: If Tina says to Wilma, "I offer to sell you my typewriter," there is no valid offer. The communication lacks definiteness.

    c. *Communication of offer:* An offer must be communicated to the intended party.

    EXAMPLE: Tina writes a note, "Dear Wilma: I offer to sell you my only typewriter for $25." There can be no offer unless the note is communicated to Wilma.

    EXAMPLE: Ordinarily a catalog entry, newspaper advertisement, or magazine advertisement is regarded merely as an invitation for offers and is not itself regarded as an offer.

2. *Termination:* A valid offer may be terminated in the following ways:

    a. *Lapse of time:* If the expiration date contained in the offer has passed, the offer is terminated. If there is no express expiration date, the offer expires after the passage of a reasonable time.

    b. *Revocation:* As a general rule, the offeror may revoke the offer anytime prior to acceptance. There are three main exceptions to this rule:

       (1) *Option to purchase:* If the offeror has granted an option to purchase, the offer cannot be revoked for the period stated in the option. An option is a promise not to revoke an offer in return for something of value. Consideration must be present for there to be an option.

(2) *Firm offer:* If a merchant promises, in a signed writing, to hold open an offer to buy or sell goods for any period less than three months, the offer cannot be revoked during the stated time period. If the stated time period exceeds three months, the offer nevertheless becomes revocable after three months. This exception is known as the merchant's *firm offer*. It does not require consideration. Because this exception is statutory, each element must exist or the exception does not apply.

(3) *Reasonable time:* If the offeror should have known that the offeree would change his/her position in reliance on the offer for a unilateral contract, the offeror will not be allowed to revoke until the offeree has had a reasonable time to complete the performance.

> EXAMPLE: *Peggy says to Pat, "I will pay you $5,000 if you run all the way across the state." In reliance on the promise, Pat began to run across the state. After nearly 24 hours, Peggy announces that she is revoking the offer. Peggy must allow Pat a reasonable time to complete performance. Peggy should have known that Pat would rely on the offer. It would be unfair to allow her to revoke before Pat has an opportunity to complete his performance.*

c. *Rejection of offer:* When the offeree rejects the offer, the offer is terminated. A mere inquiry on the part of the offeree does not amount to a rejection.

EXAMPLE: *Mike says to Peter, "I offer to sell you my bicycle for $20." Peter responds, "$20 seems rather high. Would you consider $15?" Peter has not rejected the offer.*

(1) *Rejection:* The offeree rejects an offer when he/she expresses an unwillingness to accept the offered terms.

> EXAMPLE: *Mike says to Peter, "I offer to sell you my bicycle for $20." Peter responds, "No, I really don't want to buy it for that price." Peter has rejected the offer.*

(2) *Counteroffer:* A counteroffer by the offeree operates as a rejection. The counteroffer stops the original offer and starts a new offer.

> EXAMPLE: *Mike says to Peter, "I offer to sell you my bicycle for $20." Peter responds, "I offer you $15 for your bicycle." Peter has rejected the original offer, causing it to terminate. He has also made an offer of his own, known as a counteroffer.*

d. *Death or insanity:* The death or insanity of either party automatically terminates the offer (unless there is a valid option in effect).

e. *Destruction of subject matter:* If the subject matter of the offer is destroyed, the offer is automatically terminated.

f. *Illegality of the offer:* If an offer that is legal when made later becomes illegal because of a change in the law, the offer is terminated.

> EXAMPLE: *The Metropolis Mineral Company offers to sell four grams of cryptonite to Luthor for $20,000. Before Luthor accepts, however, the legislature enacts a law outlawing the sale of cryptonite. The offer is terminated at the time the law becomes effective.*

3. *Acceptance:* A clear expression by the offeree to the offeror of an agreement to the terms of the offer constitutes an acceptance.

   a. *Clarity of acceptance:* An acceptance must be positive and clear.

   b. *Acceptance of terms of offer:* An acceptance cannot vary the terms of the offer in any way. Common law requires that the acceptance "mirror" the terms of the offer.

      (1) *Counteroffer:* An attempted acceptance that varies from the terms of the offer will likely be interpreted as a counteroffer, which terminates the original offer.

      (2) *Battle of forms:* The Uniform Commercial Code (UCC) greatly relaxes the mirror-image requirement of the common law where the sale of goods is involved. Under its battle of forms section, the UCC provides that when the sale of goods is involved, the acceptance need not mirror the terms of the offer so long as the intent to accept the terms offered is clearly expressed. This means that the offeree can add terms, modify terms, or ask that terms be deleted so long as the acceptance is not made *conditional* on the requested changes becoming part of the contract.

         > EXAMPLE: *Company A writes to Company B, "We offer you 1,000 business cards of the quality of the enclosed sample with your letterhead imprinted for $50." Company B responds, "We accept your offer if you will include two card-carrying cases as shown on page 44 of your catalog." There is no contract. Even under the UCC's liberalized rule, the attempted acceptance fails because the offeree made acceptance conditional on the additional term. Use of words such*

as "if" or "provided that" or "so long as" have the effect of making acceptance conditional.

> EXAMPLE: Company A writes to Company B, "We offer you 1,000 business cards with your letterhead imprinted for $50." Company B responds, "We accept your offer. Include two card-carrying cases as shown on page 44 of your catalog." There is a contract for the 1,000 cards. The acceptance is not conditional. The reference to the cases is a proposal which Company A is free to reject. (For further discussion of the "battle of forms" provision, see Chapter 4, Sales, Section B-3-c.)

c. *Communication of acceptance:* If an acceptance is sent through an authorized means of communication, it is effective upon being sent. If it is sent through an unauthorized means of communication, it is not effective until it is received.

   (1) *Authorized means of communication:* Any means of communication specifically approved by the offeror is authorized. Unless the offeror indicates otherwise, any reasonable means of communication that is at least as reliable and as prompt as that used by the offeror is an authorized means. Thus, the offeree should use the same or better means of communication than the offeror used.

   > EXAMPLE: Pam writes to Diane, "I offer to sell you my typewriter for $30." The offer is mailed on May 1. On May 3 Diane receives the offer and writes, "I accept." The acceptance is mailed on May 3. On May 4 Pam mails a note to Diane in which she says, "I revoke my offer." On May 5 Pam receives Diane's acceptance. On May 6 Diane receives Pam's attempted revocation. There is a contract. The acceptance, having been sent through an authorized means of communication, is effective upon being sent (May 3). The revocation cannot be effective until it is received. Because it was received after the acceptance had become effective, it is of no consequence.

   > EXAMPLE: Pam writes to Diane, "I offer to sell you my typewriter for $30. Your acceptance must be by phone on or before May 5." Diane writes, "I accept." Diane mails the acceptance on May 4. Pam receives the acceptance on May 6. There is no contract. The acceptance was not effective upon being sent because the mail was not an authorized means of acceptance according to the terms of the offer.

   (2) *Receipt of first communication:* If the offeree first responds

by sending a rejection and follows by sending an acceptance, the acceptance is not effective upon being sent. The first communication received by the offeror is effective.

EXAMPLE: Pam writes to Diane on May 1, "I offer to sell you my typewriter for $30." On May 3 Diane receives the offer and writes, "I will not pay $30. I offer you $20." On May 4 Diane writes, "I accept your offer of May 1." On May 5 Pam receives Diane's rejection. On May 6 Pam receives Diane's acceptance. There is no contract. The rejection was effective upon receipt. It terminated the offer.

    d. *Silence as acceptance:* Ordinarily, silence will not constitute an acceptance. Under some special circumstances, however, silence may be interpreted as an expression of acceptance.

EXAMPLE: The Supreme Carpeting Company employed Jack as a salesperson. Although Jack had no authority to bind the company to a contract, his job was to solicit orders. Jack solicited an order from Irv for carpeting for a large office building owned by Irv. Jack assisted Irv in filling out the detailed order form, and Jack carried the form back to the company's headquarters for approval. Supreme held Irv's order for eight weeks without acting on it. The court will probably find a contract was formed between Irv and the Supreme Company. Irv's order was an offer. Because Supreme's salesperson solicited the offer, under the circumstances Supreme was obligated to respond to Irv within a reasonable time. The company's silence is interpreted as acceptance of the offer.

C.   **Types of Contracts**

The basic types of contracts are quasi contracts, unilateral contracts, bilateral contracts, express contracts, implied contracts, formal contracts, and simple contracts.

    1. *Quasi Contract:* The so-called quasi contract is not a contract in the true sense because there is no mutual assent. The law imposes an obligation under some circumstances where there is no agreement between the parties to prevent an injustice from occurring. Frequently a quasi contract is found to exist to prevent unjust enrichment of a party.

EXAMPLE: Neal owed $100 to Mike for the repayment of a loan from Mike. Without knowing that Mike had moved, Neal went to Mike's former apartment. Finding no one home, Neal placed the $100 in a plain folder and left it inside the door. Ozzi, the new occupant of the apartment, returned home later and found the money. Upon discovering what happened, Neal demands that Ozzi return the money. The law *imposes a duty on Ozzi to return the money to Neal. Ozzi would be unjustly enriched if he were allowed to keep the money.*

2. *Unilateral Contract:* A unilateral contract is one in which the offer is accepted by performance of the requested act. In a unilateral contract the offer invites acceptance only by performance of the requested act, not by a return promise.

   EXAMPLE: *Tim's dog, Lassie, has disappeared. Tim offers to pay $100 to anyone who returns Lassie to him. Jeff learns of the offer and promises Tim that he will find the dog and return it. There is no contract. The offer can only be accepted by actual performance. If Jeff returns Lassie to Tim, there is a unilateral contract.*

3. *Bilateral Contract:* A bilateral contract involves an exchange of promises. The offer is accepted by a return promise from the offeree. Unless the offer provides that acceptance is to be by actual performance, a promise to perform will usually suffice as an acceptance.

   EXAMPLE: *Jean says to Debbie: "I offer you $10 to shovel my sidewalk. Will you agree to do it?" Debbie says, "Yes, I accept." A bilateral contract has been formed. Jean invited acceptance by return promise.*

   If it is not clear whether an offer is for a unilateral or bilateral contract, the courts will find a bilateral contract was intended.

4. *Express Contract:* An express contract is one in which the parties express their agreement in words. It may be written or oral.

5. *Implied Contract:* An implied contract is one in which the parties' agreement is expressed by their conduct instead of by their words.

   EXAMPLE: *Harold drove his car to a self-service gas station. Without saying a word, he filled his tank with gasoline. The station attendant watched as Harold pumped the gasoline. By their conduct, the parties formed an implied contract for the sale of the gasoline. By his actions, Harold promised to pay the listed price of the gasoline he pumped into his tank.*

6. *Formal Contract:* A formal contract is one that complies with a specific form required by law for contracts of that particular type. Negotiable instruments, for instance, must meet certain specific requirements. (See Chapter 5, Negotiable Instruments.)

7. *Simple Contract:* All contracts that do not come within the narrow category of formal contracts are called simple contracts.

D. Statute of Limitations

The law of each state establishes a time period within which suits for breach of contract must be brought. If the suit is not brought within the relevant time period following the breach, the right to sue for a remedy is lost. A typical statute of limitations requires that a suit based on an oral contract must be brought within five years of the breach and that a suit based on breach of a written contract must be brought within ten years of the breach.

E. Statute of Frauds

The law that requires certain types of contracts to be in writing is generally known as the *statute of frauds*. When the statute of frauds applies, the contract cannot be enforced in court unless it is in writing and signed by the party being sued.

1. *Sale of Land:* Contracts for the sale of land are covered by the statute of frauds.

2. *Sale of Goods:* A contract for the sale of goods for $500 or more requires a writing.

3. *Promise in Consideration of Marriage:* A promise to give goods or money in return for a promise to marry must be in writing to be enforceable.

    EXAMPLE: *Jones says to Anderson, "If you marry me, I will give you $10,000." Jones' promise is not enforceable unless it is in writing and signed by Jones.*

4. *Promise to Perform for Another Party:* A promise to be responsible for the obligation of another party must be in a signed writing to be enforceable. (This promise is called a *surety promise*.)

    EXAMPLE: *Sam accompanies Wilbur to the bank and tells the banker, "Give Wilbur the loan he wants. If he fails to pay, I will pay." Sam's promise is not enforceable unless it is in writing and signed by him.*

    EXAMPLE: *Gary accompanies Herman into a clothing store and tells the clerk, "Give him the shirt he wants. I will pay." Gary's promise need not be in writing to be enforceable because he has assumed direct responsibility for the debt. Had he said, "If he does not pay, I will," a writing would be required because his obligation would be secondary or indirect.*

5. *Contracts That Cannot Be Performed within One Year:* Contracts that cannot be performed within one year are covered by the statute of frauds.

Contracts

      a. *Time for contract performance:* The time runs from the time the contract is entered into, not from the time actual performance is to take place.

      EXAMPLE: On May 1 Tina hires Melba to work in Tina's store for six months beginning on January 2. The contract must be in writing because it cannot be performed within one year from the date it was made.

      b. *Contract performance within one year:* If the contract could possibly be performed within one year, it is not covered by the statute of frauds.

      EXAMPLE: David hired Phil to write a dictionary. Even though it is most unlikely that the dictionary can be completed within the year, it is possible. The contract, therefore, is not covered by the statute of frauds. Here the law considers possibilities, *not* probabilities.

6. *Promise of Responsibility for Obligation of Estate:* A promise from one who is the court-appointed manager of the estate of a deceased person to be personally responsible for an obligation of the estate must be in writing and signed.

EXAMPLE: James died while owing money to Bob. James's son, James Jr., was appointed by the court to manage his deceased father's estate. The estate does not have enough money to pay the debt owed to Bob. James Jr. promised to pay the debt himself. His promise is not enforceable unless it is in writing and signed by him.

F. Assignment of Rights and Delegation of Duties

Sometimes a person who was not a party to the formation of the original contract acquires rights or undertakes responsibilities provided for in the contract.

1. *Assignment:* An assignment is a transfer of a contract right to one who is not a party to the contract. One who makes assignment is known as an *assignor*. One to whom an assignment is made is known as an *assignee*.

      a. *Assignable contract rights:* Most contract rights are assignable. The law provides, however, that certain rights are nonassignable. The contract may state that it is nonassignable. The prohibition on assignment of certain types of rights is for the protection of the nonassigning party to the contract.

(1) An assignment that materially increases the burden or risk of the nonassigning party is prohibited.

EXAMPLE: The Acme Pest Control Company contracted with Tim to spray Tim's house each time a roach was discovered. Tim is not permitted by law to assign his rights under the contract to Joe who owns a house in a different location. Such an assignment changes the risk of Acme. It was willing to make such a contract regarding Tim's house but may not have been willing to enter such a contract for Joe's home. Moreover, if Joe's home is larger or considerably farther away from Acme's headquarters, Acme's burden of performance would also be increased.

(2) Rights that are highly personal in nature cannot be assigned.

EXAMPLE: Dr. Jones contracted to perform cosmetic surgery on Myron's face for $2,000. Myron cannot assign his rights under such a contract.

EXAMPLE: Hank, a lawyer, contracted to make a will for Wilma. Wilma cannot assign her rights to another person.

(3) An assignment that is specifically outlawed by a statute cannot legally be made. For instance, some statutes prohibit wage assignments.

(4) A mere statement in a contract that there can be no assignment does not necessarily mean that no assignment can be made. The assignor would be in breach of the contract and, therefore, liable for any damages caused to the nonassigning party, but an assignment could still be made.

b. *Gratuitous assignment:* The law does not require that there be consideration in order for an assignment to be valid. An assignment made without consideration is known as a *gratuitous assignment*.

EXAMPLE: Jake owes $100 to Sandra. Sandra assigns her right to receive the money to Carla. Even though there was no bargained-for exchange between Sandra and Carla, the assignment is nevertheless valid.

c. *Enforcement of assigned rights:* The assignee can enforce the assigned rights against the nonassigning party.

EXAMPLE: Al contracted to purchase a boat from Bob for $300. Bob delivered the boat to Al. Under the contract Al was obligated to pay the purchase price within six months. Bob assigns right to receive the $300 to Carl. If Al fails to pay within the six-month period, Carl can sue Al to enforce his right to receive the money.

(1) *Full performance of contractual duties:* If the nonassigning party has already rendered full performance of the contractual duties to the assignor, the assignee cannot require a second performance of them.

(2) *Notification to nonassigning party:* If, however, the nonassigning party has been notified of the assignment and still renders performance to the assignor, he/she may be required to perform again for the assignee.

EXAMPLE: Wanda owes $50 to Gloria. Gloria assigns her right to receive the money to Sally. Before being notified of the assignment, Wanda pays the $50 to Gloria. Wanda has a good defense against a suit brought by Sally. If Wanda had paid the money to Gloria after receiving notice of the assignment, Wanda would not have a valid defense to a suit brought by Sally.

(3) *Assignment of contract rights only:* The assignor cannot assign greater rights than he has under the contract. The assignee merely stands in the shoes of the assignor.

2. *Delegation:* A delegation is a transfer of one's contractual obligation to another person. It may involve all of one's obligations under a contract or only part of them.

   a. *Nondelegation of duties:* Some duties may not be delegated.

   (1) *Duties requiring skill or judgment:* Duties that involve the exercise of skill or judgment cannot be delegated.

   EXAMPLE: Wayne hired Omar to paint a portrait of Wayne. Omar cannot delegate his duty to paint the portrait because it involves a special skill.

   EXAMPLE: Roger hired Bill to serve as the chief strategist for Roger's political campaign. Bill cannot delegate his duties because they require the exercise of judgment.

   EXAMPLE: Curt hired Daryl to mow Curt's lawn. Daryl can delegate his duty because it does not require special skill or judgment.

   (2) *Delegation prohibited by contract:* If delegation is prohibited

Contracts

in the contract, a party cannot delegate duties.

  b. *Novation:* The delegating party remains responsible for performance of the contractual duties unless there is a novation. If the nondelegating party expressly agrees to release the delegating party from further responsibility and accepts the delegating party's promise to perform, <mark>a novation has occurred.</mark>

  EXAMPLE: The Gold Star Disposal Company contracted with Dan to pick up and remove garbage from Dan's farm house twice per week. Gold Star delegated this duty to the Victory Disposal Company. Victory failed to pick up Dan's garbage. Dan can successfully sue Gold Star because the delegation did not relieve Gold Star of its contractual obligations.

  EXAMPLE: Assume in the above situation that Dan had expressly agreed to release Gold Star from its obligations in return for Victory's promise to perform the same duties. Dan could then successfully sue only Victory.

G. **Breach of Contracts—Remedies**

When a party fails to perform its contractual obligations, the issue of what constitutes an appropriate remedy becomes relevant. A party breaches a contract when, without justification, it fails to perform its obligations under the terms of the agreement. The nonbreaching party is entitled to a remedy as compensation for the loss suffered as a result of the breach. The most commonly sought remedies are money damages, specific performance, and restitution.

  1. *Money Damages:* The nonbreaching party may sue to recover the amount of money required to put the property in as good a position as it would have been in had there been no breach (that is, had the contract been performed as promised).

  EXAMPLE: Howard contracted to paint Don's car for $300. Howard failed to paint the car. Don hired someone else to paint the car for $450. Assuming that $450 was a reasonable price negotiated in good faith, Don is entitled to recover $150 from Howard.

    a. *Nominal damages:* If a party cannot prove that a loss was suffered as a result of the breach, only nominal damages are awarded. Nominal damages are a small amount, often one dollar, which the court grants to recognize that a breach of contract did in fact occur, but that no real loss was proven.

    EXAMPLE: If in the above situation Don hired someone else to *paint his car for $300, he could only recover from Howard the value of the time and effort he expended to find someone else to paint the car.*

    b. *Liquidated damages:* At the time they enter into the contract, the parties may agree on the money damages to be paid in the event of a breach. These predetermined damages are known as *liquidated damages*. The courts will enforce a liquidated-damages clause only if the stated damages bear a close relationship to those which could be reasonably expected to occur in the event of a breach. If the liquidated-damages clause amounts to a penalty for the breaching party further than an attempt to compensate the nonbreaching party reasonably, it will not be enforced.

2. *Specific Performance:* The nonbreaching party may sue for a court order requiring the breaching party to perform its contractual duties. In order to obtain specific performance, the nonbreaching party must convince the court that no amount of money damages will put it in the position it would have been in had there been no breach.

EXAMPLE: Cindy contracted to sell her home to Paula. Cindy breached the contract. If Paula sues for specific performance to require Cindy to complete the sale, Paula will succeed. The law recognizes that no two pieces of land are the same and, therefore, money damages would be inadequate. Given any amount of money, Paula could not buy property the same as Cindy's.

EXAMPLE: George contracted to sell 20 pounds of salt to Myron for $20. If George breaches the contract, Myron will not succeed in obtaining specific performance because money damages would be adequate.

3. *Restitution:* The nonbreaching party may sue to require the breaching party to return what it received under the contract.

EXAMPLE: Linda contracted to sell her antique bicycle to Floyd for $800. Under the terms of the agreement, Floyd took possession of the bicycle and was to pay the purchase price in four installments. Floyd breached the contract by failing to make the payments. Linda may sue for restitution and recover the bicycle from Floyd.

EXAMPLE: Ann contracted to purchase a gold ring from Bernice. In compliance with the terms of the contract, Ann paid $400 for the ring. Bernice breached the contract by failing to deliver the ring. Ann may sue for restitution and recover the $400 she paid to Bernice.

Chapter 3: Review Questions

PART A: Multiple-Choice Questions

DIRECTIONS: Select the best answer from the four alternatives. Write your answer in the blank to the left of the number.

_____d_____ 1. George is employed by the City of Greenville as a street commissioner. In the course of his work for the city, George uses a concrete mixing machine owned by the city. Bob, a citizen of a nearby town, offered to rent the machine from George for one day at a cost of $150. When George rejected the offer because he feared losing his job for leasing city property to an unauthorized person in violation of a city ordinance, Bob offered to pay a rental of $250. George accepted the offer. Bob returned the machine after using it, but he refused to pay the $250 to George. If George sues Bob to enforce the contract

    a. George will succeed in collecting the $250.
    b. George will succeed in collecting only a reasonable amount.
    c. George will succeed in collecting the fair rental value of the equipment.
    d. George will not succeed in collecting anything from Bob.

_____c_____ 2. For months Matt has attempted to purchase an antique car owned by Paul. Matt's latest offer of $5,000 was rejected by Paul. The next day Matt observed Paul leaving a theater which was showing an X-rated movie. Matt took a picture of Paul and threatened to circulate the picture at Paul's workplace if Paul did not contract to sell the car to Matt. Fearing that he would lose his job if the picture was circulated, Paul signed a contract to sell the car to Matt for $5,500. When Paul refused to deliver the car, Matt sued him for breach of contract.

    a. Matt will win because the agreement is in writing and signed by Paul.
    b. Paul will win because his agreement was obtained by fraud.
    c. Paul will win because his signature was obtained by duress.
    d. Paul will win because his signature was obtained by undue influence.

_a_

3. Jane offered to sell her television to Becky for $200. Jane told Becky that the television was two years old and that a new picture tube had just been installed. Relying on these statements, Becky agreed to purchase the television. Two days later Becky learned that the set had its original picture tube. Becky sues Jane, seeking the return of the sale price.

   a. Becky will succeed in having the sale set aside. She must return the set, and Jane must return the $200.
   b. Becky will not succeed in recovering the money because the agreement involved a mutual mistake.
   c. Becky will not succeed in recovering the money because of the legal principle of "buyer beware."
   d. Becky could only succeed in recovering the money if she is a minor.

_d_

4. Mona, who is a nurse, offered her friend Rona $100 if Rona would lose 25 pounds. Mona showed Rona a study that indicated that weight loss would improve her health. Rona accepted Mona's offer. She lost 25 pounds. Mona, however, refused to pay Rona the $100. Mona claims the weight loss was good for Rona but that she received no benefit from it. Rona sues Mona to collect the $100.

   a. Mona will win the suit because there was no consideration.
   b. Mona will win the suit because the agreement violates public policy.
   c. Mona will win the suit because there was no bargained-for exchange of something of value.
   d. Rona will win.

_d_

5. Judy's mother was hospitalized from May 1 to June 1 while Judy was in Europe on business. Upon her return to town, Judy visited the hospital. She told the head of the hospital's billing department that she was so thankful her mother had been properly cared for over that month that she would pay the bill if her mother failed to pay. Later, however, Judy refused ta pay the bill. The hospital brings suit against Judy based on her promise to pay.

   a. The hospital will win because there was no consideration.
   b. The hospital will win because Judy promised to answer for the debt of another person.
   c. Judy will win because undue influence is present.
   d. Judy will win because there was no consideration.

Contracts

___a___

6. Bill hired Jim to panel Bill's basement. The written contract provided that Jim would remove the wallpaper and install a specified kind of paneling for $1,700 including labor. After Jim had removed the wallpaper and paneled half of the basement, he refused to complete the job unless Bill promised to pay him an additional $100. Jim realized the job was taking longer than expected. Bill promised to pay the additional $100. Upon completion of the work, however, Bill refused to pay the extra $100. Jim sues Bill to collect the $100.

   a. Bill will win because there was no consideration.
   b. Bill will win because the agreement to pay the $100 was illegal.
   c. Jim will win because there was a mutual mistake as to how long the job would take.
   d. Jim will win because Bill is guilty of fraud in promising to pay the $100 which he never intended to pay.

___c___

7. The accountancy firm of Wilson, Jones, and Smith contracted to purchase all pencils which the firm needed for the coming year from the Sharp Pencil Company at a price of 7 cents per pencil. One month into the year covered by the contract the firm began purchasing pencils from another company at 5 cents per pencil. Sharp sues the firm for breach of contract.

   a. Sharp will lose because the firm's promise was illusory.
   b. Sharp will lose because there was no consideration.
   c. Sharp will win because the firm's promise is enforceable.
   d. Sharp will win because the firm is guilty of fraudulent misrepresentation.

___b___

8. Mike who is 15 years old contracted to buy a set of golf clubs for $85 from Sam who is 45 years of age.

   a. The contract is void.
   b. The contract is voidable by Mike.
   c. The contract is voidable by Sam.
   d. The contract is voidable by either Sam or Mike.

___d___

9. Rick who is 15 years of age ran away from home. He checked into a hotel one evening when the temperature dropped to 10 degrees. The next day Rick notified the hotel clerk that he was a minor and claimed that he owed the hotel nothing because he was disaffirming the contract. The hotel clerk argued that Rick was legally obligated to pay the $92 per night fee which the hotel charges all its guests. Who is correct?

   a. Rick is correct. The law allows him to disaffirm.
   b. The hotel clerk is correct. Because lodging was a necessary item to Rick, he is obligated to pay the contract price.
   c. The hotel clerk is correct. Rick's minority is irrelevant.
   d. Neither party is correct.

___d___ 10. Mary, a 17-year-old high school student, contracted to purchase stereo equipment from National Sales. Under the terms of the contract, Mary was to pay $10 per month for 45 months. After reaching 18, the age of majority in her state, Mary continued making the monthly payments for another five months. Mary then notified National that she was disaffirming the contract, National argues that Mary cannot disaffirm.

   a. National is correct because a minor can disaffirm only during minority.
   b. National is correct because Mary ratified the contract upon making the first payment after her 16th birthday.
   c. National is correct because the stereo equipment is a necessity.
   d. National is correct because Mary has ratified the contract.

___a___ 11. Jack wrote a note to Todd which read, "Todd, I offer to sell you my calculator for $10. (Signed) Jack." Jack placed the note on a table in his own home. Later that evening Todd made an unannounced visit to Jack's house. While Jack was in the kitchen getting refreshments, Todd found the note and read it. When Jack reentered the room, Todd laid out a $10 bill and said, "I accept." Is there a contract?

   a. No, because there was no valid offer.
   b. No, because there was no valid acceptance.
   c. No, because there was no consideration.
   d. Yes, there is a contract.

 12. Alice, a college professor, offered to sell her desk to Brenda for $350. Alice promised to hold the offer open for one week. The next day, however, Alice sold the desk to Rupert for $420. When Alice told Brenda of the sale later that same day, Brenda took $350 to Alice and said, "I accept your offer." Brenda claims she has contracted to purchase the desk. Alice claims the offer to Brenda has been revoked. Who is correct?

   a. Brenda is correct. Alice was legally obligated to hold the offer open for a week as promised.
   b. Alice is correct. The offer was revoked when Alice told Brenda of the sale.
   c. Alice is correct. The offer was revoked when Alice refused to take Brenda's $350.
   d. Brenda is correct. Alice's offer was a firm offer which cannot be revoked for three months.

Contracts 65

_____ c _____

13. Sally, a book company sales agent, wrote to Tom, a book store purchasing agent, "I offer to sell you 300 volumes of *How to Become a Millionaire* for $900. This offer will remain open for two months. (Signed) Sally." A week later, however, before Tom had responded to the offer, Sally phoned Tom and told him that she revoked the offer. Tom argues that Sally cannot revoke for the two-month period. Sally claims she can revoke any time prior to acceptance. Who is correct?

   a. Sally is correct.
   b. Tom is correct because there was a valid option.
   c. Tom is correct because there was a merchant's firm offer.
   d. Neither party is correct. Sally can revoke after the passage of a reasonable time.

_____ d _____

14. Alex said to Barry, "I offer to sell you this briefcase for $30." Barry responded, "I offer you $25 for it." Alex said, "No, that is not enough." Barry then said, "O.K., I accept your offer." Is there a contract at this point?

   a. Yes, there is a contract.
   b. No, because there is no consideration.
   c. No, because the offer was not in writing.
   d. No, because the offer had terminated before Barry's attempted acceptance.

_____ d _____

15. Frank wrote to Jenny, "I offer to sell you my lawn mower for $50." Jenny wrote back, "I accept. Include a gallon of gasoline." Is there a contract?

   a. No, because the attempted acceptance does not match the terms of the offer.
   b. No, because the parties are not merchants.
   c. Yes, because the acceptance was mailed.
   d. Yes, because the acceptance was not conditional.

_____ c _____

16. On May 1 Sandy wrote to Burt, "I offer to sell you my banjo for $50." On May 3 Burt received Sandy's offer and wrote back, "I accept your offer." On May 4 Sally sold the banjo to Ed. She phoned Burt on May 4 and told him the offer was revoked. On May 5 Sandy received Burt's letter of acceptance. Is there a contract between Sandy and Burt?

   a. No, because the offer was revoked before the acceptance was received.
   b. No, because performance became impossible when Sandy sold the banjo to Ed on May 4.
   c. Yes, because the acceptance became effective on May 3.
   d. Yes, because the offer was made prior to May 3.

___d___ 17. On June 1 Al wrote to Bob, "I offer to sell you my window fan for $25." On June 3 Bob received Al's offer and wrote to Al, "No, thank you. Your price is higher than I can pay." On June 4 Bob changed his mind and wrote to Al, "I accept your offer." On June 5 Al received Bob's letter of rejection. On June 6 Al received Bob's letter of acceptance. Is there a contract between Al and Bob?

   a. Yes, because the acceptance was effective upon being mailed.
   b. Yes, because the offer had not been terminated on June 6 when the acceptance was received.
   c. No, because the rejection was effective when mailed on June 3.
   d. No, because the rejection was effective on June 5 before the acceptance was received.

___a___ 18. Mike lost his watch. He placed an ad in the local newspaper which read, "I offer $20 to anyone who returns my watch to me." It included a description of the watch and his address. Ken read the ad and later found the watch. He returned it to Mike and collected the reward. What kind of contract existed between Mike and Ken?

   a. Unilateral contract
   b. Bilateral contract
   c. Quasi contract
   d. Formal contract

___d___ 19. Curt agreed to purchase a small strip of land from Dick for $499. The agreement was not put in writing. Curt later denied that he had made such an agreement. Dick sues Curt to enforce the agreement.

   a. Dick will win. The contract need not be in writing because less than $500 is involved.
   b. Dick will win. The statute of frauds does not apply to sales of land.
   c. Curt will win because there was no consideration.
   d. Curt will win because the agreement was not in writing and signed by him.

_____ 20. Clyde owned and operated a restaurant. He contracted to purchase 400 dozen plates from Susan. Susan failed to deliver the plates. Clyde sues Susan. Clyde seeks specific performance. Will the court order specific performance?

   a. Yes.
   b. Yes, but only if Clyde proves that Susan breached the contract.
   c. No, because specific performance cannot be awarded in a breach of contract suit.
   d. Yes, but only if money damages are inadequate.

Contracts

PART B: Matching Sets

Matching Set 1

Match each fact statement (21-24) with the appropriate element of a valid contract (A-D). Write the letter of your response in the blank to the left of the number.

ELEMENTS

A. Consideration
B. Capacity
C. Legality
D. Mutuality of Assent

FACT STATEMENTS

___B___ 21. Requires attainment of age of 18 and freedom from mental deficiency.

___D___ 22. An agreement between the parties.

___C___ 23. Applies to both subject matter and purpose.

___A___ 24. A bargained-for exchange of something of value.

Matching Set 2

Match each fact statement (25-28) with the appropriate legal term (A-D). Write the letter of your response in the space to the left of the number.

LEGAL TERMS

A. Duress
B. Undue Influence
C. Fraud
D. Misrepresentation

FACT STATEMENTS

__B__ 25. Taking unfair advantage of a high level of trust in a close relationship.

__C__ 26. An intentionally false statement of a significant fact.

__D__ 27. An innocently false statement of a significant fact.

__A__ 28. An improper threat used to obtain assent.

Matching Set 3

Match each fact statement (29-32) with the appropriate type of contract (A-D). Write the letter of your response in the blank to the left of the number.

TYPES OF CONTRACTS

A. Quasi
B. Unilateral
C. Bilateral
D. Implied

FACT STATEMENTS

__C__ 29. An exchange of promises.

__A__ 30. Lacks mutual assent, but prevents unjust enrichment.

__D__ 31. Conduct rather than words expresses the agreement.

__B__ 32. Performance of the requested act constitutes acceptance of the offer.

Contracts

Matching Set 4

Match each fact statement (33-36) with the correct remedy (A-C). Write the letter of your response in the space to the left of the number.

REMEDIES

A. Money Damages
B. Specific Performance
C. Restitution

FACT STATEMENTS

___C___ 33. A return by the party who breached a contract of that which it received under the contract.

___A___ 34. An amount calculated to place the nonbreaching party in as good a position as it would have been in had there been no breach.

___B___ 35. A court order requiring the breaching party to carry out its contractual duties.

___B___ 36. Awarded only after a showing that money damages would be inadequate.

PART C: Case Problems

DIRECTIONS: For each of the questions relating to the case problems, select the best answer from the four alternatives. Write the letter of your answer in the blank to the left of the number.

Case 1

Ted and Mary were robbed of all their cash and belongings while vacationing in a large city. Since they had left home without traveler's checks or credit cards, they contacted Jane, a friend who lived in the city. On her way to work Jane accompanied Ted to a camera shop and told the proprietor, "Let him pick out any camera under $300, and I will pay for it on the way back home this afternoon." She then took Mary to a clothing store and told the clerk, "Mary will select the clothes she wants up to $400. If she doesn't pay, I will." The next day she accompanied Mary to a furniture store where Mary ordered an $800 couch to be delivered in 30 days. Jane told the salesperson, "I will pay for it."

_____a_____ 37. Assume the camera shop sues Jane to recover the $250 sale price of the camera Ted selected and took home.

   a. The camera shop will win because Jane's promise was a direct promise to pay for goods under $500.
   b. The camera shop will win because the goods are valued at under $1,000.
   c. Jane will win because her promise was to pay for the debt of another.
   d. Jane will win because the camera's value is more than $200.

_____c_____ 38. Assume the clothing store sues Jane to collect the $350 sale price of the clothing Mary selected and took home. The correctly reasoned answer is

   a. the clothing store will win because Jane's promise was a direct promise to pay for goods under $500.
   b. the clothing store will win because the goods are valued at under $500.
   c. Jane will win because her promise was to pay for the debt of another and was not in writing.
   d. Jane will win because the promise to pay for the debt of another is never enforceable.

_____d_____ 39. Assume the furniture store sues Jane for the price of the couch. The correctly reasoned result is

   a. the furniture store will win because Jane's promise is a direct promise to pay.
   b. the furniture store will win because the price of the couch is under $1,000.
   c. Jane will win because her promise is indirect.
   d. Jane will win because her promise to pay for goods over $500 is not in writing.

Case 2

Sandra owned an antique coffee grinder that Tony, Randall, and Kathy each wanted to buy. On June 1 Sandra mailed to each of the interested parties an offer to sell the item for $300. On June 3 each of the interested parties received the offer. On June 3 Tony mailed a note which read, "$300 is too high. I offer $250." This was received by Sandra on June 4. On June 3 Randall mailed the following response, "Would you consider $250?" Also, on June 3 Kathy wrote, "I do not have $300 to spend. Sell it to someone else." On June 4 Sandra received Randall's note but did not receive Kathy's because it had been mailed to an incorrect address.

Also, on June 4 Tony, Randall, and Kathy, acting independently of one another, each mailed the following communication: "I accept your offer of June 1. Enclosed is my money order for $300." On June 5 Sandra received Kathy's first response. On June 6 she received all of the responses mailed on June 4.

Contracts

___d___ 40. With whom does Sandra have a contract?

   a. Tony
   b. Randall
   c. Kathy
   d. Randall and Kathy

___a___ 41. If Sandra had hand delivered the following note to each of the other parties on June 3, "My offer of June 1 is hereby revoked," the delivery of the note would

   a. revoke the offer.
   b. have no effect.
   c. revoke the offer only if delivered before the other party's receipt of the offer.
   d. revoke the offer only as to Tony and Kathy.

Case 3
On May 1 Joan loaned $200 to Todd. The loan was payable with 5 percent interest on January 30. On July 1 Joan assigned her right to receive the money to Ann. Todd was not notified. On January 30 Todd paid the required amount to Joan. On February 1, Ann demands that Todd pay her.

___c___ 42. The correct outcome is

   a. Todd must pay Ann.
   b. Ann may collect from Todd and then from Joan.
   c. Ann may recover the money from Joan.
   d. Ann is not entitled to any recovery.

___b___ 43. If Todd had been notified of the assignment on January 29

   a. it would make no difference.
   b. Todd could be required to pay Ann even after he paid Joan.
   c. Todd cannot be required to pay twice.
   d. Ann is not entitled to any recovery.

Contracts

Chapter 3: Solutions

PART A: Multiple-Choice Questions

Answer   **Refer to Chapter Section**

1. (d)   [A-1-c] The agreement is illegal. A city ordinance prohibits the leasing of city property to unauthorized persons. Because the agreement is illegal, it is not an enforceable contract. George, therefore, will lose his suit. (George and Bob could be prosecuted for violating criminal statutes. That possibility, however, is unrelated to George's suit for breach of contract.)

2. (c)   [A-2-b(1)] Matt's threat to circulate the picture caused Paul to lose free will. His apparent agreement to the terms of the sale was obtained by duress. Paul feared the loss of his job if the picture was released. Matt's conduct did not amount to undue influence because there was no close relationship between the parties. There was no fraud because Matt did not make a false representation to Paul.

3. (a)   [A-2-b(3), (4)] Becky will succeed in having the agreement set aside. Jane's statement that the set had a new picture tube was a false statement of fact. It was reasonably relied upon by Becky. If Jane knew her statement was false, it amounts to fraud. If Jane reasonably believed her statement was true, it amounts to an innocent misrepresentation. In either event Becky is entitled to have the agreement set aside. She will be required to return the television and will be entitled to the return of the money.

4. (d)   [A-3-a] Rona will win because all the elements required for a valid contract are present. Rona surrendered her right to maintain her weight. She performed the act requested by Mona. Whether Mona received anything of value is unimportant. The fact that Rona benefited from the weight loss is unimportant.

5. (d)   [A-3-d] Judy will win because there was no consideration. The care which the hospital rendered to her mother had already been performed. There was, therefore, no bargained-for exchange. Moreover, Judy merely told the hospital employee that she would pay the bill if her mother failed to pay. Since this is a promise to answer for the debt of another person, the law requires that it be in writing. There was no evidence to support a claim of undue influence.

6. (a) [A-3-e] There was no consideration to support Bill's promise. Jim was doing nothing in return for the extra $100. He was merely doing what he had already contracted to do. He was legally obligated to perform his contractual duties. There is nothing illegal if parties to a contract voluntarily agree to change its terms so answer (b) is incorrect. There is nothing in the facts to indicate that there was a mutual mistake as to how long the job would take so answer (c) is incorrect. Likewise, fraud will not provide a basis for Jim to prevail because Bill's statement did not induce Jim to enter into a contract. Jim had already entered into the contract to do the job for $1,700.

7. (c) [A-3-g] A promise to buy all of the goods that a party needs or requires is enforceable. The Uniform Commercial Code imposes a standard of good faith, thus making the quantity involved in such a promise reasonably certain. Had the promise been to buy all the pencils the firm wanted or desired, it would have been illusory and, therefore, unenforceable. As stated, the promise provides a basis for consideration. Thus, answers (a) and (b) are incorrect. Alternative (d) is incorrect because there is no evidence that fraudulent statements led to the formation of the contract.

8. (b) [A-4-a(1), (4)] A contract entered into by a minor is voidable at the option of the minor. The minor may elect to enforce the contract against the adult. Mike may avoid the contract by disaffirming it during his minority or within a reasonable time after reaching his majority.

9. (d) [A-4-a(1), (5)] Rick is allowed to disaffirm, but since lodging was a necessity to him, he must pay the reasonable value of the lodging. The reasonable value may differ from the $92 which the hotel charges its customers.

10. (d) [A-4-a(6)(a), (b)] By making five monthly payments after reaching majority and remaining in possession of the stereo equipment, Mary has ratified the contract. It is also true that more than a reasonable time has passed since she reached her majority. Mary, therefore, cannot now disaffirm. Answers (a) and (b) are incorrect because they do not account for the fact that a minor may disaffirm a contract for the sale of goods within a reasonable time after reaching majority. Answer (c)

Contracts

is incorrect because stereo equipment is not a necessary item.

11. (a)   [B-1-c] The offer was not communicated to Todd with Jack's intent. Since Jack had not sent the note, there is a chance he would reconsider it and not communicate it to Todd. When Todd found and read the note in Jack's house, he learned of the note's contents without Jack intending for him to learn of it at that time. The law requires that an offer be communicated with the intent of the offeror. Answers (b) and (c) are not as correct as answer (a). It is true that without a valid offer there can be no acceptance and no consideration. In this case, the only reason acceptance and consideration are lacking is that there is no valid offer. Answer (a), therefore, is the best answer. Answer (d) is clearly wrong because without the offer there can be no acceptance and, therefore, no contract.

12. (b)   [B-2-b] As a general rule, the offeror may revoke the offer at any time prior to acceptance. Alice told Brenda of the sale to Rupert before Brenda tendered the money and indicated her intent to receipt. Answer (c) is incorrect because the offer had already been revoked. Moreover, an offer cannot be revoked if it has been accepted. Answers (a) and (d) are incorrect because there is no merchant's firm offer. Alice was not a merchant. As a professor, she did not sell desks regularly. There was no option because Brenda did not give anything of value to Alice in return for Alice's promise to hold the offer.

13. (c)   [B-2-b(2)] All of the elements of a merchant's firm offer are present. Sally is a merchant (she sells books on a regular basis). Her offer is in writing. It is an offer to sell goods. It is signed by her, and it contains a promise that the offer will be held open for a period of time. The offer is not revocable for two months. Answer (b) is incorrect because there was no consideration for an option.

14. (d)   [B-2-c(2)] Barry made a counteroffer which terminated Alex's original offer. Answer (c) is incorrect because there is no requirement that such agreements be in writing. Answer (b) is incorrect because, were it not for the termination, consideration would be present.

15. (d)   [B-3-b(2)] Since this is a contract for the sale of goods, the Uniform Commercial Code applies. So long as the offeree expresses an intent to accept the offer and does not make acceptance conditional on new or different terms, acceptance is effective. In this case, the acceptance is not conditioned upon the additional term. Answer (b) is incorrect because the parties need not be merchants for this rule to apply. Answer

(c) is incorrect because the timing of the acceptance is not critical in this case. There was no rejection or revocation.

16. (c) [B-3-c(1)] The mail was an authorized means of communication since it was used by the offeror and there was nothing in the offer to indicate that the mail would be unacceptable. The acceptance, therefore, was effective upon being sent. Since the offer was accepted on May 3, the attempted revocation on May 4 was of no legal effect.

17. (d) [B-3-c(2)] Because the offeree's first response was the sending of a rejection, the acceptance was not effective upon being sent. In such a case, whichever communication arrives first is the one which is effective. Since the rejection was received before the acceptance was received, the rejection governs and there is no contract.

18. (a) [C-2] The only way that Mike's offer could be accepted was by performance. It was, therefore, a unilateral offer. When Ken performed the requested act, he accepted the offer. Answer (b) is incorrect because there was no exchange of promises. Answer (c) is incorrect because the parties did intend to contract. Answer (d) is incorrect because the agreement did not conform to any specific form required by law. For instance, no negotiable instruments were involved.

19. (d) [E-1] A contract for the sale of land must be in writing and signed by the party being sued. The $500 requirement applies only when goods are involved so answer (a) is incorrect. Answers (b) and (c) are clearly incorrect.

20. (d) [G-2] Specific performance is only available in cases where money damages are inadequate. In this case Clyde could only get specific performance if he could prove that the plates he contracted for were so unique that he could not purchase similar plates with any sum of money. It is extremely doubtful that Clyde can prove that. He will be limited to receiving money damages in his suit.

Contracts

PART B: Matching Sets

Matching Set 1

21.	(B)	[A-4]
22.	(D)	[A-2]
23.	(C)	[A-1]
24.	(A)	[A-3]

Matching Set 2

25.	(B)	[A-2-b(2)]
26.	(C)	[A-2-b(3)]
27.	(D)	[A-2-b(4)]
28.	(A)	[A-2-b(1)]

Matching Set 3

29.	(C)	[C-3]
30.	(A)	[C-1]
31.	(D)	[C-5]
32.	(B)	[C-2]

Matching Set 4

33.	(C)	[G-3]
34.	(A)	[G-1]
35.	(B)	[G-2]
36.	(B)	[G-2]

PART C: Case Problems

37. (a) [E-2] Jane's promise was a direct promise to pay for the camera. The promise was not conditional. Since the goods are valued under $500, there is no requirement for the promise to be in writing.

38. (c) [E-4] Jane's promise was to pay for the debt of Mary. It was not a direct promise to pay. Rather, the promise was conditional on Mary's failure to pay. Since the promise was to pay for Mary's debt, the law requires that it be in writing.

39. (d) [E-2] Although Jane's promise was a direct promise to pay, the law required that it be in writing because the value of the goods exceeds $500.

40. (b) [B-3] Randall's first communication was a mere inquiry which did not constitute a rejection of the offer. His second communication was a valid acceptance. Kathy and Tony had rejected Sandra's offer in their first communications which Sandra received before she received their attempted acceptances.

41. (a) [B-2] Generally, an offer may be revoked by the offeror any time prior to its acceptance. Sandra's actual delivery of the revocation before any of the offerees had accepted was a valid revocation.

42. (c) [F-1-c] Todd was not notified of the assignment before he performed his obligation fully. He cannot, therefore, be required to perform twice.

43. (b) [F-1-c(2)] Once he is notified of the assignment, Todd must honor it or risk being required to pay twice.

CHAPTER 4
Sales

OVERVIEW

The Uniform Commercial Code is a set of laws dealing with a wide range of business applications such as the sale of goods (this chapter), commercial paper (in Chapter 5), and security interests in personal property (Chapter 6). The UCC is a model act which has been adopted in part or in whole by all *states* (not federal government) except that Louisiana has enacted commercial laws which incorporate only certain articles of the UCC. The UCC was created to promote greater uniformity in interstate commercial transactions.

Sales is the term which applies to Article II of the Uniform Commercial Code. Article II is the specialized law of contracts developed for the sale of *goods* (not contracts for the sale of land, services, or stock). While some basic concepts of common law contracts carry over into sales, the candidate should be aware of those significant alterations or variations such as the firm offer, the "battle of forms," changes in existing contracts, risk of loss, liberal provisions as to required contract terms, and the significance of whether the seller and/or buyer are merchants.

In studying this area, the candidate should attempt to visualize practical applications of sales law. For example, think of the purchase of a new car (a good). The new car dealer is a *merchant*. The buyer chooses (*identifies*) which car he or she wishes to purchase. Because the seller is a merchant of the kind of goods involved, the potential liability for loss (*risk of loss*) will be with the merchant until *delivery*. Thus, the merchant is responsible for any damages and/or destruction prior to delivery regardless of whether the buyer has paid for the car or whether the buyer has received title. Various *warranties* will apply unless properly disclaimed and/or limited.

The candidate should be familiar with the basic definitions and applications of Article II. In addition, the types of warranties under sales law and product liability (negligence, strict liability) should be understood.

DEFINITION OF TERMS

BATTLE OF FORMS. A typical situation in business wherein agreement has been reached by the parties through the use of printed forms with the terms on buyer's forms and seller's forms not being identical. The UCC rule between merchants states that additional terms in the offeree's acceptance will be binding unless the offer precluded such additions, the terms would materially alter the offer, or the offeror objects to the additional terms within a reasonable amount of time.

BULK TRANSFER. Any transfer not in the ordinary course of business of a major portion of the assets, materials, or inventory of an enterprise.

COVER. Discretionary right of the buyer to secure substitute goods upon the seller's failure to perform.

CURE. Seller's right to remedy nonconforming delivery where time yet remains for contract performance or seller reasonably believed buyer would accept nonconforming delivery and buyer did not.

DISCLAIMER. A seller's statement that the sale of goods is without warranty(ies).

FIRM OFFER. A written offer by a merchant stating that the offer will be held open for a period of time, not to exceed three months.

FREE ON BOARD (FOB). Delivery term which designates the place the seller must deliver the goods at seller's expense, for example, FOB Chicago; the seller pays for shipping and has the risk of loss to the place named as the destination.

GOOD FAITH. Acting in good faith; defined as being "honesty in fact" and observing reasonable commercial standards.

GOODS. All things which are movable at the time of identification to the contract for sale (in essence, tangible personal property other than money).

MAGNUSON-MOSS WARRANTY ACT. An act passed by Congress to provide federal modification of the state UCC warranty rules as applied to consumer goods.

MERCHANT. A person who deals in the kind of goods being sold or who holds himself out as possessing expertise as to the good(s) involved or who hires an agent who has expertise with regard to the good(s) involved.

NEGLIGENCE. Liability to the manufacturer and/or seller due to the failure to exercise reasonable care.

OPEN TERMS. Terms that need not be expressly stated.

PRODUCTS LIABILITY. The term used to describe the potential liability of any business involved in the manufacture, distribution, and/or sale of a product (good).

RISK OF LOSS. The allocation of loss for damages and/or destruction used to designate which contracting party should bear the financial loss if damage and/or destruction should occur prior to complete performance of the sales contract.

STRICT LIABILITY. Liability to a manufacturer and/or seller of a product because of its inherently dangerous nature.

WARRANTY. Any affirmation of fact (expressed or implied) by the seller to the buyer which becomes a part of the sales contract.

A. Sale of Goods

Article II of the Uniform Commercial Code is the state-adopted statutory law in regard to contracts for the sale of goods. Article II has been adopted in every state except Louisiana. Article II follows the same basic approach as common law contracts, such as the elements necessary to form a contract. Where in conflict, however, Article II, if applicable, supersedes the common law.

1. *Goods:* All things that are movable at the time of identification to the contract for sale are known as *goods*. In essence, a good is tangible personal property other than money.

    a. *Intangible property:* Negotiable instruments (checks, notes), security investments (mortgages), and investment securities (bonds, stock certificates) are intangible property, not goods.

    b. *Crops and timber:* Contracts for the sale of crops and timber are sales of goods, regardless of who is to sever them.

    c. *Land:* Contracts concerning sale of land are clearly not goods.

    EXAMPLE: *John Owner contracts to have Carl Builder build a new home on Owner's lot. Although goods will have to be purchased to build the home, the contract is considered to be a contract primarily for services.*

    d. *Performance of services:* Contracts for performance of services (for example, plumbing) are not sales of goods.

2. *Elements of Contract for Sale of Goods:* The same essential elements of a valid enforceable contract at common law (included in Chapter 3) carry over to contracts for the sale of goods under Article II. These elements include

    a. *Mutual assent:* Offer plus acceptance.

    b. *Consideration:* Something of legal value.

    c. *Capacity:* Age and/or mental.

    d. *Legal objective:* Purpose of the contract.

    e. *Writing:* A writing if the sale of goods is $500 or more.

3. *Good Faith:* Good faith (described as "honesty in fact") is required in all contract aspects for all parties under the UCC.

4. *Contract for Sale Other Than Goods:* Where a contract is not for the sale of goods, then common-law contract principles will apply.

5. *Modifications to Sales Contracts:* Although the essential elements of common-law contracts do carry over to sales, there are many UCC modifications.

    EXAMPLE: *A sales contract can be modified without any new consideration as long as both parties to the contract agree in good faith. For example, if the buyer agrees, the seller of toner for a copier machine could charge more than the original contract to reflect higher wholesale costs to it. This is not true for common-law contracts.*

B. **Creation of the Sales Contract**

1. *The Offer:* As in contracts, the offer is made by the offeror and must be communicated to the offeree.

2. *Firm Offer:* An offer by a merchant may be considered a *firm offer*—in essence, an irrevocable offer without the need of consideration—if the following conditions exist:

    a. *Merchant offer:* The offer is made by a merchant (a person who regularly deals in the kind of goods involved).

    b. *Writing:* The offer is in writing.

    c. *Time period for offer:* The merchant gives assurance that the offer will be held open for a period of time not to exceed three months.

    EXAMPLE: *The Globe Company sends a written offer to the Ajax Office Products Store offering to sell them the new Marvel Word Processor. If the offer gives Ajax ten days to accept, then the offer will be considered a firm offer and irrevocable for ten days.*

3. *The Acceptance:* In order for the sales contract to be valid, the offer must be accepted by the offeree.

    a. *Manner of acceptance:* The manner of acceptance must be of the same medium of communication as the offer, or better.

    EXAMPLE: *Xerox Corporation mails an offer to General Motors. General Motors may send the acceptance by mail or better (telegram or telex, if possible).*

Sales

- b. *Mirror-image acceptance:* A mirror-image acceptance (an acceptance exactly in response to the offer), as in common law, is not required. Additional terms are considered as proposals to be added to the contract unless the "battle of forms" applies.

- c. *Battle of forms:* A problem sometimes occurs between merchants where a form contract offer is accepted by the offeree by the usage of the offeree's form contract acceptance. *Between merchants,* additional terms in the acceptance become part of the contract *unless:*

    (1) These additional terms are precluded by terms of the offer, or

    (2) They materially alter the offer, or

    (3) Notice of objection to the additional terms is given within a reasonable time to the offeree.

    EXAMPLE 1: ABC Company orders ten reception chairs from Cajun Chair Company. Although ABC ordered wheat-colored chairs with brown arms, Cajun accepted, based on the delivery of wheat-colored chairs with black arms. Whether such alteration is material or not is ultimately a question of fact. To be safe, ABC should notify Cajun promptly if this is believed to be a material alteration.

    EXAMPLE 2: Use the same facts as above, but ABC's offer stated that Cajun should agree to ship wheat-colored chairs with black arms or none at all. Now Cajun clearly could not accept by promising to ship chairs with black arms.

- d. *Offer requiring prompt shipment of goods:* An offer that calls for prompt shipment of goods by the offeree may be treated as a *bilateral* contract by giving the offeror an acceptance or as a *unilateral* contract by shipping the goods promptly.

- e. *Notice of acceptance required:* Where the offeror would not otherwise have reasonable means to know if the offeree has commenced a unilateral acceptance or not, the offeree is required to send notice that he/she is in the process of accepting.

- f. *Shipment of nonconforming goods:* A shipment of nonconforming goods (goods that for some reason do not comply with the sales contract) meant by the shipper as an acceptance, without notice of such nonconformity, results in an acceptance and, at the same time, a breach of contract allowing the buyer to recover damages. If shipped with that nonconforming notification, then it is treated as an *accommodation,* a counteroffer, and the buyer may accept or reject.

4. *The Sales Contract:*

   a. *Required terms:* The UCC is much less restrictive than the common law as to required information to form a contract. The following information is required:

   (1) The names of the parties to the contract.

   (2) The quantity of the subject matter to the contract.

   b. *Permissible open terms:* As long as contractual intent is found, the UCC is quite liberal in permitting open terms (terms that need not be expressly stated). The following open-term presumptions apply if not defined in the sales contract:

   (1) *Price:* The price will be assumed to be a reasonable price.

   (2) *Time and place for performance:* Performance is due at a reasonable time where the goods are located, generally at the seller's place of business.

   (3) *Buyer's rights of inspection:* The buyer has the right to inspect the goods prior to payment unless the order is a c.o.d. order. (*Inspection* refers to the process of looking over the goods to the contract prior to accepting them.)

   (4) *Passage of the risk of loss:* Passage depends on FOB terms, but the risk generally passes with the possession of goods. (*Risk of loss* means who would suffer the loss if the goods were damaged or destroyed.)

   (5) *Passage of title:* Title generally passes upon payment for the goods. Title will often be reflected only by a sales receipt.

   c. *Required writing:* A contract for the sale of goods amounting to $500 or more must be in writing to be enforceable *except* in the following circumstances:

   (1) *Confirmation of oral contract:* Between merchants, a *written confirmation* of an oral contract, which is signed and sent by one to another, will be enforceable against either merchant if the receiver has knowledge of the confirmation and fails to object within ten days.

   EXAMPLE: Barbara orders 40 boxes of computer paper for

Sales

$625 by telephone from Hoefer Products. Hoefer sends an order confirmation by mail to Barbara. This will serve as their written agreement unless Barbara objects within ten days of receipt.

(2) *Admission:* An admission, to the extent of the quantity admitted.

EXAMPLE: Anne orally agrees to purchase ten chairs from Bonnie for $100 each. Later Anne writes Bonnie that "our contract for ten chairs at $100 each is unenforceable because it was oral." The contract is now in writing!

(3) *Special manufacture of goods:* The goods are being specially manufactured. Such goods being produced for the buyer are not suitable for sale in the ordinary course of the seller's business. In order for the contract to be enforceable, the seller must be recognized in the industry for manufacturing or purchasing these types of goods.

EXAMPLE: The Misplaced Yankee Pizza Parlor orders $1,200 worth of yo-yos with the parlor's logo on them. Because of their unsuitability for regular sale, the yo-yo manufacturer would probably be able to enforce the oral contract.

d. *Parol evidence rule:* Courts will bar the attempt to introduce evidence to vary, alter, or contradict matters allegedly orally agreed upon prior to or simultaneously with the creation of the contract unless fraud or an equivalent defense is alleged.

EXAMPLE: Suzanne agrees to buy the red Firebird if the dealer will include special pinstripes. The parties inadvertently fail to include the pinstripes in the sales contract. Suzanne would be precluded from recovery by the parol evidence rule.

e. *Contract interpretation:* Where ambiguity exists, a party may introduce evidence for purposes of clarification. Two common examples are:

(1) *Past conduct of business representative:* Precedents established in procedures that are used in handling business transactions.

EXAMPLE: In the past, the parties treated order solicitations taken by route salespersons as being subject to the approval of the home office. This past conduct could be shown in determining whether an acceptance occurred in a present case involving a route salesperson.

(2) *Trade usage:* The normal usage, way, or the practice within the industry.

EXAMPLE: "Delivery during May-June" has been interpreted by usage of trade in the retail clothing industry to mean 40 percent of the fall order received in June, 40 percent in July, and the final 20 percent in August.

5. *Identification:* Identifying the good(s) to the contract (selecting which good will be sold) may be done by either the seller or the buyer. Identification creates a "special property interest." In essence, this means the buyer can now get insurance to cover against loss or damage to the goods.

EXAMPLE 1: Gene is a buyer for a new Corvette. Gene will be the one making the identification, selecting which Corvette he desires to purchase of the Corvettes at the dealer's lot.

EXAMPLE 2: Olivia orders hiking boots from a mail-order business. In this case the seller will select which boots of the kind and size Olivia ordered will actually be sent to her.

C. **Transfer of Title/Risk of Loss**

1. *Passage of Title (Legal Ownership):* Unless the parties agree otherwise, title (legal ownership) generally passes upon the seller's delivery of goods to the buyer. (See specific applications under C-2.)

   a. *Sale of goods by nonowner:*

      (1) *Void title:* If the seller has a void title (stolen goods, no legal title), then the buyer also gets a void title (no title). In other words, neither a thief nor any subsequent taker from a thief gets or can pass good title.

      EXAMPLE: Rod steals Mack's sailboat and later sells it to Gary. Although Gary is a good-faith purchaser, pays value, and does not know of the theft, Mack can recover his boat. Gary could sue Rod for the return of his money.

      (2) *Entrustment:* The UCC recognizes an exception if a good is left with a merchant who deals in such goods, entrustment. If so, the merchant may transfer possession and ownership to a good-faith purchaser for value during the ordinary course of business.

Sales 87

> *EXAMPLE: Jane takes her television set into a television store for repair. If the store should sell Jane's television to Paul (whether by accident or not), then Paul will get good title if he was a good-faith purchaser for value. Jane's only remedy is against the store.*

    b. *Goods formerly owned by minor:* A minor who sells a good has the right to disaffirm the sales contract and recover the good if done while a minor or reasonable time after reaching legal age *and* the good has not been purchased by a third party in good faith, for value, and without notice of the minor's claim.

> *EXAMPLE: Susan, a minor, sells her ten-speed bike to Mary. Later, Mary sells the bike to Stacy. If Stacy purchased without notice of Susan's voidable title, she will prevail against Susan. Note that at common law Susan would have prevailed against any subsequent purchaser.*

    c. *Bulk sales:* A *bulk sale* is a transfer of substantial amount or all of seller's inventory to another, not in the ordinary course of business. (Note: This section is covered in Article VI of the UCC.) A bulk-sale purchaser does not get good title unless the following can be shown:

        (1) The buyer must secure a list of creditors from the seller, and

        (2) The buyer must notify creditors of proposed purchase, and

        (3) The buyer must wait for ten days after notice to pay or take possession of goods, or

        (4) The buyer will get only voidable title as to existing creditors.

2. *Risk of Loss:* The term *risk of loss* refers to which contracting party should bear the financial loss if damage and/or destruction should occur to the goods prior to complete performance of the sales contract.

> *EXAMPLE: A ships 20 cartons of books to B via Ace Transit. En route the cartons are destroyed without fault by either A or B. As between A and B, who should suffer the loss? Risk-of-loss rules determine who suffers the loss.*

Risk of loss is not dependent on title or whether the buyer has made payment. Parties may specifically allocate risk of loss in the sales contract. The general rule, if not specified, is that the risk of loss is on the breaching party.

    a. *Merchant seller:* With a merchant seller, the risk of loss does not shift until tender (being ready to perform) and delivery of goods. For a nonmerchant seller, risk of loss shifts upon tender alone.

EXAMPLE: Karen purchases a new Firebird from Morgan Pontiac. Karen pays for the car in the morning and is to return at 1:00 P.M. to take delivery. The dealer is ready to deliver (tender) at 1:00 P.M., but Karen is late. The car is subsequently damaged at no fault of the dealer. Risk of loss is still with the dealer, a merchant.

EXAMPLE: If Karen had purchased the car from a private party, not a car dealer, the risk would have shifted upon tender, with the seller being prepared to deliver the car at 1:00 P.M.

b. *Sale-on-approval contracts:* These contracts are primarily for the buyer's personal usage.

  (1) Buyer may return goods even if the contract goods conform to the contract.

  (2) Risk of loss and title are considered to be still with the seller until the buyer accepts the goods.

  (3) Buyer's creditors cannot get a lien against the goods until acceptance by the buyer occurs.

c. *Sale or return:* In this case, the goods are primarily bought for resale.

  (1) The buyer may return the goods, at his/her expense, even though the goods are conforming (are as they are supposed to be).

  (2) The risk of loss and the title are with the buyer.

  (3) The buyer's creditors can reach goods (place a lien against them) unless proper notice and/or filing is provided by the seller.

d. *Consignment goods:* When goods are sold on consignment, they are given to a dealer for the dealer to sell for the owner. They are treated as a "sale or return" transaction.

e. *Shipment contracts (FOB some location):* FOB ("free on board") signifies that the seller pays for shipping and has the risk of loss to the place named after the FOB destination.

  (1) *Destination contracts (FOB buyer's place of business):* The seller has the risk of loss and title until tender (delivery) at

Sales

     the buyer's place of business.

  (2) *Shipment contract (FOB seller's place of business):* The risk of loss shifts from the seller to the buyer and the buyer pays for shipping when the seller does the following:

    (a) The seller ships substantially conforming goods (substantially as ordered).

    (b) The seller makes appropriate shipping arrangements with a carrier.

     EXAMPLE: Seller fails to arrange for a refrigerated shipping truck and produce rots en route. Seller bears loss if refrigerated truck was appropriate.

    (c) Notice of shipment is sent to buyer.

 f. *"Delivery without any movement of goods":* Such delivery occurs when a bailee (public warehouseman) is in possession of the goods concerned. Risk of loss shifts to the buyer when

  (1) document of title (essentially the evidence of title) passes from seller to buyer, or

  (2) the bailee acknowledges the buyer's rights, or

  (3) the bailee receives direction from the seller to release the goods to the buyer.

D. Warranties

Warranties are representations of fact and/or promise. In essence, warranties are guarantees.

1. *Warranty of Title:* The seller assures the buyer that the seller has good title to pass to the buyer. In particular, the seller warrants that the following are true:

 a. *Proper transfer:* There is a proper transfer of goods to the buyer.

  EXAMPLE: Thief steals a bike and sells it to Sara. Sara gets no title as the bike is stolen. Sara would have to give the bike to the rightful owner. Thief would be liable to Sara for the loss.

 b. *No infringement:* Seller warrants that there is no infringement of any trademark, patent, copyright, or similar right of a third party, unless the buyer has provided the specifications.

EXAMPLE: Novelty Shop orders 25 Chicago Cubs T-shirts from Austin Supply. Austin will have breached warranty if the shirts are sold without proper licensing.

    c. *Legal use of ideas or rights:* No improper infringement (illegal usage of another's ideas or rights) has occurred, unless the buyer provided the specifications.

2. *Express Warranty:* Any affirmation of fact or promise (written or orally stated) which is a basis of the bargain is called an *express warranty*. This warranty serves as a factor in the decision to buy. The seller need not have intended to make a warranty for an express warranty to occur. An express warranty does not include "puffing" (sales talk).

EXAMPLE: "This 1990 Cadillac is the best used car that you could hope to buy." An express warranty exists as to the year and make of the car—1990 Cadillac. The rest is "puffing."

No formal words, such as warranty or guarantee, are required. If a sample, model, or description is used, then the goods must be of the same general quality.

EXAMPLE: Farmer shows a sample of his apple crop to a grocery store. The farmer warrants that the apples delivered for resale will be substantially of the same choice and grade as the sample apples shown.

3. *Implied Warranty of Merchantability:* The implied warranty of merchantability warrants that goods are fit for ordinary purposes. This warranty occurs automatically if the seller is a merchant who deals in goods of the kind sold or holds himself or herself out as knowledgeable.

EXAMPLE: A lawn chair should withstand a person of reasonable weight.

The implied warranty of merchantability also warrants that the product is adequately contained, packaged, and labeled. This type of warranty applies to food sold if an item found in the food is not to be reasonably expected or is a foreign substance.

EXAMPLE: A cherry pit is reasonably to be expected in a piece of cherry pie but not in a lemon pie.

4. *Implied Warranty of Fitness for a Particular Purpose:* In this case, the seller must have actual knowledge of the buyer's particular purpose and requirements for which the goods are to be utilized. There is no requirement that the seller be a merchant seller.

Sales

      a. *Reliance on seller's recommendation:* The seller must have reason to know that the buyer is relying on the seller's choice and/or recommendation.

      b. *Reliance on seller's expertise:* The buyer must *actually* rely upon the seller's expertise, since the buyer must not have superior knowledge.

      EXAMPLE: Glenn goes to the Arctic Ski Shop to purchase cross-country skis. Glenn tells the salesperson that he knows nothing about skis but desires to be equipped with good, reliable skis that will require little care. Glenn could recover his money if the skis proved unsuitable.

5. *Appropriate Plaintiffs:* Persons who may sue for warranty defects must be deemed *appropriate plaintiffs.* Such plaintiffs normally include

      a. *Purchaser(s):* The person(s) who actually purchased the goods.

      b. *Purchaser's family:* Members of the purchaser's immediate family.

      c. *Guests:* Guests who are injured by the product while in the purchaser's home.

      EXAMPLE: Purchaser's child is injured by a defective item bought by the parent. A suit could be brought on behalf of the child if a warranty violation exists.

6. *UCC Disclaimers:* A warranty disclaimer is a seller's statement, oral or written, that the sale of goods is without warranty(ies).

      a. *Disclaimers for implied warranty of merchantability:*

          (1) May be oral or written.

          (2) Must be conspicuous if written.

          (3) Must actually state "merchantability" in the disclaimer if "as is" is not utilized.

      b. *Disclaimers for implied warranty of fitness for particular purpose:*

          (1) Must be in writing.

          (2) Must be conspicuous.

(3) Require no special or formal words.

c. *As-is disclaimers: As is* may be utilized to disclaim the implied warranties. *As is* refers to an item just the way it exists, with all faults or defects.

7. *Magnuson-Moss Warranty Act:* This federal law supersedes the UCC in its application to sales of consumer goods costing $10 or more to consumers. The purpose of the act is to improve the adequacy of warranty information and make such information more understandable to the consumer.

   a. *Warranty:* The act does *not* require the making of a written warranty, but if a warranty is made, then the following will apply:

      (1) The seller must disclose fully and conspicuously, in simple language, the terms and conditions of the warranty.

      (2) The act prohibits the exclusion of implied warranties if a warranty is given.

      (3) The act requires a consumer warranty, if given, to be stated as *full* or *limited warranty*.

   b. *Full warranty:*

      (1) The seller/warrantor promises to fix or replace the good during its lifetime if the product becomes defective.

      (2) Warranty protection extends to any person to whom the product is transferred and/or any injured party.

   c. *Limited warranty:*

      (1) The seller provides less than a full warranty.

      (2) Implied warranties may not be limited other than as to duration of time applicable.

      (3) If the time the full warranty is effective is the only limitation to the full warranty, then the seller may label the product in this way:

         "Full 6-month warranty"
         "Full 90-day warranty"

Sales

E. Remedies

1. *Right to Cure:* A seller is given the *right to cure* (to make correct) a nonconforming delivery of goods if either of the following conditions exist:

    a. *Time remaining for performance:* Time still remains before time for performance has passed.

    EXAMPLE: Seller ships ten red chairs to buyer. Buyer objects and points out that the contract said blue chairs. If sufficient time for delivery still remains, the seller may redeliver with a correct order of blue chairs.

    b. *Nonacceptance of tender:* Seller reasonably thought buyer would accept a nonconforming tender, and buyer did not accept.

    EXAMPLE: In the preceding example, if seller is out of blue chairs and reasonably believed from past transactions that the red chairs would be satisfactory to buyer, the seller can correct with a redelivery of blue chairs (if now possible).

2. *Seller's Remedies, Buyer at Fault:* If the buyer is at fault, the seller has several options.

    a. *Suing the buyer:* The seller must identify the goods, if not already done, and can sue the buyer for the price of the goods.

    b. *Stopping or withholding delivery:* The seller may stop or withhold delivery of the goods.

    c. *Recovery of damages:*

    (1) The seller may recover damages for the loss incurred, including expenses, less expenses saved by not having to complete contract performance.

    (2) The seller may recover profits lost because of the breach only in exceptional cases.

    d. *Canceling the contract:* The seller may cancel the contract.

3. *Buyer's Remedies for Seller's Breach:* A seller's breach of contract may result in several different forms of remedies.

    a. *Cover:* If the seller has indicated repudiation or inability to perform the contract before the time of performance, the buyer may choose to cover (acquire substitute goods).

(1) The buyer has no duty to cover.

(2) The buyer may recover the additional costs less any costs saved by the seller's breach.

EXAMPLE: Seller informs buyer of inability to perform. Buyer acquires substitute goods for $400 more but will save $125 in shipping costs by the seller's nonperformance. The net damages are $275.

b. *Recovery of damages:* A buyer may recover damages for any direct losses attributable to the seller's breach. Most often the damages will be similar to the preceding example concerning cover.

c. *Specific performance:* Money damages are presumed to be appropriate. If the goods are unique, however, the buyer may seek specific performance. Specific performance means the seller will be ordered to go through with the contract. What is unique is left up to court determination.

EXAMPLE: A contract to purchase a 1988 Grand Prix automobile would not be unique. A contract for a 1929 Ford Roadster would more likely be found unique.

d. *Canceling the contract:* The buyer may be able to cancel the contract if the seller fails to perform or indicates that he or she will not perform.

F. Products Liability

Products liability is the term used to describe the potential liability of any business involved in the manufacture, distribution, and/or sale of a product (good). It is quite common to read in the newspaper of large lawsuit recoveries for defective products sold, such as automobiles or drugs. Three theories are utilized in product liability cases: negligence, strict liability, and warranty liability.

1. *Negligence:* Negligence is the failure to exercise reasonable care. To recover, the plaintiff must show that the defendant owed a duty to the plaintiff and breached this duty. The breach directly caused damages to be suffered. The plaintiff must have suffered injury as a result of the defendant's negligence in

   a. *Design of the product,* and/or

   b. *Manufacturing of the product,* and/or

      c.   *Packaging of the product,* and/or

      d.   *Labeling of the product.*

The injured party need not have been the purchaser of the product (no privity of contract required).

EXAMPLE: A pedestrian is injured when struck by a car. Evidence establishes that the car manufacturer was negligent in design of the braking system which caused the accident. The pedestrian could recover from the car manufacturer.

2. *Strict Liability:* The product must be an inherently dangerous product. Negligence of the defendant need not be proven to win, and privity of contract is not required to be shown. Also, no intent to produce or sell a defective product need be proven. The injured party must establish that the following conditions exist:

    a.   *Defective product:* The product was defective when it left the seller's control.

    b.   *Injury to plaintiff:* The defect caused the plaintiff's injury.

    c.   *Unreasonably dangerous product:* The defect caused the product to be unreasonably dangerous in usage.

    d.   *No material alteration of product:* The product was not materially altered after leaving the seller's control.

    e.   *Product use:* The product was being used as contemplated by the manufacturer.

EXAMPLE: Carl purchases an electric saw from Sears. To speed up his sawing, Carl removes the saw blade guard. Carl could not now recover for injuries suffered if he cuts his hand.

A court may award punitive damages (punishment) where the defendant's defective product or the defendant's conduct is found by a court to be highly unconscionable.

EXAMPLE: Auto manufacturers have had to pay punitive damages for such matters as poorly placed gas tanks (causing fires in rear-end collisions) and inherently defective suspension systems.

The injured party may sue the retailer, the wholesaler, and/or the manufacturer of the defective product.

3. *Warranty Liability:* (See Section D of this chapter.)

4. *Multiple Theories of Recovery:* The same product defect might permit recovery by multiple theories of recovery. Negligence is generally the most difficult to establish.

Sales

Chapter 4: Review Questions

PART A: Multiple-Choice Questions

DIRECTIONS: Select the best answer from the four alternatives. Write your answer in the blank to the left of the number.

_____c_____ 1. The Office Supply Corporation sent a written offer to Beck offering to sell Beck ten file cabinets at $100 each. Office Supply gave Beck sixty days to accept.

    a. Office Supply may revoke the offer at any time as it received no consideration.
    b. Office Supply's offer is not revocable for three months.
    c. Office Supply's offer would be revocable if oral.
    d. The offeree must be a merchant for a firm offer to be found.

_____c_____ 2. Baker and Martin, both merchants, orally agree that Baker will sell to Martin five display cases at $100 each.

    a. This contract need not be in writing as an insufficient dollar amount is involved.
    b. No consideration is necessary to form a binding sales contract.
    c. A writing would not be required if the display cases are to be specially manufactured.
    d. The sales contract would be unenforceable if without an established time and place for performance.

_____d_____ 3. The Western Lounge orders eight bar stools for prompt shipment from the Cleveland Chair Company. Cleveland may properly do any of the following except

    a. reject the offer.
    b. promptly ship the bar stools without an acceptance response.
    c. send an acceptance response.
    d. cure the offer.

4. Which of the following statements is true about identification?

   a. Only the seller can identify the goods.
   b. Upon identification the buyer gets an insurable interest.
   c. Title is passed to the buyer upon identification.
   d. Only conforming goods can be identified.

5. Karen takes her watch to a jeweler to be fixed. A burglar steals the watch from the jeweler's place of business and sells it to Bob at a football game. Bob was a good-faith purchaser for value without knowledge of the theft. Karen seeks the watch.

   a. Karen will win.
   b. Karen will lose as she entrusted the watch.
   c. Bob has voidable title to the watch.
   d. A good-faith purchaser for value will always prevail.

6. Miller Company sends a written offer to Ajax Company ordering 15 blue widgets. Ajax Company accepts but makes minor alterations. A contract will have resulted if

   a. Miller made no objection.
   b. Miller made a firm offer.
   c. Ajax did not use its own acceptance form.
   d. Ajax acted in good faith.

7. An appliance store sells a television set to Betsy with Betsy retaining the right to return the set if not satisfied at the end of ten days. A thief steals the set from Betsy's apartment prior to the passing of the ten days.

   a. The transaction is a sale on approval so the risk of loss is with Betsy.
   b. The transaction is a sale or return so the risk of loss is with Betsy.
   c. The transaction is a sale on approval so the risk of loss is with the store.
   d. The transaction is a sale or return so the risk of loss is with the store.

8. Daniels, of Denver, and Carey, of Dallas, entered into a contract whereby Daniels was to sell and ship widgets to Carey, FOB Denver. Risk of loss during transit is

   a. with Daniels if Daniels arranged the shipping contract.
   b. with the carrier.
   c. with Daniels if Daniels is a merchant dealing in goods of the kind involved.
   d. with Carey unless Daniels shipped substantially nonconforming goods.

Sales

9. Seller sends nonconforming goods to buyer. The time for performance has expired. Buyer could easily cover but refuses to do so.

   a. A buyer must cover if reasonably possible.
   b. A buyer need not cover even if reasonably possible.
   c. The seller must be allowed the right to cure.
   d. The buyer's action demonstrates a lack of good faith so seller would prevail.

10. Express warranties

    a. must be intentionally made.
    b. are only made by merchants.
    c. may be oral.
    d. are "full warranties."

11. Gary sells Phil a car for $2,500. The contract says the car is sold *as is*. Accordingly

    a. there is no warranty of title.
    b. Gary disclaimed the warranty of fitness of merchantability.
    c. Gary should have mentioned merchantability.
    d. the disclaimer is dependent upon whether Gary is a merchant of cars.

12. Your company purchases a new delivery truck from Champion Motors. The vehicle is involved in an accident after the right front wheel mysteriously falls off while the driver is making an ordinary delivery trip. Assuming the problem was an inherent defect from the time the truck left the factory, your company might reasonably expect to prevail on each count below *except*

    a. breach of express warranty suit against Champion Motors.
    b. products liability against the truck manufacturer.
    c. breach of implied warranty of particular purpose suit against the truck manufacturer.
    d. negligence of Champion Motors in originally servicing the truck at time of sale.

PART B: Matching Sets

Matching Set 1

Match each principle of law (13-17) with the appropriate statement of applicable law (A-B). Write the letter of your answer in the blank to the left of the number.

STATEMENTS OF APPLICABLE LAW

A. Applicable to both Common Law and UCC Article II
B. Applicable only to UCC Article II

PRINCIPLES OF LAW

_____ 13. Firm offer to sell a copier machine.

_____ 14. Mutual assent to the formation of a contract.

_____ 15. Gap fillers to permit enforcement of contract.

_____ 16. Statute of frauds.

_____ 17. Implied warranty of merchantability.

Sales

Matching Set 2

Match each principle of law(18-22) with the appropriate statement of merchant status (A-B). Write the letter of your answer in the blank to the left of the number.

STATEMENTS OF MERCHANT STATUS

A. Rule dependent upon whether one or both contracting parties is a merchant.
B. Merchant status is not important to rule's application.

PRINCIPLES OF LAW

_____ 18. Good faith.

_____ 19. Firm offer.

_____ 20. Express warranty.

_____ 21. Battle of forms.

_____ 22. Confirmation of oral contract.

PART C: Case Problems

DIRECTIONS: For each question related to the following case problem, select the best answer from the four alternatives. Write your answer in the blank to the left of the number.

Case 1

You have been asked to order $600 of computer paper from Freeport Supply Company. You call Freeport Supply's 800-number, order the paper, and instruct them to bill your company. Freeport Supply agrees.

_____ 23. Which action listed below would be the best step Freeport Supply Company could take to bind your company's performance?

    a. Send a confirmation of order statement.
    b. Identify the goods to the contract.
    c. Limit the applicable warranties on the paper.
    d. Cure.

_____ 24. Assume that a proper written contract exists for the computer paper. Freeport Supply temporarily runs out of the ordered paper so they send the next grade paper to your company. This paper is simply not acceptable to your company.

    a. If the paper was the best alternative paper available to Freeport Supply, you must accept it.
    b. Freeport Supply may have a right to cure.
    c. Freeport Supply could have avoided any legal problems by simply telling your company that they had run out of the proper paper and could not deliver as per the contract.
    d. This is an example of a bulk sale.

_____ 25. Assume Freeport Supply does not correct the order. Your company returns the paper, and you have had to order substitute paper from Western Supply Company. You have not paid Freeport Supply anything. The substitute paper costs $700.

    a. Ordering substitute paper from another source is called cure.
    b. You ought to be able to recover $700 in damages from Freeport Supply.
    c. This is an example of entrustment.
    d. You ought to be able to recover $100 in damages from Freeport Supply.

Sales

Chapter 4: Solutions

PART A: Multiple-Choice Questions

	Answer	Refer to Chapter Section
1.	(c)	[B-2] This is an example of a valid firm offer because Office Supply Corporation is a merchant, the offer is in writing, and there is a time certain (60 days). Consideration is necessary in order to make a valid firm offer. A firm offer is irrevocable for the time stated or three months, whichever is less.
2.	(c)	[B-4-c(3)] The general rule is that a contract for the sale of goods for $500 or more must be in writing, regardless of whether the seller and/or buyer is a merchant. An exception exists, however, where specially manufactured goods constitute the subject matter of the sales contract.
3.	(d)	[B-3-d] Under the UCC, an offer requesting prompt shipment can be accepted by prompt shipment or by an acceptance. If the former, a unilateral contract exists, while in the latter a bilateral contract results.
4.	(b)	[B-5] Identification is the process whereby specific goods are associated with the sales contract. Upon identification, the buyer gets a special property interest and an insurable interest (meaning he or she may legally insure the goods). Either a seller or a buyer may identify the goods involved.
5.	(a)	[C-1-a(1), (2)] Karen's delivery of her watch to the jeweler for repairs is an entrustment. The burglar gets no title, and no purchaser of the watch thereafter can improve on the title.
6.	(a)	[B-3-c] This problem illustrates the battle of forms. Where merchants are involved, an acceptance with minor changes becomes part of the contract unless the offeror precluded the same terms in the offer or objects within a reasonable time after the receipt of the acceptance. A contract may be found even though the offer was made on the seller's form and the acceptance was made on the buyer's form.
7.	(c)	[C-2-b] The sale was a sale on approval; the television set was for Betsy's personal use. The risk of loss was with the seller

until the ten days elapsed or Betsy accepted.

8. (d) [C-2-e] The terms of shipment call for a shipment *contract* whereby the risk of loss shifts to the buyer when the seller arranges a proper carrier contract and delivery to the carrier of substantially conforming goods.

9. (b) [E-1] The seller's right to cure exists prior to expiration of time for performance. The buyer need not cover even though it would be done easily enough.

10. (c) [D-2] Express warranties may be oral.

11. (b) [D-6-b] *As is* is an appropriate disclaimer for either implied warranty. *As is* does not disclaim the warranty of title.

12. (c) [D-4] Your company might reasonably expect to recover from either the car dealer or manufacturer on the basis of express warranty, implied warranty of merchantability (not fit for its ordinary purpose), negligence, or strict liability. However, the implied warranty of particular purpose probably would not have arisen.

Sales 105

PART B: Matching Sets

Matching Set 1

13. (B) [B-2] Firm offer was unknown at the common law.

14. (A) [A-2(a)] Same basic elements to form a contract.

15. (B) [B-4-b] UCC only; common law demanded greater inclusion of specifics before enforcing contract.

16. (A) [A-2-e] There are some UCC-only exceptions, but the statute of frauds, as such, applies to both.

17. (B) [D-3] Implied warranties are a creation of the UCC.

Matching Set 2

18. (B) [A-3] Good faith, honesty in fact, is required of every contracting party in every contract.

19. (A) [B-2] The firm offer is good only if made by a merchant offeror of the goods involved. (Note: It does not matter whether the offeree is a merchant.)

20. (B) [D-2] Any seller can make an express warranty. It does not matter whether Sears is the seller or you are the seller at your annual garage sale.

21. (A) [B-3-c] There are two battle-of-the-forms rules, one between merchants and one for all other types of contracts (those that include a merchant or no merchants).

22. (A) [B-4-c(1)] Between merchants, a written confirmation of oral contract sent by one contracting party to the other will suffice for a required writing under the UCC.

PART C: Case Problems

23. (a) [B-4-c(1)] A written confirmation in the form of a memorandum from one merchant to another suffices for the lack of a prior writing under the statute of frauds section of the UCC. Without such a confirmation, your company might have attempted to void the transaction for the lack of a writing.

24. (b) [E-1] A seller may have the right to cure if the seller delivers nonconforming goods, they are rejected, and there is still time before delivery is finally due to substitute the proper goods.

25. (d) [E-3-a] You ought to be able to recover $100 in damages: $700 cover price less $600 contract price.

CHAPTER 5
Negotiable Instruments

OVERVIEW

In the modern business world the use of checks, drafts, and promissory notes is taken for granted. Yet, if such instruments were not available, business transactions would, by necessity, be based on the actual transfer of cash. If cash were required, the risk and inconvenience of transporting the money would retard the conduct of business. Moreover, credit would become more difficult to arrange, and efforts to finance transactions would be hampered.

It is the use of negotiable instruments as substitutes for money that makes today's streamlined transactions possible. This chapter presents the fundamentals of the law of negotiable instruments. The candidate should become familiar with the concept of negotiability and the elements it requires, the types of negotiable instruments, the requirements for a valid transfer of such instruments, and the defenses which the law recognizes against the holder of such instruments.

DEFINITION OF TERMS

BEARER. One who is in possession of a negotiable instrument.

CASHIER'S CHECK. A check drawn by a bank on itself.

CERTIFICATE OF DEPOSIT. An instrument in which a bank acknowledges the receipt of money and its obligation to repay the money on a certain date.

DRAFT. A negotiable instrument which contains an unconditional order directing another to pay a certain sum of money.

DRAWEE. A party who is ordered by the terms of a draft to pay a certain sum of money.

DRAWER. One who issues a check or other draft.

HOLDER. One who possesses an instrument which is issued or indorsed to him/her or is payable to the bearer.

HOLDER IN DUE COURSE. A holder who has given value for an instrument and has taken it in good faith without knowledge of any defect.

INDORSEE. One who receives an indorsed instrument. (Note: The word *endorse* is commonly used in business. The word *indorse* is used in the UCC.)

INDORSEMENT WITHOUT RECOURSE. One in which the indorser disclaims liability in the event the maker or drawer fails to pay.

INDORSER. A payee who transfers an instrument by signing it and delivering it to an indorsee.

MAKER. One who signs a promissory note.

NEGOTIABLE INSTRUMENT. A written document containing a signed, unconditional promise or order to pay a certain sum of money at a specified time or upon demand to the order of a named party or to the bearer.

NEGOTIATION. The transfer of an instrument in such form that the transferee becomes a holder.

PAYEE. The party to whom a check or draft is made payable.

PROMISSORY NOTE. A negotiable instrument which contains a promise by the maker to pay a certain sum of money to another party at a specified time or on demand.

RESTRICTIVE INDORSEMENT. One which requires the indorsee to accept the instrument subject to certain specified conditions.

SIGHT DRAFT. A draft which is payable when presented for payment by the holder.

SPECIAL INDORSEMENT. One which names the party to whom the indorser makes the instrument payable.

TIME DRAFT. A draft which is payable in the future.

TRADE ACCEPTANCE. A type of draft commonly used in connection with the sale of goods in which the seller is both the drawer and the payee and the buyer is the drawee.

A. The Significance of Negotiability

Negotiability is a valued characteristic because it is possible for the recipient of a negotiable instrument to be free of many of the defenses which the promisor could assert against the original owner of the document.

1. *Legal Requirements:* The law establishes certain requirements for

Negotiable Instruments

negotiability (see Section B of this chapter). These are contained in the Uniform Commercial Code (UCC).

2. *Effect of Negotiability:* A document containing a promise which can be transferred to another party in a manner which entitles the recipient to enforce the promise without being subject to all the defenses which could be asserted against the original owner is said to be negotiable. To fully appreciate the effect of the transfer of a negotiable instrument, it should be compared to the ordinary assignment of contract rights.

   a. *Assignable contract rights:* Most contract rights are assignable (see Chapter 3: Contracts). However, the assignee is subject to the same defenses to which the assignor is subject. The assignee merely stands in the shoes of the assignor.

   EXAMPLE: Al contracted to deliver a certain rare coin to Bob in return for Bob's promise to install new carpeting in Al's living room. Bob assigned his rights in the contract to Cal. When Cal sued Al to collect the coin, Al defended on the grounds that Bob had failed to install new carpeting. Al is permitted to assert this defense against Cal. Bob's contract right was assignable, but the contract was not negotiable within the meaning of the law. Thus Cal was subject to all defenses which Al could assert against Bob.

   b. *Assignable rights free of defenses:* A document that meets all the legal requirements for negotiability is worth more to other parties because, unlike an ordinary contract, its recipient, if he qualifies as a holder in due course [see Section B-6-c(6) of this chapter], may take rights free of most defenses. It therefore involves less risk.

   EXAMPLE: Al signed a properly drawn check in the amount of $200 and delivered it to Bob in return for Bob's promise to carpet Al's living room. Bob endorsed the check and delivered it to Cal, to whom he owed $200. Cal cashed the check. Even if Bob did not carpet Al's room as he promised, Cal, assuming he took the check without any knowledge of Bob's failure to perform, is free of Al's claims.

B. **Elements of a Negotiable Instrument**

The Uniform Commercial Code (UCC) establishes the legal requirements for a negotiable instrument. If all of these requirements are not met, a document may be a contract capable of being assigned, but it is not a negotiable instrument. The difference between a mere contract and a negotiable instrument is important to those to whom the document is transferred (see

Section A-2 in this chapter).

1. *Writing:* A negotiable instrument must be in writing. The requirement serves two main functions:

    a. *Fraud:* It minimizes the risk of fraud.

    b. *Transfer:* It allows for ease and certainty in transferring the promise to other parties.

    The UCC does not require that the writing be on paper. The writing requirement will be satisfied if the material on which the writing is done is in "tangible form." The material should, of course, be of the type that is likely to last for a considerable time.

    EXAMPLE: Unhappy with his hotel room on his vacation to Hawaii, Lance paid his bill with a check he carved on a coconut. The instrument meets the writing requirement of the UCC.

2. *Signature:* In order to qualify as a negotiable instrument, a writing must be signed in accordance with the UCC.

    a. *Maker's signature:* If the instrument is a note, it must be signed by its maker.

    b. *Drawer's signature:* If the instrument is a check or a draft, it must be signed by the drawer.

    c. *Type of signature required:* A traditional signature is not required. Any mark made or adopted by a party with the intention of authenticating the writing will suffice as a signature.

    (1) An *X* or other mark will serve as a signature if it was the intent of the person making the mark to authenticate the document.

    (2) A rubber stamp which imprints a party's name may be used by the party or the party's authorized agent as the party's signature.

    (3) The signature may appear any place on the document.

3. *Unconditional Promise:* A negotiable instrument must contain an unconditional promise or order to pay.

    a. *Promise to pay:* A writing that merely recognizes a debt does not satisfy the requirement of a promise to pay.

    EXAMPLE: Don agreed to purchase Tina's lawnmower for $40.

Negotiable Instruments

Upon receiving the lawnmower, Don wrote on a piece of paper, "Tina, I owe you $40. (Signed) Don." The promise requirement is not satisfied.

    b. *Order to pay:* A check that bears the name of a bank and words such as "Pay to the order of ..." satisfies the order requirement.

        (1) The order to pay is clear and certain.

            (a) Words such as "please pay" are sufficiently clear and definite.

            (b) Words such as "I hope you will pay" or "I wish you would pay" are *not* sufficiently clear and definite.

        (2) The bank's name on the check identifies the party that must pay pursuant to the order and thus satisfies the legal requirement that the order to pay be directed to a specific, identifiable party.

    c. *Unconditional promise:* The promise must not be conditional.

        (1) If the promise states that it is subject to another agreement, the promise is conditional and does not meet the requirements for a negotiable instrument.

        (2) If the promise to pay states that payment can *only* be made from a particular source or fund, the promise does not meet the requirement for a negotiable instrument.

        EXAMPLE: Willis signed a document which read, "I promise to pay to the bearer of this note $5,000 on May 1, 1994. Payment is to be made only *from my travel account."*

            (a) Because it is possible that a specified fund will not be in existence when payment becomes due, the promise is conditional.

            (b) If the word *only* were omitted, the preceding promise would satisfy the promise requirement for a negotiable instrument.

    d. *Reference to agreement:* A mere reference to an agreement does not render a promise to pay conditional.

        (1) The instrument may contain a statement of the parties' agreement.

EXAMPLE: George writes, "I promise to pay Jane $100 on May 1 in payment of the desk she will deliver to me on that date. (Signed) George." George's promise is not conditional. He merely stated the terms of the agreement.

    (2) The instrument may contain a reference to a separate agreement so long as the promise to pay is not made conditional on the other agreement.

EXAMPLE: Susan writes, "I promise to pay Jack $35. Jack agrees to return the books he borrowed from me last semester. (Signed) Susan." Susan's promise merely refers to another agreement. Because the promise to pay is not subject to Jack's agreement to return the books, it is not a conditional promise.

4. *Specific Sum of Money:* The promise to pay must be expressed in terms of a specific sum of money.

    a. *Stated or ascertainable sum:* The sum must either be stated on the face of the instrument or be ascertainable without the necessity of referring to another source.

EXAMPLE: A promise to pay "$100 with 9 percent interest upon demand" expresses a specific sum because the interest can be calculated without reference to any other source of information.

    b. *Promise to pay money:* The promise to pay must not include a promise to pay in something other than money.

EXAMPLE: A promise to pay $300 and deliver a new light fixture will not suffice for a negotiable instrument because the promise includes a commitment to pay in something other than money.

    c. *Promise to pay in foreign currency:* The promise may be expressed in terms of a foreign nation's money. The UCC recognizes as money "a medium of exchange authorized or adopted by a domestic or foreign government as part of its currency."

EXAMPLE: Boris writes, "I promise to pay 10,000 ruples on June 1." Ruples are recognized as money in the Soviet Union, so Boris's promise states a specific sum of money.

5. *Payable at Specific Time or Upon Demand:* To meet the requirements of a negotiable instrument, the promise must make the payment due at a specific time or upon demand.

    a. *Statement of due date:* To be considered payable at a specific time,

Negotiable Instruments 113

the document must either state a certain date or express the due date in terms that allow the time to be ascertained with certainty.

EXAMPLE: Bill promises to pay "$500 sixty days after the birth of Lou's next child." The due date cannot be ascertained because the birth date of the child is uncertain.

EXAMPLE: Sally promises to pay "$200 on or before July 1, 1991." The due date is sufficiently definite. Although Sally may elect to pay before the stated date, the payment is due on July 1, 1991.

    b. *Payment upon demand:* Promises to pay *upon demand, at sight,* or *upon presentment* satisfy the requirement.

6. *Payable to Order or Bearer:* To be negotiable, an instrument must make it clear that the promisor intended for the instrument to be transferable by the promisee to another party.

    a. *Acceptable word usage:* Words such as *pay to the order of Gregg Wilson* or *payable to the bearer* satisfy this requirement.

    b. *Transfer of instrument:* If the instrument is simply made payable to a named party, it may still be transferred, but the rights of the transferee will be limited. The transferee will not be considered a holder [see B-6-c(5) and (6) below].

    c. *Parties to negotiable instruments:* The parties involved in the making and transferring of negotiable instruments are known in the law by various names. Familiarity with the basic terminology employed by the UCC is helpful in understanding negotiable instruments.

        (1) *Drawer:* A drawer is one who issues a check or other draft.

        (2) *Drawee:* A drawee is a party who is ordered by the drawer to pay a certain sum of money to a party known as a *payee.*

        EXAMPLE: Alice writes a check in the amount of $10 payable to Barb. Alice is the drawer; Barb is the payee. Alice's bank is the drawee.

        (3) *Maker:* A maker is one who signs a promissory note promising to pay a certain sum of money to another party.

        (4) *Indorser and indorsee:* An indorser is a payee who transfers the instrument by signing it and delivering it to one known as an indorsee. (An indorsee can become an indorser.)

EXAMPLE: Barb is named as the payee on a check. She signs the check and delivers it to Cathy. Barb is the indorser. Cathy is the indorsee.

(5) *Holder:* A holder is one who possesses an instrument that is issued or indorsed to that person or is payable to the bearer.

(6) *Holder in due course:* A holder in due course is one who gives value for an instrument and takes it in good faith without knowledge of any defect. A holder in due course is free of many defenses to which an ordinary assignee is subject (see Section E of this chapter).

C. Types of Negotiable Instruments

The UCC recognizes four types of instruments: checks, drafts, promissory notes, and certificates of deposit.

1. *Checks:* A check is an instrument that is drawn on a bank and is payable on demand.

2. *Drafts:* A draft is an instrument that contains an unconditional order by the drawer, directing the drawee to pay money to a payee (see Section B-6-c in this chapter).

   a. *Time draft:* A draft that is payable in the future.

   b. *Sight draft:* A draft that is payable when presented for payment by the holder.

   c. *Trade acceptance:* A special kind of draft that is commonly used in connection with the sale of goods. The seller is the drawer and the payee of the draft. The buyer is the drawee. The seller typically sells the trade acceptance after the buyer has signed it, indicating its acceptance. This allows the seller to convert the instrument into cash and allows the buyer time to make payment.

   EXAMPLE: On June 1 Midwest Industries agrees to sell a quantity of goods to Acme Incorporated. According to their agreement, Acme is to pay the $10,000 sale price within 60 days. Midwest draws a trade acceptance ordering Acme to pay $10,000 to the order of Midwest on August 1. Acme signs the instrument, indicating its acceptance. Midwest then sells the instrument. The trade acceptance is worth more to the transferee than an assignment of an account receivable because the trade acceptance renders the transferee free of most defenses that party would face as a mere *assignee. (This assumes the transferee is a holder in due course.)*

3. *Promissory Notes:* A promissory note is an instrument that contains a promise by the maker to pay a certain sum of money to another party at a specific time or on demand.

4. *Certificates of Deposit:* A certificate of deposit is an instrument in which a bank acknowledges the receipt of money and its obligation to repay the money on a certain date. The certificate of deposit also contains a statement of any interest that the bank agrees to pay.

D. **Transfer of Negotiable Instruments**

A negotiable instrument may be transferred by assignment or by negotiation.

1. *Assignment:* An assignment is a transfer of contract rights. Assignments are governed by contract law (see Chapter 3; Contracts, Section G). Because the assignee stands in the shoes of the assignor, the assignee is subject to the same defenses to which the assignor is subject. Thus, one of the main advantages of a negotiable instrument is lost when it is merely assigned.

2. *Negotiation:* Negotiation is the transfer of an instrument in such form that the transferee becomes a holder [see Section B-6-c(5) in this chapter]. Negotiation may occur in two ways.

    a. *Negotiation by delivery:* If the negotiable instrument is payable to the bearer, it is negotiated by delivery.

    EXAMPLE: Dick signed a check reading, "Pay to the order of cash, $100." He delivered the check to Mary. The act of delivery constituted negotiation. Mary became the holder.

    b. *Negotiation by indorsement and delivery:* If the negotiable instrument is payable to the order of a party, the instrument is negotiated when the named party indorses it and delivers it to a holder.

    EXAMPLE: Dick signed a check reading, "Pay to the order of Mary Johnson, $100." Mary took the check to the bank, indorsed it by signing her name on the back, and received the $100. The bank became the holder.

    (1) *Blank indorsement:* A blank indorsement is one that does not specify an indorsee. An instrument that is payable to the order of a payee becomes payable to the bearer once the payee indorses it in blank.

EXAMPLE: Mary signed a check which read, "Pay to the order of Debbie Black, $20." Debbie indorsed the check in blank by signing the back of it. The check became payable to the bearer when she indorsed it in blank.

(2) *Special indorsement:* A special indorsement is one which names the party to whom the indorser makes the instrument payable.

EXAMPLE: Ellen signed a check which read, "Pay to the order of Peter Jones, $40." Peter specially indorsed the check by writing on the back, "Pay to the order of Glen Hall. (Signed) Peter Jones."

A party who receives a negotiable instrument indorsed in blank may make it a specially indorsed instrument by writing over the signature of the blank indorser.

EXAMPLE: Ed Green received a check that had been made payable to Joe Lane. Joe Lane had indorsed the check in blank by signing his name on the back. Ed may write over Joe's signature, "Pay to Ed Green." Ed has made the check into one that is specially indorsed.

(3) *Indorsement without recourse:* An indorsement without recourse is one in which the indorser disclaims liability in the event the maker or drawer fails to pay.

EXAMPLE: Tim manages several apartments for Mike. A tenant gave Tim a check for rent. The check was made payable to the order of Tim. Instead of merely indorsing the check, Tim writes "without recourse" above his signature. This insures that Tim will not be held liable in the event the check is not paid.

(4) *Restrictive indorsement:* A restrictive indorsement is one that requires the indorsee to follow certain instructions.

EXAMPLE: Ann signed a check payable to the order of Brenda. Brenda indorsed the check on the back by writing, "Pay to Clara, provided that she graduates from college by May 30, 1995." Brenda signed beneath the statement. Clara or any subsequent holder cannot collect payment until the condition is met. (Brenda could not put such a condition in a check on which she is the drawer without making the check nonnegotiable, but she is permitted to indorse a check conditionally.)

E. Defenses

There are two main categories of defenses: personal defenses and real defenses.

1. *Personal Defenses:* Personal defenses are valid only against an ordinary holder. Personal defenses will not allow a party to avoid paying a holder in due course [see Section B-6-c(6) in this chapter].

    a. *Breach of contract:* Negotiable instruments are usually issued as a result of a contract between two parties. If a third party gives value for that negotiable instrument and takes it without any knowledge of the breach, the third party is free from the defense of breach of contract.

    EXAMPLE: Leon contracted to purchase four copy machines from True-Copy, Inc. Under the agreement Leon gave True-Copy a promissory note for $4,000 payable in two months. True-Copy sold the note to XYZ, Inc. for $3,600. When the note became due, XYZ presented it for payment. Leon claimed that because he only received three machines, he was not obligated for the full amount of the note. XYZ is free of Leon's personal defense because XYZ qualifies as a holder in due course provided that it had no knowledge of any breach at the time it acquired the note for value.

    b. *Fraud in the inducement:* A party who issues a negotiable instrument based upon a fraudulent representation (see Chapter 3: Contracts, Section A-2-b) cannot use fraud as a defense against a holder in due course.

    EXAMPLE: Based on Lloyd's representation that a certain rock had been brought from the moon to earth by astronauts, Jake agreed to purchase the rock for $5,000. Jake issued a promissory note to Lloyd in that amount. Later Jake learned that Lloyd had misrepresented the rock's origin and that in fact Lloyd had found the rock in his yard. Although Jake would have a valid defense against Lloyd or an ordinary holder, if Lloyd has transferred the note to a holder in due course, Jake must pay the note. (Jake could still sue Lloyd.)

    c. *Illegality:* If the law makes the transactions merely voidable as opposed to void, illegality is a personal defense. Most illegal agreements are voidable.

    EXAMPLE: Larry contracted to drive Bill's truck carrying Bill's furniture to Dallas in return for a promissory note from Bill in the amount of $150. Larry's driver's license had expired. He therefore could not legally perform the agreement. Larry transferred the *note to Hal who paid $125 for it. Hal had no knowledge of any illegality. Hal is not subject to the defense of illegality.*

d. *Duress and undue influence:* These are considered personal defenses so long as the abuse involved did not become so outrageous that the issuer of the instrument lost his/her will as a result of threats of physical harm.

EXAMPLE: Mike threatens to organize all of the local hardware-store owners and obtain their promise never to buy from ABC Manufacturing, Inc., unless ABC issues a note to him for $10,000 for his services as a consultant. When ABC issues the note to Mike, he quickly sells it to Irv for $9,450. Irv had no knowledge of any threat. ABC cannot assert the defense of duress against Irv who is a holder in due course.

e. *Mental incapacity:* This is not a valid defense against a holder in due course unless the incapacity is so extreme that the instrument is void rather than merely voidable.

f. *Payment of the instrument:* Upon paying the amount of the negotiable instrument, the maker should obtain the return of the instrument or at least have it marked *canceled*. If such a precaution is not taken, the instrument may come into the possession of a holder in due course against whom payment would not be a valid defense.

g. *Writing without authority:* The defense that someone acted without authority and completed an incomplete instrument is a personal defense.

EXAMPLE: Lucy asked Georgia to go to the grocery store for her and purchase the items on a grocery list. Lucy gave Georgia a check which she had signed. The check was left blank as to the payee and the amount. Georgia wrote her name in as the payee and wrote in $200 as the amount. Georgia then indorsed the check and delivered it to a holder in due course. The unauthorized completion would constitute a valid defense against Georgia or an ordinary holder but not against a holder in due course.

2. *Real Defenses:* Real defenses are valid against all holders, including holders in due course. Real defenses are sometimes referred to as universal defenses.

   a. *Forgery:*

   (1) One whose signature is forged on a negotiable instrument may use forgery as a defense even against a holder in due course.

(2) If an agent has signed a negotiable instrument on behalf of a principal, the principal may assert the signer's lack of *any* authority as a defense even against a holder in due course.

b. *Fraud in the execution:* [See Chapter 3: Contracts, Section A-2-b(3).]

EXAMPLE: Burt, a movie star, is asked by a fan to autograph a picture. Later the fan lifts the picture off the promissory note which it was covering. Burt's signature appears on the note. Since Burt was deceived as to what he was signing, he has a valid defense even against a holder in due course.

c. *Material alteration:* A material alteration of the instrument that should be apparent to a holder is a real defense.

(1) A material alteration is one that changes the amount, the interest, the date, the signature, or the parties.

(2) A correction of the maker's address is not a material alteration.

(3) A correction of the amount due in order to rectify a mere mathematical error is not a material change.

(4) A line or other mark that does not alter the parties, the amount, the interest, the date, or the signatures is not a material alteration.

(5) If an alteration is not material, it is not a defense against any holder.

(6) If an alteration is material, it is a defense against any ordinary holder. It is a defense against a holder in due course only if the alteration is apparent.

d. *A discharge in bankruptcy:* Federal bankruptcy prevails over the interest of a holder in due course. If the debt is discharged in bankruptcy court, the holder has no right to payment. (See Chapter 8: Credit, Security, and Bankruptcy, Section C-2-a.)

e. *Illegality that renders an instrument void:* If the instrument is merely voidable, it provides only a personal defense (see Section E-1-c in this chapter).

f. *Mental incompetence:* A person who has actually been found by a court to be mentally incompetent cannot issue a negotiable instrument that is enforceable against him/her. Such a person has a real defense. If at the time the instrument is signed the person has not yet been adjudged by a court to be mentally incompetent, the instrument is merely voidable and provides only a personal defense.

- g. *Threat:* If a signature was obtained by the threat of force or immediate violence, the instrument is void. This type of extreme duress provides a real defense.

- h. *Minority:* Minority is a real defense to the same extent that it is a defense to the enforcement of a simple contract.

Negotiable Instruments 121

Chapter 5: Review Questions

PART A: Multiple-Choice Questions

DIRECTIONS: Select the best answer from the four alternatives. Write your answer in the blank to the left of the number.

_____ 1. Wes contracted to deliver his motorcycle to Ed in return for Ed's promise to paint Wes's house. Ed assigned his rights in the contract to Ted. When Ted sued Wes to obtain the motorcycle, Wes defended on the grounds that Ed had not painted the house. Is Wes permitted to assert the defense against Ted?

    a. Yes, because Ted is subject to the same defenses to which Ed would be subject.
    b. Only if Ted knew that Ed had not completed painting the house at the time Ted took the assignment.
    c. No, because the contract was a negotiable instrument.
    d. None of the above.

_____ 2. Mel owed a disputed debt to the Acme Farm Implement Company. Angry and frustrated at his inability to resolve the dispute, Mel carved a check on a pumpkin and delivered it to Acme. Does the pumpkin qualify as a negotiable instrument?

    a. No, the UCC requires the writing to be on paper.
    b. No, pumpkins are among the items specifically excluded by the UCC as media for negotiable instruments.
    c. Yes, if all the elements of negotiability are met.
    d. Yes, because pumpkins are goods under the UCC.

_____ 3. Alex wrote on a slip of paper, "Barb, I owe you $55. (Signed) Alex." Is this a negotiable instrument?

    a. Yes, because all requirements of the UCC are met.
    b. No, because the signature was not notarized.
    c. No, because the promise was conditional.
    d. No, because the writing does not contain a promise to pay.

4. Jack wrote, "I promise to pay Wayne $150 if Wayne delivers his 13-inch color television set to my home by May 1. (Signed) Jack." Is this writing a negotiable instrument?

   a. Yes, because all requirements of the UCC are met.
   b. No, because the sum of money is not certain.
   c. No, because the promise to pay is conditional.
   d. No, because it is not payable to the bearer.

5. Luke wrote a check payable to the order of Sandra. The check is drawn on the First National Bank. Which of the following is true?

   a. Luke is the drawer, Sandra the drawee, and the bank the payee.
   b. Luke is the drawer, Sandra the payee, and the bank the drawee.
   c. Luke is the maker, Sandra the holder, and the bank the indorsee.
   d. Luke is the maker, Sandra the indorsee, and the bank the drawee.

6. Which of the following is a negotiable instrument?

   a. A check
   b. A time draft
   c. A trade acceptance
   d. All of the above

7. William contracted to purchase a new oven for his restaurant from the Universal Supply Company. Under the terms of the agreement, William gave Universal a promissory note for $6,000 payable in three months. Universal negotiated the note to Max in return for $5,200. When the note became due, Max presented it for payment. William claimed that the oven Universal had delivered did not comply with the contract. Is Max subject to William's defense?

   a. No.
   b. No, provided that Max had no knowledge of any breach of the contract at the time he purchased the note.
   c. Yes, because breach of contract is a real defense.
   d. Yes, because a promissory note is not a negotiable instrument.

8. Which of the following is a real defense?

   a. Fraud in the inducement
   b. Payment on the instrument
   c. Forgery
   d. Breach of contract

Negotiable Instruments 123

9. An important difference between a real defense and a personal defense is that

   a. a personal defense can be asserted against a holder in due course, but a real defense cannot.
   b. a real defense can be asserted against a holder in due course, but a personal defense cannot.
   c. a personal defense requires two witnesses, but a real defense requires only one.
   d. none of the above.

10. Susan signed a check made payable to the order of Pamela. Pamela indorsed the check by writing on the back of it, "Pay to Louise provided that she registers to vote by October 1, 1991." Pamela signed her name below the statement. Pamela has made a/an

    a. restrictive indorsement.
    b. indorsement without recourse.
    c. assignment.
    d. forgery.

11. Which of the following would not constitute a material alteration of a negotiable instrument?

    a. A change in the amount of money listed.
    b. A change in the stated rate of interest.
    c. A change in the date.
    d. A change in the stated address of the maker for the purpose of correcting it.

12. Hugh is a holder in due course of a note made by Chet. When Hugh demanded payment on the note, Chet claimed he had already paid the full amount to Greg, the previous holder. Which of the following statements is true?

    a. Chet may assert the defense against Hugh because payment is a real defense.
    b. Chet will succeed with the defense if he can prove that he actually paid the full amount to Greg.
    c. Both (a) and (b) are true.
    d. Hugh is not subject to the defense of payment.

13. Assume that in the preceding situation Hugh sued Chet on the note. Before the case came to trial, however, Chet obtained a discharge of the debt in federal bankruptcy court. Which of the following statements is true regarding Hugh's right to collect on the note?

    a. Hugh can only collect if he proves he obtained the note prior to Chet's filing for bankruptcy.
    b. Hugh can only recover if he proves that he obtained the note prior to the date on which Chet obtained the discharge in bankruptcy.
    c. Hugh can recover regardless of the timing of the bankruptcy.
    d. None of the above.

14. A material alteration of a negotiable instrument provides a defense against

    a. any holder (ordinary holders and holders in due course).
    b. only ordinary holders.
    c. ordinary holders and holders in due course if the alteration is apparent.
    d. none of the above.

15. Lenny, a delivery person for a flower shop, delivered flowers to Jim. Lenny showed Jim a receipt and asked him to sign on a certain line. While Jim went to get a pen, Lenny substituted a promissory note for the receipt. Thinking he was signing the same document he had just examined, Jim signed the note. Lenny negotiated the note to Howard, a holder in due course. When Howard demanded payment, Jim asserted the defense of fraud. May Jim's defense be used against a holder in due course?

    a. No, because fraud is a personal defense.
    b. Yes, because Lenny's conduct amounts to fraud in the execution.
    c. No, because Lenny's conduct amounts to fraud in the inducement.
    d. Yes, because Lenny's conduct amounts to duress.

Negotiable Instruments

PART B: Matching Sets

Matching Set 1

Match the type of negotiable instrument (A-D) with the appropriate statement (16-19). Write the letter of your answer in the blank to the left of the number.

NEGOTIABLE INSTRUMENTS

A. Check
B. Draft
C. Promissory Note
D. Certificate of Deposit

STATEMENTS

_____ 16. Contains bank's acknowledgement of receipt of money and its obligation to pay the money on a certain date.

_____ 17. Contains an unconditional order by the drawer, directing the drawee to pay money to a payee.

_____ 18. Contains a promise by its maker to pay a specified sum of money to another party at a specified time or upon demand.

_____ 19. Drawn on a bank and payable on demand.

Matching Set 2

Match the term describing a party to a negotiable instrument (A-D) with the correct statement (20-23). Write the letter of your answer in the blank to the left of the number.

PARTIES TO NEGOTIABLE INSTRUMENT

A. Drawer
B. Indorser
C. Maker
D. Holder

STATEMENTS

_____ 20. A payee who transfers the negotiable instrument.

_____ 21. One who signs a promissory note.

_____ 22. One who issues a check.

_____ 23. One who possesses a negotiable instrument issued or indorsed to him/her or payable to bearer.

Matching Set 3

Match the type of defense, real or personal, (A-B) with the appropriate defense (24-28). Write the letter of your answer in the blank to the left of the number.

TYPES OF DEFENSE

A. Real Defense
B. Personal Defense

DEFENSES

_____ 24. Fraud in the inducement

_____ 25. Breach of contract

_____ 26. Forgery

_____ 27. Fraud in the execution

_____ 28. Discharge in bankruptcy

Negotiable Instruments

PART C: Case Problems

DIRECTIONS: Each of the following case problems requires you to answer one or more multiple-choice questions about the case. Select the best answer from the four alternatives. Write the letter of your answer in the blank to the left of the number.

Case 1

William had several fake diamonds that he attempted to sell as real diamonds. On May 1 he sold one of these to Rita in return for a promissory note in the amount of $200. Also on May 1 he sold one to Mark in return for a promissory note in the amount of $250. On May 2 William transferred Rita's note to Wanda in return for $175. Wanda had no knowledge of any misrepresentation. On May 8 William transferred Mark's note to Barry in return for $20. Barry knew at the time of this transfer that Mark planned to sue William for misrepresentation concerning the "diamond" sale.

_____ 29. When Rita's note became due, Wanda sued Rita to collect the $200. Which is the correct result?

   a. Rita can use the defense of misrepresentation against Wanda.
   b. Rita will win because a promissory note is nontransferable.
   c. Wanda will win if she can prove that the misrepresentation was fraud in the execution.
   d. Wanda will win because she is a holder in due course.

_____ 30. When Mark's note became due, Barry sued to collect the $250. Which is the correct result?

   a. Mark can use the defense of misrepresentation against Barry.
   b. Barry can collect $20 from Mark, but not the full amount of the note.
   c. Barry will win because he is a holder in due course.
   d. Barry will win because misrepresentation is no defense in a suit based on a promissory note.

Case 2

Adam is a holder in due course of a promissory note purportedly signed by Bruce. When Adam sued to collect on the note, Bruce claimed the signature was forged.

_____ 31. Which of the following is a correct statement?

   a. Bruce can assert the defense of forgery against Adam.
   b. Bruce cannot assert the defense of forgery against Adam.
   c. As a holder in due course, Adam can collect on the note only from the party who negotiated the note to him.
   d. As a holder in due course, Adam cannot collect on the promissory note.

32. Assume that Bruce, instead of claiming forgery, claims that the note was altered after he signed it. Which of the following is correct?

   a. Any alteration will be a defense against Adam.
   b. Any material alteration will be a defense against Adam.
   c. Any apparent alteration will be a defense against Adam.
   d. Only apparent and material alterations will be a defense against Adam.

Case 3

Helen signed a draft which read, "Pay to the order of Wayne, $100." She delivered the draft to Wayne.

33. In order to negotiate the draft, Wayne must

   a. indorse it.
   b. deliver it.
   c. indorse and deliver it.
   d. Wayne cannot indorse the draft since it is payable to him.

34. Assume that Helen signed a draft which read, "Pay to bearer, $100." She delivered it to Wayne. In order to negotiate the draft, Wayne must

   a. indorse it.
   b. deliver it.
   c. indorse and deliver it.
   d. Wayne cannot negotiate the draft because it is payable to the bearer.

Chapter 5: Solutions

PART A: Multiple-Choice Questions

	Answer	**Refer to Chapter Section**
1.	(a)	[D-1] Ted is merely an assignee. As such he stands in the shoes of Ed, the assignor. Since Ed would be subject to Wes's defense, Ted is also subject to that defense. The contract did not qualify as a negotiable instrument. Among other things, the contract did not contain an unconditional promise to pay a certain sum of money.
2.	(c)	[B-1] The Uniform Commercial Code requires only that the writing be in tangible form. Since a carving on a pumpkin is tangible, this requirement is met.
3.	(d)	[B-3-a] Alex's writing merely acknowledges a debt. It does not contain an express promise to pay the money. There is no requirement that the signature be notarized.
4.	(c)	[B-3-c(1)] Jack's promise is conditioned on Wayne's delivery of the television. The writing, therefore, does not qualify as a negotiable instrument.
5.	(b)	[B-6-c] Luke, as the issuer of the check, is the drawer. The bank, as the party that is ordered to pay the money, is the drawee. Sandra, the party to whom the check is payable, is the payee.
6.	(d)	[C-1, C-2] Each of the listed instruments meets the requirements for negotiable instruments. Each is a signed writing containing a promise to pay a certain sum of money at a specific time or upon demand to the order of someone or to the bearer.
7.	(b)	[E-1-a] If Max had no knowledge of the alleged breach, he qualifies as a holder in due course and, therefore, takes free of William's defense.
8.	(c)	[E-2-a] Forgery is a real defense. Each of the others listed are personal defenses, which cannot be successfully asserted against a holder in due course.

9. (b) [E-2] Only real defenses can be successfully asserted against a holder in due course.

10. (a) [D-2-b(4)] Pamela has made a restrictive indorsement. Louise, the indorsee, must perform the stated act in order to collect payment on the check. If Pamela had been the drawer of the check, she could not include such a condition without making the check nonnegotiable. As the payee, however, Pamela may make such an indorsement.

11. (d) [E-2-c(1)] Answers (a), (b), and (c) relate to important aspects of the instrument that affect the amount due or the date the money is payable. A correction of the address of the maker, however, does not change the nature of the obligation.

12. (d) [E-1-f] Payment is a personal defense. Because Hugh is a holder in due course, he is not subject to such a defense. Chet should have insisted that Greg return the note to him when he paid Greg. At least Chet should have had the note marked canceled.

13. (d) [E-2-d] A discharge in bankruptcy is a real defense. It, therefore, applies even against a holder in due course.

14. (c) [E-2-c] A material alteration provides a valid defense against all ordinary holders. In addition, it provides a defense against a holder in due course if the alteration is an obvious one.

15. (b) [E-2-b] Since Lenny actually deceived Jim into signing something other than what he thought he was signing, fraud in the execution occurred. Unlike fraud in the inducement, fraud in the execution is a real defense. It, therefore, is valid even against a holder in due course.

Negotiable Instruments

PART B: Matching Sets

Matching Set 1

16.	(D)	[C-4]
17.	(B)	[C-2]
18.	(C)	[C-3]
19.	(A)	[C-1]

Matching Set 2

20.	(B)	[B-6-c(4)]
21.	(C)	[B-6-c(3)]
22.	(A)	[B-6-c(1)]
23.	(D)	[B-6-c(5)]

Matching Set 3

24.	(B)	[E-1-b]
25.	(B)	[E-1-a]
26.	(A)	[E-2-a]
27.	(A)	[E-2-b]
28.	(A)	[E-2-d]

PART C: Case Problems

29. (d) [E-1-b] Since Wanda gave value for the instrument and took it in good faith without knowledge of any defenses, she is a holder in due course who takes free of the personal defense of fraud in the inducement.

30. (a) [E-1-b] Since Barry did not take the instrument in good faith without knowledge of the defense, he is not a holder in due course. He is, therefore, subject to the defense of fraud in the inducement.

31. (a) [E-2-a] Forgery is a real defense that may be asserted even against a holder in due course.

32. (d) [E-2-c] Since Adam is a holder in due course, he takes free from even a claim of material alteration unless the alteration is an apparent one.

33. (c) [D-2-b] Because this instrument is payable to Wayne, he must both indorse and deliver it in order to negotiate the instrument.

34. (b) [D-2-a] Since this negotiable instrument is payable to the bearer, it is negotiated by mere delivery.

CHAPTER 6
Personal and Intellectual Property

OVERVIEW

Anything that is capable of being owned is property. Ownership includes the right to possess, control use, or transfer. Land, including attached buildings, fixtures, and crops, is called *real property* and is dealt with in Chapter 7. Property other than real property is known as *personal property*. If the property has physical existence, it is considered *tangible*. If not, it is *intangible* property (shares of stock, checks, or other such representation of value). Finally, property is either *public* (owned by the government) or *private*.

Copyright, patent, and trademark interests are also considered property. These legal interests are commonly referred to as *intellectual property*. In order to encourage creative thinking and innovative advances in technology, federal law affords the author or inventor certain protection for his/her work. For instance, one who writes a poem, book, or computer program may apply for copyright protection. One who invents a new tool or a unique design for a ballpoint pen may apply for a patent. A business may wish to obtain trademark protection for the distinctive marking it places on its products. Copyrights and patents give the protected parties the exclusive right to market and profit from their works. Anyone who violates the copyright or patent will be held liable for damages. This chapter reviews the law of personal property, including copyrights, patents, and trademarks.

DEFINITION OF TERMS

CHATTEL MORTGAGE. The legal document used when the collateral securing a loan is personal property, such as in the purchase of a car financed through a lender.

COPYRIGHT. Legal protection available to the author of a literary work. A copyright gives the author the exclusive right to use the work subject to certain legally recognized exceptions.

FAIR USE. Legally recognized exceptions to copyright protection that allow those other than the author to use the copyrighted work for certain limited purposes.

FIXTURES. Personal property so attached to real property as to become a part thereof, for example, paneling in a home; hot water heater.

INFRINGEMENT. Illegal use of patented or copyrighted work.

LITERARY WORKS. Works such as books, magazines, newspapers, plays, musical compositions, artwork, photographs, motion pictures, recordings, computer programs, data bases, and other verbal or numerical symbols that can be copyrighted by the author.

PATENT. Legal protection available to the inventor of a machine, process, product, chemical, a new variety of nonpollinating plant life, or other new useful invention. A patent gives the inventor the right to prevent others from using the patented invention in the United States and its territories and possessions.

PATENT AND TRADEMARK OFFICE. Federal agency in U.S. Department of Commerce that administers patent law.

PERSONAL PROPERTY. Everything subject to ownership which is not real property.

REAL PROPERTY. Land and permanent attachments thereto such as crops, buildings, and fixtures.

A. Classification of Property

Land, including attached buildings, fixtures, and crops, is called *real property.* Property other than real property is known as *personal property.* Personal property that is attached to real property and becomes a part of it is known as a *fixture.*

EXAMPLE: Paneling constitutes personal property when brought to a construction site. When installed in offices in a building, paneling becomes a fixture.

1. *Types of Personal Property:*

    a. *Tangible:* Personal property having a physical existence--capable of physical possession--is known as tangible personal property.

    EXAMPLES: A book, an automobile, a stereo.

b. *Intangible:* Personal property not existing in physical form--incapable of physical possession--is known as intangible personal property.

EXAMPLES:

Stock certificates only represent the ownership of stocks in a corporation. Corporate ownership is determined solely by the corporation's shareholder records.

Patents, copyrights, and accounts receivable.

2. *Acquisition of Ownership:* Individuals acquire ownership of personal property through purchase, gift, finding abandoned or lost property, and by will or descent.

   a. *Acquisition by purchase:*

   EXAMPLE: Ed buys a can of paint at the local Sears store.

   b. *Acquisition by gift:*

      (1) *Parties:*

         (a) *Donor:* Person making the gift.

         (b) *Donee:* Person receiving the gift.

      (2) *Required elements of gift:*

         (a) Present donor intent to make a gift to the donee.

         (b) Delivery of property and/or title thereto.

         (c) Acceptance of the gift by the donee.

      (3) *Types of gifts:*

         (a) *Intervivos gift:* A gift made during the donor's lifetime.

         (b) *Testamentary gift:* Personal property may be transferred through a will which becomes effective upon the death of its maker.

         (c) *Causa mortis:* This type of gift requires a fear of imminent death in the donor. If the donor survives or dies of another cause, then the gift is considered legally canceled.

EXAMPLE: Al was told by his doctor that he has terminal, inoperable cancer and is not expected to live more than 60 days. Al decides to give his antique desk to Sue and arranges to have it moved to her home. Through a medical miracle, Al survives and is completely cured. The gift is canceled.

    c. *Acquisition by finding property:*

        (1) *Abandoned property:* If property is abandoned, then the finder receives full ownership rights. Property is considered abandoned when it is obvious that the previous owner intended to relinquish ownership rights. The manner, place, and time of the previous owner's parting with the property are relevant in determining whether abandonment has occurred.

        EXAMPLE: Adam finds some Indian arrowheads while tilling his garden.

        (2) *Lost or mislaid property:* If property is lost, the finder has rights superior to everyone but the rightful owner. If property is mislaid, the owner of the premises upon which it is found has rights superior to all but the rightful owner.

        EXAMPLE: Lassie, a dog, wanders onto Hector's property. Hector would not get good title to the lost dog because title is still held by Lassie's owners.

        (3) *Other types of ownership claims:* It is often difficult to ascertain whether property is lost, mislaid, or abandoned. Much case law exists regarding determination of conflicting ownership claims to such property.

    d. *Acquisition by descent:* Personal property can be acquired by relatives of a deceased person who dies without a will by descent. Each state has its own law establishing the order of descent. This is known as the *law of intestacy.*

3. *Chattel Mortgages on Personal Property:* A chattel mortgage represents the giving of security interest in personal property, similar to that of giving a mortgage on real property. Today, UCC Article IX is in effect and governs the issuance of chattel mortgages, except in Louisiana.

B. Copyrights

A *copyright* is legal protection available to the author of a literary work. A copyright gives the author the exclusive right to use the work subject to certain legally recognized exceptions.

1. *Protection of Rights in Literary Works:* Copyright protection is available to the author of a literary work. A literary work may take various forms, such as

    - books, magazines, journals, and newspapers.
    - plays, lectures, and musical compositions.
    - artworks, photographs, and graphic designs.
    - motion pictures and recordings.
    - computer programs and data bases.
    - audio-visual displays.
    - any other verbal or numerical symbols.

2. *Protection is Not Automatic:* The author of a literary work must take certain precautions to qualify for copyright protection.

    a. *Release of work:* The author must not allow the work to be released to the public unless it bears an indication of the author's intent to copyright the work.

       (1) *Intent:* The intent may consist of the word *copyright,* the year the work is released, and the name of the author.

       (2) *Copyright symbol:* The copyright symbol © should be used on all works the author intends to copyright because it is recognized in many countries in addition to the United States.

    b. *Registration of copyright:* In order to enforce his/her rights fully in court, the author must register the copyright with the Copyright Office in the Library of Congress in Washington, D.C. This requires filing an application form, which is accepted by the Register of Copyrights.

3. *Duration of Copyright Protection:*

    a. *Author known:* Copyright protection lasts for the lifetime of the author plus 50 years.

b. *Author unknown:* If the author is unknown or if the work is done under the name of a fictitious person, the duration of copyright protection is 75 years from the date the work was first released to the public (or 100 years from the date the work was created if its creation preceded its release by more than 28 years).

c. *Work created prior to January, 1978:* If the work was created before January 1, 1978, its copyright protection is for only 28 years. (An additional 47 years of protection may be applied for upon the expiration of the first 25 years.)

4. *Nature of Copyright Protection:* The author of a copyrighted work has the right to the exclusive use of the work subject to certain legal exceptions.

   a. *Permission to use copyrighted work:* The holder of a copyright may grant permission to another party to use the copyrighted work. The permission might be obtained in return for the payment of a fee, or it might be granted without payment.

   b. *Fair uses of copyrighted work:* The law recognizes certain fair uses as exceptions to the copyright holder's exclusive right to the copyrighted work.

      (1) Copying a copyrighted work for purposes of studying it or using it in the course of one's research is permissible.

      (2) Using copyrighted material for limited purposes in a classroom for instructing students is permissible if the work is relatively short, and it would be impractical to obtain the consent of the copyright holder. If the material is a major part of the class material or if it is used from year to year, the author's consent may be required.

      (3) Other fair uses are permitted if they do not affect the potential market for the work or otherwise decrease the value of the work. If there is a question as to whether a particular use is permitted under copyright laws, a legal expert should be consulted.

5. *Enforcement of Copyrights:* A party who has violated copyright law may be prosecuted for a criminal offense or sued by the copyright holder for damages.

   a. *Criminal violation:* In a criminal case, the intentional violator may be fined or imprisoned.

   b. *Civil violation:* In a civil suit for damages, the violator will be ordered to pay damages to the copyright holder.

    c. *Court orders:*

        (1) A court may enter an order directing a party to stop a practice that constitutes a copyright violation. If the party defies the order, he/she will be subject to contempt of court proceedings (see Chapter 2: Court Procedures, Section B-1).

        (2) A court may order a party to turn over or destroy all illegal copies of copyrighted material.

    d. *Prosecution:* A violator may be prosecuted in a criminal case and sued for damages in another suit for the same violation.

C. Patents

A *patent* is legal protection available to the inventor of a machine, process, product, chemical, a new variety of nonpollinating plant life, or other new useful invention. A patent gives the inventor the right to prevent others from using the patented invention in the United States and its territories and possessions.

1. *Protection of Rights of Inventors:* One who invents or discovers a new process or machine may qualify for patent protection.

EXAMPLES:

Patent protection is also available for an inventor who manufactures a new product.

One who discovers a new chemical, a new chemical compound, or a plant may apply for patent protection.

One who invents or discovers useful improvements in existing machines, processes, products, chemicals, or plants may also apply for patent protection.

2. *New and Useful Requirement:* An invention must be new and useful in order to qualify for a patent.

    a. *Known or used:* If the invention has been known or used by others or if it is merely an obvious extension of an existing invention, it does not qualify for a patent.

    b. *Nonperformance:* If the invention does not perform the intended purpose or is otherwise not useful, it does not qualify for a patent.

3. *Obtaining a Patent:* In order to obtain a patent, the inventor must apply to the Patent and Trademark Office in Washington, D.C. The law does not require that the inventor be represented by a lawyer, but it is highly advisable that the inventor obtain expert assistance.

4. *Duration of Patent Protection:* Patent protection lasts for 17 years from the date the patent is granted.

5. *Nature of Patent Protection:* A patent gives the inventor the right to prevent others from making, using, or selling the invention in the United States and its territories and possessions.

   a. *No right to make:* A patent does not give the inventor the right to make, use, or sell the invention. The invention must comply with all relevant state and federal laws.

      EXAMPLE: Floyd invented a new kind of lawnmower and obtained a patent for it. The mower, however, does not comply with the standards of the Environmental Protection Agency. Floyd cannot legally market the mower unless he complies with all relevant laws. Mere possession of a patent does not give him the right to market the product. It only gives him the right to prevent others from using his invention.

   b. *Outside United States:* It may be possible to obtain a patent protection in other countries. The United States has entered into a treaty with many other nations for the purpose of making international patent protection easier to obtain. Expert assistance should be obtained to expand patent protection beyond the United States and its territories and possessions.

   c. *Licensing:* The patent holder may grant a license permitting another party to use the invention.

6. *Enforcement of Patent Rights:* A patent holder may sue one who infringes upon the patent.

   a. *Cease and desist:* The court may enter an order directing a party to stop a practice that constitutes patent infringement. If the party defies the order, it will be subject to contempt of court proceedings (see Chapter 2: Court Procedures, Section B-1).

   b. *Pay damages:* The court may order the infringing party to pay damages to the patent holder.

   c. *Challenge validity:* In a patent-infringement suit, the party being sued may challenge the validity of the patent.

    d. *Countersuit:* One who is threatened with a patent-infringement suit may sue the patent holder in order to obtain a court ruling on the issue.

    e. *Government use:* The government may use patented inventions without permission from the patent holder. The patent holder is entitled to receive fair compensation, however, for the use of the invention.

D. Trademarks

A *trademark* is a distinctive marking, motto, or device that is placed on products to identify their source.

1. *Qualification as a Trademark:* To qualify as a trademark, the marking, motto, or device must be distinctive and must not be merely descriptive of the product or its use.

    EXAMPLE: The maker of a new soft drink places the words A Refreshing Drink *on its beverage containers. This phrase does not qualify as a trademark because it is descriptive of the product. It would be unfair to prevent competitors from describing their beverages as refreshing drinks. If the phrase was accompanied by a distinctive design, it could, with the design, qualify as a trademark.*

2. *Registration Not Required:* A trademark need not be registered with the government in order to be protected from infringement. Registration does add to the protection of a trademark, however, by providing proof of the date of the trademark's use.

    EXAMPLE: Two businesses use the same symbol on their products. Each claims the symbol as a trademark. One of the businesses had registered its trademark with the government in 1961. The other never registered the symbol as a trademark and cannot prove it used the symbol on products prior to that time.

3. *Infringement:* The holder of a trademark is entitled to sue anyone who infringes upon it and to recover lost profits and a court order prohibiting further unauthorized use of the trademark.

Personal and Intellectual Property 143

Chapter 6: Review Questions

PART A: Multiple-Choice Questions

DIRECTIONS: Select the best answer from the four alternatives. Write your answer in the blank to the left of the number.

_____ 1. A stock certificate is personal property. Which factor listed below is a property aspect of the stock certificate?

    a. A stock certificate is considered tangible property.
    b. A stock certificate is considered intangible property.
    c. A stock certificate could be a fixture.
    d. A stock certificate is not considered property.

_____ 2. To make a valid intervivos gift, all of the following must be present except

    a. donative intent by the donor.
    b. delivery to the donee.
    c. fear of imminent death.
    d. acceptance by the donee.

_____ 3. Copyright protection may be obtained for an original work in each of the following categories except

    a. books, magazines, journals, and newspapers.
    b. computer programs.
    c. photographs.
    d. original works in each of the above categories may be copyrighted.

_____ 4. Copyright protection lasts for

    a. 17 years.
    b. 50 years.
    c. life of the author plus 50 years.
    d. forever.

5. Tom invented a new engine for automobiles that makes it possible to get 73 miles per gallon. Tom was granted a patent by the Patent and Trademark Office in Washington, D.C. When Tom attempted to sell cars with his new engine in them, however, he was informed by the Environmental Protection Agency that the engine did not conform to the applicable standards. Tom claims the patent permits him to sell the engines. Is Tom correct?

   a. Yes, because patent law prevails over other applicable regulations.
   b. Yes, because patent law prevails over administrative agency regulations, but not over other federal legislation.
   c. No, because patent laws merely give the inventor the right to prevent others from using the invention.
   d. No, because he should have obtained copyright protection.

6. Patent protection lasts for

   a. 17 years.
   b. 50 years.
   c. the inventor's life plus 50 years.
   d. the inventor's life plus 17 years.

7. Sally obtained a patent on a new ballpoint pen she invented. She discovered Hal making and selling similar pens without permission. Sally sued Hal. Which of the following is true?

   a. In the suit Hal may challenge the validity of Sally's patent.
   b. The court may order Hal to stop making and selling the pens if he is found to be violating Sally's patent rights.
   c. The court may order Hal to pay damages to Sally if he is found to be violating Sally's patent rights.
   d. All of the above.

8. At a picnic table along the side of the highway, Elmer found a map that had directions and phone numbers written upon it. Hugo claims that the map is his and can prove that he owned it on an earlier date. Elmer's interest in the map will prevail over Hugo's if it is determined that

   a. Hugo had lost the map.
   b. Hugo had abandoned the map.
   c. Hugo had mislaid the map.
   d. Hugo had made the map.

Personal and Intellectual Property

PART B: Matching Sets

Matching Set 1

Match the intangible property interest term (A-C) with the appropriate statement (9-12). Write the letter of your answer in the blank to the left of the number.

INTANGIBLE PROPERTY INTEREST TERMS

A. Copyright
B. Patent
C. Trademark

STATEMENTS

_____ 9. A distinctive marking, motto, or device placed on products to identify their source.

_____ 10. Legal protection available to the author of a literary work.

_____ 11. Legal protection available to an inventor.

_____ 12. Lasts 17 years from the date it is granted.

Matching Set 2

Match the property term (A-D) with the appropriate statement (13-16). Write the letter of your answer in the blank to the left of the number.

PROPERTY TERMS

A. Donee
B. Fixture
C. Intervivos Gift
D. Donor

STATEMENTS

_____ 13. One who gives a gift.

_____ 14. A gift made during one's lifetime.

_____ 15. Attachment to real property.

_____ 16. One who receives a gift.

Personal and Intellectual Property

Matching Set 3

Match each of the property terms (A-B) with the appropriate statement (17-20). Write the letter of your answer in the blank to the left of the number.

PROPERTY TERMS

A. Abandoned Property
B. Lost or Mislaid Property

STATEMENTS

_____ 17. Finder receives full ownership rights.

_____ 18. Owner's interest prevails over that of finder.

_____ 19. Owner intended to relinquish ownership rights.

_____ 20. Finder's interest prevails over anyone else's interest except for original owner.

PART C: Case Problems

> DIRECTIONS: For each of the questions relating to the following case problems, select the best answer from the four alternatives. Write your answer in the blank to the left of the number.

Case 1

Ann and her niece Susan were passengers on an airplane. The pilot announced that the plane had run out of gas and that an emergency landing would be attempted. Ann began crying and removed her diamond ring and gave it to Susan saying, "Here, this is for you. I'm going to be dead in a few minutes." The plane made a miracle landing, and Ann suffered only a sprained ankle. Susan refuses to return the ring.

_____ 21. Which of the following statements is true?

  a. Susan is entitled to keep the ring because the gift was completed.
  b. Susan is entitled to keep the ring because the ring was mislaid property.
  c. Ann is entitled to the return of the ring because it was a gift in contemplation of death.
  d. Ann is entitled to the return of the ring because it was a fixture.

Case 2

Bates invented a low-calorie chocolate candy formula. He called it Light Chocolate. He also wrote a book describing his seven-year ordeal in developing and perfecting the formula.

_____ 22. If Bates wants to apply for legal protection of his new formula, he should apply for

  a. copyright protection.
  b. patent protection.
  c. trademark protection.
  d. civil rights protection.

_____ 23. If Bates wishes to obtain maximum legal protection for the term *Light Chocolate* that will appear on his product, he should apply for

  a. copyright protection.
  b. trademark protection.
  c. patent protection.
  d. civil rights protection.

_____ 24. If Bates wishes to obtain maximum legal protection for his book, he should apply for

  a. copyright protection.
  b. trademark protection.
  c. patent protection.
  d. civil rights protection.

Personal and Intellectual Property 149

Chapter 6: Solutions

PART A: Multiple-Choice Questions

	Answer	Refer to Chapter Section
1.	(b)	[A-1-b] A stock certificate is intangible property--not having physical existence and incapable of physical possession.
2.	(c)	[A-2-b(3)] A fear of imminent death is only required for a gift causa mortis.
3.	(d)	[B-1] The items listed in answers (a), (b), and (c) are considered literary works subject to the copyright laws.
4.	(c)	[B-3] Copyright protection lasts for the life of the author plus 50 years.
5.	(c)	[C-1, C-5] The inventor must still comply with all other applicable laws and regulations. Patent protection only allows the inventor to prevent others from using the invention.
6.	(a)	[C-4] Patent protection lasts for 17 years.
7.	(d)	[C-6] Answers (a), (b), and (c) are correct statements regarding patent-infringement suits.
8.	(b)	[A-2-c] The finder of abandoned property prevails over the previous owner. The finder of lost or mislaid property takes subject to the previous owner's interest.

PART B: Matching Sets

Matching Set 1

9.	(C)	[D]
10.	(A)	[B-1]
11.	(B)	[C-1]
12.	(B)	[C-4]

Matching Set 2

13. (D) [A-2-b]

14. (C) [A-2-b(3)]

15. (B) [A]

16. (A) [A-2-b]

Matching Set 3

17. (A) [A-2-c]

18. (B) [A-2-c]

19. (A) [A-2-c]

20. (B) [A-2-c]

PART C: Case Problems

21. (c) [A-2-c] A gift made in contemplation of death is canceled if the donor does not die as he or she anticipated. Since Ann survived, the gift is canceled and she is entitled to the return of the ring.

22. (b) [C-1] Patent protection includes protection to the inventor of a process, product, or chemical.

23. (b) [D-1] Trademark protection is available for distinctive markings or slogans attached to products to identify their source.

24. (a) [B-1] Copyright protection is available for literary works.

CHAPTER 7
Real Property

OVERVIEW

Anything that is owned or can be owned is property. Ownership means the right to possess, control use, and/or transfer. Land, including attached buildings, fixtures, and crops, is called *real property*. Property owned other than real property is known as *personal property*. If the property has physical existence, such as a computer, it is considered *tangible*. If not, it is *intangible* property (shares of stock, checks, or other such representation of value). Finally, property is either *public* (owned by the government) or *private* (owned by individuals).

The most effective approach to studying property is to understand the distinction between the various concepts, to be able to define specific terms, and know how they relate to each other, for example, selling mortgaged property subject to the mortgage versus a sale with the assumption of a mortgage. Practical applications will help the candidate visualize the various concepts as they are presented in this chapter. For example, a husband and wife may buy a house in joint tenancy, receive a warranty deed, assume a loan, be subject to a utility company easement for electrical lines, and have the title checked to make sure no unknown liens exist. In this example, real property is both private and tangible.

Besides real and personal property, the candidate must master the distinctions between different types of deeds to real property (warranty, quitclaim), forms of ownership (estate in severalty, tenancy in common, joint tenancy, tenancy by the entirety), methods of selling mortgaged property (subject to the mortgage or assumption of the mortgage), and various methods of acquiring and/or possessing property (deed, adverse possession, gifts).

Landlord-tenancy law requires the candidate to focus upon the classifications of tenancies, rights, duties, and remedies. Fitness for use, habitability, and termination methods and reasons should be understood.

DEFINITION OF TERMS

ADVERSE POSSESSION. The taking of real property belonging to another by notorious, adverse, open, hostile, or continuous possession for a period of years, often ten to twenty years.

EASEMENT. The right of a nonowner to use a piece of land in a specific way (affirmative) or to prevent the owner from using his or her own land in a specific way (negative).

FIXTURES. Personal property so attached to real property as to become a part thereof, for example, paneling in a home, hot water heater.

FORECLOSURE. The act of the mortgagee (lender) in forcing the sale of property secured to a loan as a result of default by the mortgagor (borrower/owner of property).

GRANTEE. One to whom property is conveyed.

GRANTOR. One who conveys property.

JOINT TENANCY. Co-ownership of property whereby a deceased party's interest goes to the surviving party/ies.

MORTGAGE. The legal document used when collateral securing a loan is real or personal property.

MORTGAGEE. The lender; party to whom the mortgage is given.

MORTGAGOR. The borrower; party putting up property to secure a loan.

NOVATION. The release of a party to a contract in consideration of the assumed liability of another, that is, the substitution of a new contract for an old contract.

PERSONAL PROPERTY. Property owned other than real property.

QUITCLAIM DEED. Grantor (the party conveying the property) transfers entire interest, if any, without any warranty of title.

REAL ESTATE MORTGAGE. The giving of a certain type of security interest in land owned or being purchased by the mortgagor.

REAL PROPERTY. Land and permanent attachments thereto such as crops, buildings, and fixtures.

REDEMPTION. The mortgagor's statutory right to pay overdue payments and penalties and be restored to predefault status.

SECOND MORTGAGE. Any mortgage secured after the original (or first) mortgage.

SECURITY INTEREST. The giving of a legal interest (lien) in one's property to another to secure a loan.

TENANCY IN COMMON. Co-ownership of property whereby a deceased party's interest passes according to the will and/or inheritance laws.

WARRANTY DEED. In essence, a warranty by the grantor that the property is transferred free from all unknown defects or claims.

A. **Classification of Property**

Property means ownership; the right to possess, use, and/or transfer real and personal property. Land, including attached buildings, fixtures, and crops is called *real property*. Property owned that is other than real property is known as *personal property*.

1. *Real Property:* Land and any improvements upon or connected with the land is *real property*. Trees and crops are considered real property until severed.

    EXAMPLES OF REAL PROPERTY:

    Land, buildings, airspace above the land, minerals, and trees.

    a. *Ownership:* An owner of real property owns not only the surface but that above and below the surface. Below-surface ownership rights in minerals (oil, gas, coal, water) may be sold or leased separately from the surface real estate.

        EXAMPLE: Mary sells a firm, Black Acre, to John but retains oil and gas interests. Mary could later sell, lease, or use this retained interest.

        EXAMPLE: Golden Oil Company secures an oil lease on Gary's farm. Golden Oil will have the right to use such amount of the farm as reasonably necessary to extract the oil.

    b. *Use of airspace:* Airspace is limited to the amount that the owner may reasonably use. Government restrictions often exist which restrict the permitted height of buildings and towers.

        EXAMPLE: Building heights are restricted close to airports so as not to interfere with airplane takeoffs and landings.

    c. *Legal interest of others:* Real property is often subject to legal interests of others, for example, utility lines, easements (right of passageway), tenants.

        EXAMPLE: If Karen signs a one-year lease on March 1, she will have a right to remain in her apartment for one year even if the building is sold the very next day.

2. *Personal Property:* All other property that is not real property is called *personal property.* (See Chapter 6: Personal and Intellectual Property for complete explanation of personal property.) *Fixtures* are items of personal property which have been attached to real property so as to become a part thereof.

EXAMPLE: Bookshelves or paneling attached permanently to walls in an office.

B. **Acquisition of Real Property**

Real property may be acquired through purchase, gift, adverse possession, condemnation, lease, or forfeiture.

1. *Purchase:* This is the most common manner in which real property is transferred.

    a. *Writing required:* A writing (written contract) is required under the statute of frauds for the sale of land (and affixed buildings and fixtures thereon). The written contract sets forth the terms and conditions of sale, such as when the closing will be, the purchase price, and the actual items to pass with the property. It must be signed by the seller.

    EXAMPLE: Sharon orally agrees to purchase Ted's house. The contract is unenforceable because no writing (written contract) exists.

    b. *Conveyance of deed:* A deed is delivered by the seller to the buyer evidencing the sale of the property. The deed represents title to the property.

    c. *Recording of deed:* The buyer records the deed in the county courthouse so as to provide public record of ownership. The failure to record the deed would allow the seller to resell the property to another buyer if the third party purchaser bought in good faith, for value, and without notice of prior sale.

2. *Gift:* The voluntary giving of the property to another without charge is called a *gift.* For a gift to be considered a *valid* gift, the following elements must be present:

    a. *Intent to make a gift by donor (giver):* The donor intends to make an unconditional present gift.

    EXAMPLE: Roger tells Eugene that he is to have Roger's farm when Roger dies. This is not a present intent.

Real Property

b. *Delivery of a deed to donee (recipient):* Delivery of a deed may be directly to the donee or to someone who accepts the gift on behalf of the donee (constructive delivery).

c. *Acceptance of the gift by donee:* Acceptance is generally presumed where not otherwise indicated.

3. *Adverse Possession:* The taking of property from another without consent or payment may legally be accomplished by adverse possession. Acquisition by adverse possession must be

   a. *Notorious:* The adverse possessor is actually using the property.

   b. *Open:* The adverse possession is obvious in actual usage. If the usage is not sufficiently visible, then adverse possession is not possible.

   EXAMPLE: James erects a garage which extends four feet onto his neighbor's property. If no consent and/or objection occurs, the land belongs to James after the number of years set by statute.

   c. *Adverse:* The possession is without permission. In essence, the taker by adverse possession is a squatter who is trespassing. Therefore, no adverse possession may occur where the person is present with consent.

   EXAMPLE: Alvin was a tenant for 23 years in a house owned by John. Alvin has no right to the house.

   d. *Hostile:* The adverse possessor is a trespasser, using the property without permission of the owner.

   e. *Under a claim of right:* The adverse possessor must actually claim ownership over a period of time. The statutory requirement of years of adverse possession before the property may legally be taken varies by state from five to twenty years. The "tacking" of years toward meeting this statutory requirement is possible.

   EXAMPLE: James (see example under B-3-b) lived at his property for 11 years and then sold it to Elizabeth. If the adverse possession period is 20 years total, Elizabeth would have to possess the property only 9 more years.

C. Types of Deeds

Deeds represent the giving of written title from the seller to the buyer. Specific types of deeds include quitclaim deeds, warranty deeds, and special warranty deeds.

1. *Quitclaim Deed:* The grantor (seller) conveys all he or she owns, if anything, in the property.

   EXAMPLE: Kathi could give Sandy a quitclaim deed to the White House. Sandy would get no legal interest, however, because Kathi does not have any legal interest to give.

   a. *No warranties made:* If the grantor owns nothing, then the grantee (buyer) receives nothing. If the grantor owns a house and conveys by quitclaim deed, then the grantee receives good and rightful title.

   b. *Representation of ownership:* The grantor could be independently liable from the deed for misrepresentation or fraud in the inducement concerning false representations of ownership, if any exist.

   EXAMPLE: Brenda has no real-property warranty obligations to Evan if she gives Evan a quitclaim deed to a farm that she claims to own but actually does not own and wants to convey to him legally. Brenda may, however, yet face tort liability for fraud.

2. *Warranty Deed:* In essence, a warranty deed represents a warranty by the grantor (the property seller) that the property is transferred free from all unknown defects or claims.

   a. *Warranties by grantor:* In the warranty deed, the grantor warrants that:

      (1) He/she owns the property being transferred.

      (2) He/she has the right to convey the property.

      (3) The property is free from undisclosed encumbrances such as easements or mortgages.

      (4) Grantee's legal right to possession will not be disturbed.

      (5) The title to the property is good.

      EXAMPLE: Carl acquires Black Acre, a farm, from Robert by warranty deed. If Robert did not actually own Black Acre, then Carl would have a right of recovery against Robert.

   b. *Purchaser's knowledge of legal interests:* A purchaser of property is charged with knowledge, whether actually known or not, of any legal interest properly recorded against the property in the county courthouse, any defect in title evident from an inspection of the property being sold, or the zoning.

Real Property

EXAMPLE: An electric power line runs across the back lot line of Al's property. If the power line is evident, then the buyer would be charged with knowledge. Thus, a buyer should carefully inspect the property.

EXAMPLE: If the electric power line (above) was a buried cable, then the purchaser of the property would be charged with knowledge of it if the easement (right of passage) was recorded in the county courthouse. Thus, a buyer should carefully inspect the legal title at the county courthouse.

3. *Special Warranty Deeds:* These instruments are also known as bargain and sale deeds. All warranties of the general warranty deed described above are covered. The warranties, however, apply only to the time during which the grantor actually owned the property.

D. **Types of Ownership**

Real property is either owned by a sole owner (only one person or entity owns the property) or by multiple owners (more than one person or entity owns the property). When there are multiple owners of the property, ownership may be characterized by joint tenancy, tenancy by the entirety, tenancy in common, community property, or tenancy in partnership.

1. *Joint Tenancy:* Joint tenancy exists when there is simultaneous (concurrent) ownership of property by two or more owners with a right of survivorship. The owners must acquire their interest at exactly the same time and must be clearly designated in the deed as joint tenants.

    a. *Equal undivided interests:* Each joint tenant owns an equal undivided interest with equal rights of possession.

    EXAMPLE: If there are two joint tenants for a particular piece of real property, each one owns one half, regardless of which joint tenant, if either, paid greater moneys toward the purchase. If there are three joint tenants, each would own one third.

    b. *Conveyance of interest:* A joint tenant may convey his/her interest to another. The transferee becomes a tenant in common (see Section D-2 in this chapter) with the remaining joint tenant(s).

    EXAMPLE: A, B, and C own a farm in joint tenancy. A sells his undivided one-third interest to X. X is a tenant in common as to B and C but as to the remaining two-thirds interest B and C remain joint tenants.

- c. *Survivorship:* The surviving joint tenant(s) automatically receives the interest of a joint tenant who dies. A will has no effect.

    EXAMPLE: Kyle and Peter own a farm in joint tenancy. Kyle's will says that Kyle's son is to receive Kyle's share of the farm when Kyle dies. Peter would prevail.

- d. *Statement of joint tenancy:* When receiving real property in joint tenancy, the joint tenants must be sure this is clearly stated. If they do not, then the ownership of the property will be presumed to be tenancy in common.

2. *Tenancy in Common:* Concurrent ownership exists by two or more owners with no right of survivorship. Surviving co-owners do not receive the property.

    - a. *Undivided interest:* The owners have an undivided interest (like joint tenancy).

    - b. *Equality of interest:* Ownership need not be equal (unlike joint tenancy).

        EXAMPLE: A may own two thirds while B owns one third of a farm.

    - c. *Survivorship:* When a tenant in common dies, his/her share passes by will or by descent to heirs. There is no legal right by the surviving co-owner to the property unless will or descent would so direct.

    When ownership interest is not clear, it is presumed to be a tenancy in common. This is the most common means of ownership where no family connection exists.

3. *Tenancy by the Entirety:* A joint-ownership interest exists between husband and wife. This type of ownership is *not* recognized in all states.

    - a. *Conveyance of interest:* Tenancy by the entirety is essentially like a joint tenancy, except that a spouse may not sell his/her share without the consent of the other.

    - b. *Survivorship:* The surviving spouse receives the property as in joint tenancy.

    - c. *Termination:* Tenancy by the entirety is terminated by a divorce.

4. *Community Property:* Property that is owned by husband and wife is called *community property*. Community property is recognized in only eight states.

Real Property

        a. *Survivorship:* Owners have the right of survivorship (as in joint tenancy).

        b. *Ownership:* Property acquired during marriage automatically becomes community property (one half belonging to each spouse).

5. *Tenancy in Partnership:* In a partnership, each partner has a certain property interest. The partners are tenants in partnership.

        a. *Undivided interest:* Each partner has an undivided interest with equal rights of possession (as in other types of ownership).

        b. *Survivorship:* The right of survivorship is to the remaining partner(s). A deceased partner's family only has a right to the value of the decedent's partnership share.

E. Mortgages

In general, a mortgage represents a nonpossessory interest (lien) in real property that is given to secure a debt. People often confuse mortgages so as to believe that lenders are giving home mortgages. In fact, lenders are lending money that is secured by the house, the mortgaged property. Thus, the borrower is the *mortgagor* because he/she is giving a mortgage (interest in the property to secure a loan) to the lender, the *mortgagee.* A mortgage must be in writing because an interest in land is being conveyed. If the mortgagor defaults on the mortgage, not making required payments, a mortgagee may foreclose on the mortgage (deprive the mortgagor the right to redeem the property).

Property that is already subject to a mortgage may be mortgaged again if a lender is willing to take a second mortgage for security. The second mortgage is, of course, junior to the original mortgage. Only if the first mortgage is fully satisfied can the holder of the second mortgage recover anything.

F. Easements

In general, an easement is a nonpossessory interest in the land of another to either use (affirmative easement) or prevent usage (negative easement) in a particular manner.

EXAMPLE: As shown in Figure 7-1, John has a right to cross Sarah's land to reach his cabin on a lake. This right is called an affirmative easement.

Figure 7-1
Illustration of Easement

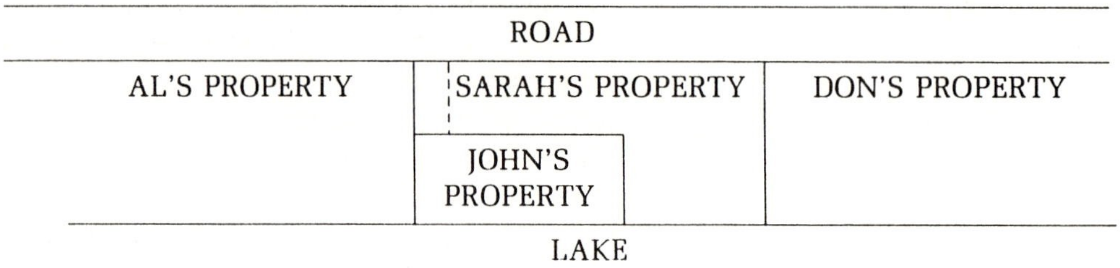

	ROAD	
AL'S PROPERTY	SARAH'S PROPERTY	DON'S PROPERTY
	JOHN'S PROPERTY	
	LAKE	

EXAMPLE: John has the right to receive sunlight crossing Sarah's property. This is a negative easement, referring to the prevention of land usage by the grantor in a way detrimental to the grantee. Sarah would not be allowed to build a tall structure that would block the sunlight crossing John's property.

1. *Characteristics of an Easement:*

   a. *Nonpossessory:* The easement only provides access across another individual's property.

      EXAMPLE: In the example illustrated in Figure 7-1, John may use his access right across Sarah's property but could not erect a garage, plant a garden, or substantially alter the passageway as to usage or size.

   b. *Maintenance:* The easement must be maintained by the individual who has the right to use the property.

      EXAMPLE: John must maintain the easement.

   c. *Interference:* The property owner may not interfere with the use of the easement.

      EXAMPLE: Sarah may not interfere with John's use of the easement passageway.

2. *Types of Easements:*

   a. *Easement appurtenant:* The right to pass over one property to get to another is known as easement appurtenant. Property subject to the easement is the *servient* land (Sarah's property in the example) while the *served* property (John's) is the dominant property. The right to use the easement runs with the land.

Real Property

EXAMPLE: A purchaser of John's property acquires the right to use the easement.

b. *Easement in gross:* The personal right of usage of land which is not tied to a second piece of land is called an easement in gross. Utilities generally have such easements for their lines across land.

c. *The nature of easements:* The creation of an easement interest may occur in one of three ways:

(1) *Express grant or resolution:* This easement must be in writing.

(2) *By necessity:* This is only possible where an owner of land divides the land into two or more parcels without providing a means of access. (A buyer is not to be left landlocked by the seller.)

EXAMPLE: If Sarah had sold John his property without mention of any right of passageway across her property, he would still have a legal right because of a necessity (see Figure 7-1).

(3) *By prescription:* By continuous adverse passage, the adverse passer secures a right of passage over property of another without consent or payment. Although not an interest in land, this right of passage is achieved in a similar manner as adverse possession of land. The adverse passage must be

(a) *Notorious:* The adverse passer must be actually using the property, and it is publicly known that the adverse passer is doing so.

(b) *Open:* The use of the property must be sufficiently visible.

(c) *Adverse:* The use of the property is without permission of the owner.

(d) *Hostile:* The adverse passer is a trespasser, using the property without the permission of the owner.

EXAMPLE: Henry gives Patti permission to go across his property on her horse. Patti can get no adverse passage right (prescriptive easement) as her passage is with Henry's consent.

The required number of years necessary to secure a

prescriptive easement may be gained by "tacking" as in adverse possession cases. The adverse passer gets the right of passageway, a nonpossessory interest, versus actual possession rights that the adverse possessor gets.

EXAMPLE: If Bill builds his garage five feet over onto Harry's property without permission and the required years go by without action by Harry, Bill is considered to actually own the five feet. Thereafter, Bill can do anything with it that one normally can do with land. A prescriptive easement would have given Bill a right of passageway forever over Harry's land but not legal title to the land nor usage other than passage alone.

    d.   *Termination of an easement:*

        (1) *Lapse:* The termination of time permitted to the passer has occurred.

        (2) *Abandonment:* Nonusage of the easement has occurred. Generally abandonment requires an affirmative act besides nonusage.

        (3) *Merger:* Dominant and servient parcels of land have been united.

             EXAMPLE: Sarah purchases John's property.

        (4) *Misuse of easement:* The easement is being used for an improper purpose.

G. The Landlord-Tenant Relationship

Property owners may lease or rent property to others. A contract known as a lease outlines the conditions of such a relationship. Most states have specific statutes regulating the landlord-tenant relationship. Below appear the general common law rules which have been changed in many places by statutes.

    1.   *The Nature of the Lease:* A lease is both a contract and a conveyance of *real property.* The *lessee* (the renter) secures possession rights for a given period of time from the *lessor* (the landlord). A lease is not required to be in writing if it will be completed within one year's time. The lease is not terminated by the death of either the lessor or lessee. A purchaser of a building takes subject to any existing leases.

Real Property 163

2. *Types of Leasehold Estates:*

   a. *Estate for years:* Tenancy is for a fixed time only, but not necessarily for only one year.

   EXAMPLE: A lease of a warehouse for 60 days is an estate for years *as a lease for a set period of time.*

   b. *Periodic tenancies:* Tenancy for a specified period of time, which will continue for similar periods of time until terminated, is known as periodic tenancy. Timely notice must be provided to terminate such leases.

   EXAMPLE: A month-to-month lease.

   c. *Tenancy at sufferance:* This type of tenancy occurs when a tenant holds over (stays) beyond the lease termination date or date otherwise agreed as to the termination date.

3. *Rights of Landlord:*

   a. *Rent:* The landlord receives the rent.

   b. *Lease term:* If tenant stays beyond the lease, the landlord may

   (1) Evict the tenant.

   (2) Treat the tenant as a holdover with period-to-period lease.

   c. *Abandonment of lease:* If the tenant wrongfully abandons the lease, the landlord:

   (1) May do nothing and sue for rent as it comes due, or

   (2) Rent the property and hold the tenant liable for any deficiencies in rent money.

   Note: In some states, a landlord must show evidence of having tried to rent the lease premises (known as mitigation of damages).

4. *Duties of Landlord to Tenant:*

   a. *Implied warranty of habitability:* Warranty to the tenant that the premises are fit for human occupancy (generally applies only to residential leases).

   EXAMPLE: The warranty is breached where landlord rents

apartment without heat in the winter.

    b. *Providing safe common areas:* The landlord must provide safe areas such as stairways and hallways.

    c. *Warranty of quiet enjoyment:* The warranty of quiet enjoyment is a warranty to the tenant that the landlord has the legal right to lease out the premises and that the tenant will not be removed without just cause during the term of the lease.

    d. *Termination of lease by tenant:* A breach of the landlord's duties does not legally permit the tenant to terminate the lease. Many courts, however, are finding *constructive eviction* where an apartment becomes uninhabitable. In essence, this means the tenant may move out without further legal duties to the landlord.

5. *Tenant's Transfer of Interest:*

    a. *Assignment:* The transfer of a tenant's entire interest in a lease is an assignment.

        (1) *Novation:* The original tenant, the assignor, is still liable unless there is a novation from the landlord. *Novation* is the release of a party to a contract in exchange for another being liable.

        (2) *Tenant liability:* The new tenant, the assignee, becomes personally liable to the landlord.

    b. *Sublease:* The transfer of less than the tenant's entire interest to the sublettor is known as a sublease.

        (1) *Tenant liability:* As in assignment, the assignor (the original tenant) is still liable on the lease.

        (2) *Binding terms:* The assignee is not personally liable to the landlord for a sublease. The terms and conditions of the lease are still binding upon the assignee, however.

A landlord may prohibit either subleasing or assignment, or both, if so stipulated in the lease. If just subleasing is prohibited, however, the tenant may still assign the lease, and vice versa.

EXAMPLE: Ginger's lease prohibits her from assigning the lease to her apartment. She is not prohibited from subleasing, however.

Chapter 7: Review Questions

PART A: Multiple-Choice Questions

DIRECTIONS: Select the best answer from the four alternatives. Write your answer in the blank to the left of the number.

_____ 1. Howard signs a ten-year lease for a building with Anderson. Howard agrees in the lease not to assign it. The lease could be terminated if

   a. Howard dies.
   b. Anderson sells the building to Quincy.
   c. Howard sublets the building to Morkle.
   d. Howard assigns the lease without permission.

_____ 2. Fernando has a year's lease with Maria, the landlord. Connie has agreed to take over Fernando's lease, and Maria has agreed to release Fernando from his lease obligations.

   a. Fernando received a novation.
   b. Fernando would not have been liable any longer to Maria regardless of her release.
   c. Connie would not have been personally liable on the lease if Fernando had not been released.
   d. This is an example of a sublet.

_____ 3. Curt just purchased a cabin on a lake from Milton. Although there was a passageway to the highway via Milton's property, Milton had traveled the old hunter's path across Jason's property. Jason has now erected a barrier across this passageway.

   a. Since Curt would not have used the hunter's path for sufficient time, no prescriptive easement could exist.
   b. If Curt's own passageway got washed out, he could use Jason's path because of necessity.
   c. Milton could have gained a prescriptive easement only if he was an adverse passer.
   d. A prescriptive easement would have to be in writing to be effective.

4. John mortgaged his farm to Delta Bank. Delta Bank recorded the mortgage. When John defaulted, it was learned by Delta Bank that John had earlier given a mortgage to Alex.

   a. If Alex failed to record, then Delta Bank would prevail over Alex.
   b. If Alex failed to record, then John would prevail over Alex.
   c. If both Alex and Delta Bank properly file, then they will share foreclosure proceeds, if any, on a pro rata basis.
   d. In both cases, John was the mortgagee.

5. The following must be created by a writing, if created by an express grant, *except*

   a. an easement.
   b. a six-month lease.
   c. a mortgage.
   d. a quitclaim deed.

6. A six-month lease is an example of

   a. periodic tenancy.
   b. tenancy at sufferance.
   c. estate for years.
   d. an easement.

7. Gen gave First Federal a mortgage for a $75,000 loan. Gen defaulted on the loan.

   a. First Federal may foreclose on the mortgage.
   b. Because Gen has defaulted, she could not redeem the property.
   c. First Federal was the mortgagor.
   d. Gen's mortgage could have been oral.

8. Which of the following actually represents legal title to property (meaning ownership of the property)?

   a. A contract to sell the property.
   b. An easement to cross the property.
   c. A deed received at closing.
   d. Title insurance.

Real Property

_____ 9. Assuming you have the choice about which deed you will receive from a seller, your best choice would be a/an

   a. quitclaim deed.
   b. general warranty deed (sometimes simply called warranty deed).
   c. special warranty deed.
   d. implied warranty deed.

_____ 10. All of the terms listed below are elements of adverse possession *except*

   a. notorious.
   b. open.
   c. hostile.
   d. permission.

PART B: Matching Sets

Matching Set 1

Match each fact statement (11-15) with the appropriate declaration of law (A-B). Write the letter of your answer in the blank to the left of the number.

DECLARATIONS OF LAW

A. Matter which requires a writing to be enforceable
B. Matter which may be oral and enforceable

FACT STATEMENTS

_____ 11. Express grant of an easement.

_____ 12. The granting of a quitclaim deed.

_____ 13. The granting of a real estate mortgage.

_____ 14. A contract for the sale of a home.

_____ 15. The lease of an apartment for a semester while at school.

Real Property

Matching Set 2

Match each fact statement (16-20) with the appropriate type of ownership (A-B). Write the letter of your answer in the blank to the left of the number.

TYPES OF OWNERSHIP

A. Tenancy in Common
B. Joint Tenancy

FACT STATEMENTS

_____ 16. Al, Beth, and Calvin are joint tenants in a farm. Al conveys his undivided interest to Don. Between Beth and Calvin, they will now own the farm jointly as _____.

_____ 17. Referring to #16, as between Don and Beth/Calvin, Don has a _____ interest.

_____ 18. Ed and Fran owned undivided interests in a lake cabin. Ed's will left his share of the cabin to Jason. However, when Ed died, a court determined that Fran was to receive his ownership rights. Ed must have had a _____ interest.

_____ 19. Kelly and Lynn own undivided interests in a vacation condominium. Kelly owns 60 percent and Lynn 40 percent. They probably own the condominium as _____.

_____ 20. Martha and Nancy inherited a farm as equal undivided owners. The will is unclear as to how they are to own the land. A court would most likely find that they have _____ interests.

PART C: Case Problems

DIRECTIONS: For each of the questions related to the following case problem, select the best answer from the four alternatives. Write your answer in the blank to the left of the number.

Case 1
Cindy and David Brix, newlyweds, are buying their first home together from a person transferred to a new location, Ben Smith. They are unsure of what to expect at their first home closing or the legal significance of several matters which will be involved in the closing. They have sought your assistance.

_____ 21. Which item below is unlikely to be involved at the closing?

    a. A lease for the home.
    b. A bill of sale for the personal property to be transferred with the home.
    c. A note from Cindy and David to a lender.
    d. A deed from Ben Smith.

_____ 22. Cindy and David are to receive a special warranty deed. This means that

    a. defects in title prior to Ben Smith's ownership will not be covered.
    b. it is likely that defects existed prior to Ben Smith's ownership.
    c. their deed will be considered more valuable than both a general warranty deed and a quitclaim deed.
    d. the deed assures the same ownership interest as if a quitclaim deed had been received.

_____ 23. Cindy and David will own their home as tenants by the entirety. This type of ownership is

    a. recognized in all states.
    b. another name for community property.
    c. quite similar in operation to joint tenancy.
    d. quite similar in operation to tenancy in common.

Chapter 7: Solutions

PART A: Multiple-Choice Questions

	Answer	Refer to Chapter Section
1.	(d)	[G-5] A lease which restricts assignment can be terminated by the landlord if the tenant assigns the lease without the landlord's approval.
2.	(a)	[G-5-a] Fernando received a novation when Maria agreed to release him and look only to Connie.
3.	(c)	[F-2-c] To gain a prescriptive easement, one must be an adverse passer, not having consent. There may be "tacking," the adding of the years Milton used the property to Curt's time. To tack, there must not have been any interruption of usage.
4.	(a)	[B-1-c and E-1] Delta Bank would win if it otherwise had no knowledge of the prior mortgage. John is still liable to Alex.
5.	(b)	[G-1] A writing is not required for the lease because it will be completed within one year's time. An express grant easement, mortgage, or quitclaim deed must be in writing.
6.	(c)	[G-2-a] A lease for a stated duration is an *estate for years* even though it may be less than a year in length.
7.	(a)	[E] A mortgagee may foreclose on a mortgage in a situation where the mortgagor defaults on the mortgage.
8.	(c)	[C] A deed represents the seller's passing of ownership to the buyer. The buyer records the deed in the courthouse for the county where the property is located to give official notice to third parties.
9.	(b)	[C-2] A general warranty deed, often simply called a warranty deed, provides the greatest protection to the buyer and is the most respected by lenders.
10.	(d)	[B-3-c] No adverse possession may occur where the person is present with consent.

PART B: Matching Sets

Matching Set 1

11. (A)   [F] A grant of an easement is the giving of right of passageway. It must always be in writing.

12. (A)   [C] All deeds must be in writing to be enforceable since they represent the actual conveyance of title to real property.

13. (A)   [E] Because an interest in land is being conveyed, a mortgage must be in writing.

14. (A)   [B-1-a] A writing is required since a contract for the sale of real property is for a conveyance of real property.

15. (B)   [G-1] A lease for a semester is a lease for less than one year. Therefore, it would not have to be in writing to be enforceable.

Matching Set 2

16. (B)   [D-1-b] The joint tenancy relationship between Beth and Calvin has not been broken. As to each other, they will continue to be joint tenants of a 2/3 nonpossessory interest.

17. (A)   [D-1-b] Since Don did not acquire his ownership interest with Beth and Calvin, he cannot be a joint tenant with them.

18. (B)   [D-1] A joint tenancy interest passes automatically to the surviving joint tenant(s). A will of the decedent will have no effect upon passage of ownership.

19. (A)   [D-2-b] Joint tenancy interests must be equal. Therefore, Kelly and Lynn could not be joint tenants.

20. (A)   [D-2] When there is a genuine question as to whether a joint tenancy or tenancy in common exists, a court will rule the latter.

PART C: Case Problems

21. (a)   [G] A lease will seldom be involved in the sale of a home from a person who has been living in the home.

22. (a)   [C-3] The special warranty deed operates exactly like the warranty deed except that it applies only to the time during which the grantor actually owned the property.

23. (c)   [D-3-b] Upon the death of Cindy or David, if still married at death, the property will automatically go to the survivor as in joint tenancy.

CHAPTER 8

Credit, Security, and Bankruptcy

OVERVIEW

This chapter focuses upon the lending of money. Every day millions of credit transactions (the lending of money) take place. In fact, statistics indicate that an individual is likely to have made at least one credit transaction this past week. Some typical examples include purchasing gasoline with an Exxon credit card, a new jacket with a VISA card, or a new car with local bank financing. A common thread exists for all three examples: a borrower borrows money from a lender now with the promise, implied or express, to repay the borrowed money (the principal) later, often with interest.

This chapter has three major thrusts:

Credit. Government regulations providing protection for consumer credit transactions, including the borrowing of money, the reporting of credit history, billing and collection practices.

Security. Ways in which lenders can best protect themselves against the default of the borrower.

Bankruptcy. The federal process of relieving debtors from continued liabilities where the debtor has gotten too deeply in debt to be able to pay debts as they come due.

The candidate should understand

1. The purposes of the various consumer credit protection laws, their similarities and their differences.

2. The potential risks encountered by a lender and the basic ways in which a lender might be able to protect itself.

3. The purpose of the bankruptcy laws, the available chapters of bankruptcy relief, and the basic bankruptcy process.

DEFINITION OF TERMS

ARTICLE 9. The article of the Uniform Commercial Code (UCC) dealing with secured transactions.

ATTACHMENT. The process of securing a security interest in collateral against the debtor. Attachment requires the giving of value by the secured party, a legal interest in the collateral by the debtor, and a security agreement unless property is pledged.

BANKRUPTCY. A procedure governed by federal law that provides a means of obtaining relief for debtors and for the uniform and fair treatment of creditors.

BANKRUPTCY PETITION. A document filed in the bankruptcy court to commence a bankruptcy proceeding.

CONSUMER PURPOSE (under Truth in Lending Act). The borrowing of money for personal, family, or household purposes.

EQUAL CREDIT OPPORTUNITY ACT. Federal act, administered by the Federal Trade Commission, designed to promote equal opportunity in the securing of credit.

FAIR CREDIT BILLING ACT. Federal act, administered by the Federal Trade Commission, which provides consumer protection against incorrect and/or unfair billing practices.

FAIR DEBT PRACTICES ACT. Federal act, administered by the Federal Trade Commission, which regulates the manner in which creditors can attempt to collect consumer debts.

FEDERAL TRADE COMMISSION (FTC). A federal administrative agency whose primary responsibility is to keep business competition fair.

FINANCING STATEMENT. A document summarizing a security agreement which is filed in a designated place of public records, generally a courthouse.

LIQUIDATE. To settle debts by distributing the debtor's assets. Liquidation usually involves selling property to obtain cash for the purpose of paying creditors.

MORTGAGEE. The party to whom a mortgage is given, the lender.

MORTGAGOR. The party giving a mortgage to secure the borrowing of money, the borrower.

PERFECTION. The process by which the insured party gains protection against third parties.

SECURED CREDITOR. One who extends credit to another where the debtor's promise to repay is tied to legally recognized property of the debtor.

SECURITY AGREEMENT. An agreement whereby the debtor gives to the creditor an interest in personal property to secure a loan. Unless the creditor retains the

Credit, Security, and Bankruptcy 175

collateral, the security agreement must be in writing.

SECURITY INTEREST. A legally recognized interest of a creditor in certain property of the debtor.

SECURED TRANSACTIONS. Article 9 of the UCC which deals with security interests in personal property.

TRUSTEE. A person appointed by the court in a bankruptcy case who has the duty of managing the bankrupt party's property.

TRUTH IN LENDING ACT (TILA). A federal act, administered by the Federal Trade Commission, designed to provide consumers with information about the costs of borrowing money prior to the actual commitment to borrow.

A. Credit

Credit involves the borrowing of money. Credit is regulated by both state and federal governments.

1. *Credit Regulations:* Because of the perceived unfairness of bargaining power between consumer borrowers and commercial lenders, credit regulations designed to protect consumer borrowers have been created by both state and federal governments. These regulations are generally of two types:

   a. *Usury regulations:* Usury regulations focus upon the amount lenders may charge for credit. Usury regulations are a matter of state, not federal, law.

   EXAMPLE: It is not unusual for a state to regulate the maximum amount that a consumer can be charged in annual interest for a bank credit card, such as VISA or MasterCard.

   b. *Process regulations:* Process regulations are those regulations applicable to the process of borrowing money, being eligible for credit, the keeping and reporting of credit history. Both state and federal process regulations exist.

   EXAMPLE: It is a violation of federal regulations to deny credit to a creditworthy consumer because of race or sex.

   Note: Only federal process regulations will be reviewed in this chapter.

2. *Truth in Lending Act:* The purpose of the Truth in Lending Act (TILA), administered by the Federal Trade Commission (FTC), is to provide consumers with information about the costs of borrowing money prior to the actual commitment to borrow money for a consumer purpose.

a. *Agency authority:* The FTC has primary authority for the act where powers are not specifically delegated or assigned to another agency or commission.

EXAMPLE: The Federal Reserve Board promulgated the regulations to implement TILA.

b. *Consumer purpose:* The borrowing of money must be for a consumer purpose (defined to be for personal, family, or household purposes only).

EXAMPLE: Catherine wishes to borrow $3,500 to purchase a new computer system for her floral store. Although Catherine may own the store, the primary purpose is a business purpose.

EXAMPLE: Harold wishes to borrow $2,000 to purchase a computer for his home to maintain household records, write letters. This would be a consumer purpose. This borrowing would be subject to TILA.

c. *Disclosure requirements:* A borrower protected under TILA is to be provided full information about costs of borrowing (finance charges, annual percentage rate of interest) at the time of application for a consumer loan. This permits the consumer to shop around for the best credit opportunity.

EXAMPLE: Georgia is seeking to borrow money to purchase a new home. The lender must provide information such as closing costs, possible cost of securing the loan (often called points), and the annual interest rate.

d. *Limitations of the act:* TILA does *not* regulate the amount lenders may charge for credit.

e. *Credit card limitations:* TILA limits consumer liability for unauthorized usage of one's credit card to $50.

EXAMPLE: Billy's wallet is stolen by a thief. The thief uses Billy's American Express card to purchase $600 of new clothing. Billy is liable only for the first $50.

f. *Remedy for violation:* Both civil and criminal penalties are possible under TILA for breach of the act.

3. *Equal Credit Opportunity Act:* The purpose of the Equal Credit Opportunity Act (ECOA) is to make credit available to all worthy applicants without regard to race, marital status, religion, or sex (among detailed factors).

a. *Need for the act:* Too often creditors historically denied credit to creditworthy individuals because of noncredit factors, most often race (black applicant) or gender (female applicant). ECOA was enacted for the purpose of eliminating such noncredit discrimination. (To date, ECOA has not totally eliminated such abusive actions.)

b. *Definition of income:* Creditors are required to consider alimony, separate maintenance, and/or child support as income if presented by the borrower. The creditor may, however, evaluate the credit worthiness of such income. In addition, income from regular part-time employment is to be considered.

EXAMPLE: Connie is to receive $1,000 per month alimony from Charles. Connie may elect to have her alimony payments counted as income. The lender, however, may discount the payments as income if Charles is habitually late and/or misses payments.

c. *Denial of credit:* A consumer borrower who is denied credit has the right to be told the specific reason(s) for being denied.

EXAMPLE: Michelle is denied a credit card with J.C. Penney. Michelle has a right to know why she was denied.

d. *Remedies:* Civil remedies are possible.

4. *Fair Credit Reporting Act:* The purpose of this act is to regulate consumer credit reporting agencies.

   a. *Consumers' credit histories:* A lender's best means of evaluating a prospective borrower's likelihood to repay a debt properly is to review the borrower's previous credit history. Such credit history is regularly gathered and maintained in credit bureaus around the country. Obviously it is very important to a potential borrower that information held by a credit bureau is accurate and kept confidential.

   b. *Proper purpose:* The act provides specific rules to ensure confidentiality and proper usage of information. Proper usage of the information will generally relate to one of the following:

      (1) The borrowing of money.

      (2) Application for life insurance.

      (3) Seeking an employment position of responsibility.

         EXAMPLE: A credit bureau providing you information on

your neighbor simply to satisfy your curiosity would be in violation of the act.

    c. *Denial of credit:* A consumer denied credit because of an adverse credit report has the right to review the report for accuracy.

    d. *Corrections:* A consumer may challenge any portion of the report which is considered erroneous. If the credit bureau does not correct or remove the objected material, the consumer has the right to provide a one-paragraph retort which will become a part of the credit record.

    EXAMPLE: Sally may want to have stated on her record that she quit paying her membership contract to her health club because it closed the facility near her and no other facility was available within 25 miles.

    e. *Distribution:* A consumer has the right to learn who has requested his or her credit record and when.

5. *Fair Debt Collection Practices Act:* The general purpose of this act is to prevent abusive practices in the collection of consumer debt.

    a. *Debt-collection methods:* The act prohibits illegal, unconscionable, or harassing debt-collection methods.

    EXAMPLE: A bill collector is prohibited from representing himself as an attorney if he is not. Continuous calls at all hours of the day are prohibited.

    b. *Remedies:* A collector may be subject to a civil action for violation of the act.

B. Security

A lender contemplating the lending of money or the giving of credit to a borrower must be concerned with the borrower's ability to repay the loan. A borrower's promise, while subject to a breach of contract action for nonpayment, may not offer adequate protection.

1. *Types of Security:* The most common forms of security are suretyship, security interest in personal property, and security interest in real property.

    a. *Suretyship:* The lender may not lend money unless a third person, a surety, agrees to pay the note if the borrower does not.

    b. *Security interest in personal property:* Article 9 of the Uniform Commercial Code (UCC) covers security interest in personal property.

    c. *Security interest in real property:* State mortgage laws govern security interest in real property.

    A creditor may require more than one means of security.

    EXAMPLE: Robin is attending Penn State. She wishes to buy a new Mustang. It is likely that a lender will require Robin to find a surety, most often a parent, and provide a security interest in personal property, putting up the Mustang as collateral.

2. *Suretyship:* (See Chapter 3: Contracts, Section E-4)

3. *Security Interest in Personal Property:* Article 9 of the UCC covers situations involving the giving of a security interest in personal property to secure a debt. Article 9 applies to *all* items of personal property, not just goods.

EXAMPLE: Article 9 applies to a transaction where a borrower puts up 100 shares of IBM stock to secure a loan. (Stock is considered intangible personal property, not a good.)

    a. *Attachment:* For a creditor to gain a security interest in personal property of the borrower, the borrower must give a security interest.

    EXAMPLE: Ray buys a new Sears television set for $400 by using his Sears credit card. Ray's usage of the credit card, by itself, gives Sears no security interest in the television. This means Sears has no right to recover the television set from Ray if he fails to pay his Sears charge card bills.

    To gain a security interest

    (1) the secured party (the creditor) must give value. *Giving value* means that the secured party obtains the rights to the personal property that is attached in return for the binding agreement to extend credit to the debtor.

    EXAMPLE: Sears permits Ray to purchase the television set on credit.

    (2) the debtor must have rights in the collateral.

EXAMPLE: Someone stealing Ray's television set would have no rights in the collateral in a subsequent loan situation.

(3) the debtor must have given the secured party a security agreement, which must be written if the secured party does not retain possession of the collateral. A security agreement, if written, must

(a) be signed by the debtor.

(b) state the giving of the security interest.

(c) contain a sufficient description of collateral.

b. *Perfection—protecting a security interest:* A security interest is not binding upon a third party unless perfected. Perfected means protection. Protection *may* be possible against one or more of the following: other creditors, the trustee in bankruptcy, and third party purchasers.

Perfection can occur in one of the following ways:

(1) *Attachment alone:* If the secured property is consumer goods and the secured party provided the credit permitting the purchase, the secured party will be considered perfected as to other creditors and the trustee in bankruptcy by attachment alone. This situation is commonly called a purchase-money security interest (PMSI) in consumer goods.

EXAMPLE: Ray bought the television set from Sears as shown in the previous examples. Sears will not prevail if Ray sells the television set to an unknowing good-faith purchaser at a later garage sale.

(2) *Attachment and possession:* The property is purchased and a security interest is given to a creditor. In addition, the creditor (secured party) retains the property.

EXAMPLE: Karin puts up 100 shares of IBM stock as collateral to secure a loan. The secured party retains the stock.

(3) *Attachment and filing:* A secured party files a financing statement (a document summarizing the security agreement) in the proper office, generally at the courthouse in the county where the personal property is located.

EXAMPLE: If Sears were to file a financing statement concerning Ray's television set, then they would prevail even as to purchasers at a garage sale. (For practical and economic reasons, it is unlikely that Sears would.)

(4) *Caveat:* The filing of a financing statement does not mean that the secured party will always prevail. There are priority rules and coverage exceptions that go beyond the scope of the review contained in this module. The basic rule as to competing financing statements is that the first to file wins.

EXAMPLE: One of the coverage exceptions is that a bank providing inventory financing cannot invoke its lien against a purchaser in the ordinary course of business, such as a buyer of a new Ford from a Ford dealer's new car lot.

c. *Forfeiture of collateral:* A borrower putting up collateral to secure a loan risks losing that collateral for nonpayment of the loan.

EXAMPLE: If Sears did have a security agreement as to Ray's television set, then it could repossess the television if Ray fails to properly pay for it.

d. *Lien on collateral:* Where a secured party's lien in personal property is perfected against third party purchasers, the lien will prevail against even a good-faith purchaser for value. To be sure, a third-party purchaser should check the appropriate official record of UCC filings.

EXAMPLE: Assuming Sears perfected its security interest in Ray's television set by filing a financing statement, even an unknowing, good-faith purchaser for value at a garage sale would buy subject to Sears' right to recover. (Again, it is not likely that Sears would have done this just for a television set.)

4. *Real Property as Collateral:* When real property is put up as collateral, it is called the giving of a mortgage. Mortgages were introduced in Chapter 7: Real Property, Section E.

   a. *Parties to a mortgage:*

      (1) *Mortgagor:* The person putting the real estate up as collateral is called the mortgagor.

      EXAMPLE: Gwen is borrowing $75,000 from First Federal to purchase a house. Gwen is putting the house up as collateral to secure the loan (her note). Gwen is the mortgagor.

(2) *Mortgagee:* The party to whom the mortgage is given is the mortgagee.

EXAMPLE: In the foregoing example, First Federal is the mortgagee.

b. *Granting of mortgages:* A person may grant more than one mortgage on the same piece of land. The mortgage that is properly filed first is considered the first mortgage, the second to be filed the second mortgage.

EXAMPLE: After purchasing her home, Gwen borrows $5,000 from State Bank to finance the construction of a garage. State Bank will have a second mortgage if First Federal is already properly filed.

c. *Filing of mortgage:* In order for the mortgage to be binding upon third parties, the mortgagee must properly file the mortgage in the courthouse in the county where the land is located.

EXAMPLE: If First Federal forgot to file its mortgage from Gwen, then State Bank may gain first-mortgage standing when it properly files its mortgage.

d. *Priority of filing:* States have different rules as to who should prevail if more than one mortgagee exists. The most common rule is the *race-notice rule* (the first mortgagee to file in the courthouse without notice of another mortgage will prevail).

EXAMPLE: Under race notice, State Bank would not prevail in priority over First Federal if it knew of the earlier mortgage.

e. *Sale of mortgaged property:* A mortgagor may generally sell the mortgaged property, but the property will still be subject to the mortgagee's lien and the assignor will generally continue to be liable on the note.

EXAMPLE: Mel purchases Gwen's house by paying her $10,000 and assuming her mortgage notes to First Federal and State Bank. Gwen will still be liable on the original note unless specifically released by the lenders.

f. *Foreclosure:* A mortgagee may foreclose property subject to a mortgage if the mortgagor defaults or fails to pay the applicable note in a timely manner. Foreclosure means putting the property up for sale to satisfy the owed debt.

g. *Redemption:* A mortgagee will generally have the right to redeem,

certain property. This property is said to be exempt. A debtor may elect to use the exemptions recognized by state law.

(b) *Appointment of trustee:* The bankruptcy court may appoint a trustee to administer the debtor's estate. The trustee gathers the debtor's nonexempt property and converts it to cash under the court's supervision.

(3) *Filing of bankruptcy petition:* The filing of a bankruptcy petition causes an automatic stay that applies to all other legal proceedings affecting the bankrupt party's property.

(a) This stay causes a suspension of any legal actions to which it applies.

(b) The stay is effective until the bankruptcy case ends or the bankruptcy judge sets aside the stay.

(4) *Distribution to creditors:* The debtor's liquidated estate is distributed to creditors according to the priorities established under federal bankruptcy law.

(a) *Payment to secured creditors:* Secured creditors have the right to recover the property in which they have a security interest. A *secured creditor* is one who extended credit to the debtor in return for a legally recognized interest in certain property of the debtor.

(b) *Payment of administrative expenses:* As to the nonexempt property that is not the subject of a security interest, administrative expenses are paid first. These consist of the trustee's compensation, the fee of the bankrupt party's lawyer, and other expenses involved in gathering and liquidating the debtor's property.

(c) *Special priorities:* Bankruptcy law recognizes other special priorities such as claims for wages up to $2,000 for work performed within 90 days of the bankruptcy and claims for federal, state, and local taxes.

(d) *Payment to unsecured creditors:* Unsecured creditors who are not covered by a special priority are paid out of what is left of the bankrupt's estate.

(5) *Discharge for debtor:* When the distribution of the debtor's estate is completed, the debtor is granted a discharge from any further obligation on the outstanding debts.

purchase back the foreclosed property, for a period of time after foreclosure.

C. **Bankruptcy**

A bankruptcy case is governed by federal law. The procedure for a bankruptcy case differs from that of an ordinary lawsuit.

1. *Purposes of Bankruptcy:* Federal bankruptcy law is designed to accomplish two major goals: equality in treatment of creditors and relief for debtors.

   a. *Equality in treatment of creditors:* Uniformity and equality in the treatment of creditors is a goal of bankruptcy law. In the absence of federal legislation, each state would be free to establish its own bankruptcy law.

   b. *Relief for debtors:* Providing a fresh start for debtors whose situation is nearly hopeless is another purpose of bankruptcy law. This allows the debtors to escape from a lifetime of indebtedness and to become productive citizens.

2. *Types of Bankruptcy:* There are various types of bankruptcy proceedings. More common types of bankruptcy include the straight bankruptcy, the business reorganization, and the repayment plan.

   a. *Straight bankruptcy:* A straight bankruptcy is one in which the debtor's assets are converted into money, which is distributed to the creditors.

      (1) *Nature of bankruptcy:* A straight bankruptcy may be voluntary or involuntary.

         (a) *Voluntary bankruptcy:* A voluntary bankruptcy proceeding is one filed by the debtor.

         (b) *Involuntary bankruptcy:* An involuntary bankruptcy proceeding is one filed by creditors seeking to have a debtor declared bankrupt. A debtor who is generally not paying debts as they become due will be declared bankrupt.

      (2) *Liquidation of property:* In a straight bankruptcy, the debtor's property is collected and liquidated.

         (a) *Exempt property:* The bankrupt party is entitled to keep

(a) Certain debts cannot be discharged. Included in this category are debts for certain taxes, alimony and child-support obligations, damages resulting from the debtor's willful conduct, debts for certain educational loans, and fines imposed on the debtor.

(b) If the debtor is found to have been guilty of fraudulent conduct, no discharge will be granted.

(6) *Payment of discharged debts:* A debtor may agree to pay debts that have been discharged. Such an agreement is known as a *reaffirmation agreement.* Bankruptcy law establishes certain requirements for such agreements. These requirements, which include obtaining the bankruptcy judge's approval, must be met in order for the agreement to be enforceable.

b. *Business reorganization:* A business reorganization is another type of bankruptcy proceeding.

(1) *Continuation of business operations:* In a business reorganization bankruptcy, a business is allowed to remain open during the proceedings.

(2) *Reorganization plan:* The goal of this type of proceeding is to achieve a plan whereby the business can eventually pay its creditors and survive. The plan may involve a change in management or may result in a liquidation.

(3) *Resolution of firm's difficulties:* A committee of the debtor's creditors is formed to examine the state of the business and to attempt to arrive at a workable plan for resolving the debtor's financial difficulties.

(4) *Nature of bankruptcy:* A business reorganization bankruptcy may be voluntary or involuntary.

(5) *Discharge:* When all the terms of the reorganization have been met, the debtor is discharged.

c. *Repayment plan:* A repayment plan is another type of bankruptcy proceeding.

(1) *Availability:* This type of bankruptcy is available to an individual who has a regular income and debts that are less than a certain amount specified in the federal bankruptcy law.

(2) *Appointment of trustee:* In a repayment plan, a trustee is appointed to administer the debtor's future income.

(3) *Payment time period:* The plan may consist of allowing the debtor more time in which to pay debts or may provide for the payment of less than the full amount of the debts.

(4) *Approval of plan:* The plan must be approved by the bankruptcy judge.

(5) *Discharge:* When all the terms of the plan have been met, the debtor is discharged.

Chapter 8: Review Questions

PART A: Multiple-Choice Questions

DIRECTIONS: Select the best answer from the four alternatives. Write your answer in the blank to the left of the number.

_____ 1. The FTC's regulation of consumer credit is intended to accomplish all of the following *except*

   a. regulate the amount lenders can charge consumers for borrowing money.
   b. prevent discrimination in lending because of sex.
   c. allow consumer challenge to errant credit report information.
   d. make creditors specify to consumers the reason credit was denied.

_____ 2. Usury can best be defined as

   a. an improper method of debt collection.
   b. a matter dealing with the process of granting credit.
   c. a limitation on the amount which can be charged for credit.
   d. a matter covered by the Truth in Lending Act (TILA).

_____ 3. The Truth in Lending Act

   a. applies to both consumer and nonconsumer loans.
   b. requires disclosure of the costs of securing credit.
   c. limits credit card losses to $100.
   d. permits only civil, not criminal, actions.

_____ 4. The Equal Credit Opportunity Act

   a. requires a creditor to fully recognize alimony, separate maintenance, and child support.
   b. requires a creditor to make a loan to certain people, including women and blacks.
   c. makes it discretionary with the lender as to whether to give the reasons for denial of credit.
   d. would apply to someone claiming denial of credit on the base of religious practices.

5. The Fair Credit Reporting Act would probably permit each of the following *except*

   a. permit an employer to check on candidates being considered for the company's comptroller position.
   b. permit a consumer to learn the creditworthiness of a health club.
   c. permit a health insurance company to learn of the creditworthiness of a life insurance applicant.
   d. permit a lender to check the creditworthiness of a consumer loan applicant.

6. All of the following are forms of credit security *except*

   a. credit card purchase.
   b. suretyship.
   c. security agreement.
   d. mortgage.

7. Attachment requires that

   a. the transaction involve a consumer good.
   b. the collateral subject matter involve real property.
   c. the creditor possess the collateral.
   d. a security agreement has been agreed to by the parties.

8. Perfection is best described as

   a. protection against all third parties.
   b. the security obligation of the debtor to the creditor.
   c. protection against persons or parties other than the debtor.
   d. the process of filing a financing statement.

9. Which of the following must be a written document?

   a. Security agreement
   b. Perfection
   c. Attachment
   d. Financing statement

10. To gain a security interest, the secured party must

    a. file a financing statement.
    b. give value.
    c. sign the security agreement.
    d. have rights in the collateral.

Credit, Security, and Bankruptcy

11. Race-notice is the most common form of

    a. foreclosure procedure.
    b. resolving filing priorities.
    c. state redemption procedures.
    d. procedure to bind the mortgagor.

12. Which of the following is *not* true regarding bankruptcy?

    a. Uniformity and equality in the treatment of creditors is a goal of bankruptcy law.
    b. Providing a fresh start for debtors whose situation is nearly hopeless is a purpose of bankruptcy law.
    c. A bankruptcy case may be heard in a federal court or in a state court.
    d. A straight bankruptcy may be voluntary or involuntary.

13. Which of the following kinds of debts can be discharged in bankruptcy?

    a. Alimony
    b. Child support
    c. Fines
    d. Credit card bills

14. Dick has filed for bankruptcy. Among his creditors is Elmer who sold Dick an air compressor on credit and obtained a security interest in the compressor. Dan is another creditor. Dan loaned Dick $300 in return for Dan's promise to repay the money. The federal government is also a creditor because Dick owes money for federal taxes. Which of the following statements is true?

    a. Elmer has the right to recover the air compressor regardless of whether there is sufficient money to pay Dan or the federal taxes.
    b. Dan is entitled to be paid the debt owed him before Elmer is allowed to recover the air compressor.
    c. Dan is entitled to be paid the debt owed him before the federal taxes are paid.
    d. Dick will be able to discharge his federal tax liability.

PART B: Matching Sets

Matching Set 1

Match each fact statement (15-18) with the correct UCC term (A-B). Write the letter of your answer in the blank to the left of the number.

UCC TERMS

A. Attachment
B. Perfection

FACT STATEMENTS

_____ 15. Primary purpose is to secure collateral as to debtor.

_____ 16. Primary purpose is to protect collateral as to third parties.

_____ 17. Filing a financing statement is generally required unless the creditor retains possession of the collateral.

_____ 18. A security agreement must exist for this to occur.

Credit, Security, and Bankruptcy

Matching Set 2

Match each fact statement (19-22) with the correct bankruptcy statement (A-B). Write the letter of your answer in the blank to the left of the number.

BANKRUPTCY STATEMENTS

A. Debt would probably be discharged in bankruptcy.
B. Debt would probably not be discharged in bankruptcy.

FACT STATEMENTS

_____ 19. Debtor originally secured loan by misrepresenting his or her actual liabilities.

_____ 20. Debtor owes child-support payments.

_____ 21. Debtor owes $400 to a health club for membership.

_____ 22. Debtor caused $25,000 damages to Willard's property from a car accident in which debtor was found to have been negligent.

Credit, Security, and Bankruptcy

PART C: Case Problems

DIRECTIONS: For each of the questions about the following case problem, select the best answer from the four alternatives. Write the letter of your answer in the blank to the left of the number.

Case 1

Beth Johnson sought a charge card from Acme Department Stores. Beth listed as income her secretarial job income, income from a weekend second job at a local department store, and child-support payments from her ex-husband. Beth was denied the card because of "insufficient income and irregularity of credit payments." Acme had only considered Beth's secretarial income and told her the irregularity of credit payments history came from the local credit bureau. Beth learned from the credit bureau that the Towering Oaks Country Club has her listed as being deficient in membership payments, a membership which the divorce judge ruled was the property and responsibility of her former husband. Towering Oaks has refused to change the report.

_____ 23. Acme Department Stores should have considered as income

   a. only Beth's regular income from her secretarial job.
   b. the child-support payments, to the extent regularly received.
   c. the full amount of the child-support payments if originally ordered by a judge.
   d. only her full-time and part-time jobs as child-support payments are not income.

_____ 24. Beth's concern with the incorrect report of the Towering Oaks Country Club would best be resolved by which of the following acts?

   a. Equal Credit Opportunity Act
   b. Truth in Lending Act
   c. Fair Credit Reporting Act
   d. Fair Debt Collection Practices Act

_____ 25. Beth's best initial action to counter the incorrect report of the Towering Oaks Country Club would be

   a. sue the Towering Oaks Country Club.
   b. seek to have the divorce court judge order her ex-husband to make his delinquent payments.
   c. sue the credit bureau for damages.
   d. insist the credit bureau allow her to provide her defense to the Towering Oaks claim.

Chapter 8: Solutions

PART A: Multiple-Choice Questions

	Answer	**Refer to Chapter Section**
1.	(a)	[A-2-d] The amount a creditor may charge consumers for borrowing is a matter of usury law.
2.	(c)	[A-1-a] Usury laws limit what creditors can charge consumers for credit.
3.	(b)	[A-2] The TILA is intended to allow consumers to know what it will cost to borrow and pay back the loan before the borrower agrees to the loan.
4.	(d)	[A-3] The ECOA prohibits discrimination in lending on the basis of the borrower's religious beliefs or affiliation.
5.	(b)	[A-4-b] Although the prospective health club member may want to know the creditworthiness of the club before paying the membership fee, this information would not properly be available.
6.	(a)	[B-1] A credit card purchase does not involve credit security; it is an unsecured debt.
7.	(d)	[B-3-b] Attachment requires that there be a security agreement, which must be written if the creditor is not to retain possession of the collateral.
8.	(c)	[B-3-b] Perfection permits the creditor to be protected against parties other than the debtor.
9.	(d)	[B-3-b(3)] A financing statement must be in writing to be able to be recorded.
10.	(b)	[B-3-a(1)] The creditor must give value in order to gain a security interest.
11.	(b)	[B-4-d] Race-notice is the most common form of filing rule regarding which filing takes priority over competing filings.
12.	(c)	[C] Bankruptcy is governed by federal law. Only federal courts have jurisdiction over bankruptcy cases.

13. (d) [C-2-a(5)(a)] Alimony, child support, and fines are among the kinds of debts that cannot be discharged in bankruptcy. Charge card expenditures can be discharged.

14. (a) [C-2-a(4)(a)] Elmer, as a secured creditor, has the right to recover the air compressor in which he has the security interest. Because Elmer has a valid security interest, it does not become a part of the debtor's estate.

PART B: Matching Sets

Matching Set 1

15. (A) [B-3-a] Attachment primarily relates to the debtor.

16. (B) [B-3-b] Perfection primarily relates to parties other than the debtor, except for the PMSI in consumer goods.

17. (B) [B-3-b(3)] Filing is required where neither a PMSI in consumer goods or retention of collateral by the creditor is involved.

18. (A) [B-3-a(3)] Attachment requires a security agreement which may be oral if the creditor retains possession of the collateral.

Matching Set 2

19. (B) [C-2-a(5)(b)] This debt would be nondischargeable.

20. (B) [C-2-a(5)(a)] Child-support payment obligations cannot be discharged in bankruptcy.

21. (A) [C-2-a(4)(d)] This would be a common example of an unsecured debt that could be discharged in bankruptcy.

22. (B) [C-2-a(5)(a)] Accidents resulting from negligence are dischargeable. In contrast, damages resulting from intentional tortious conduct are not dischargeable.

PART C: Case Problems

23. (b) [A-3-b] A creditor must recognize child-support payments but is allowed to evaluate the regularity of payment.

24. (c) [A-4] The Fair Credit Reporting Act is the best act for Beth to use to address the improper report from the Towering Oaks Country Club.

25. (d) [A-4-d] The best initial action would be for Beth to have inserted into her credit history her one-paragraph rebuttal of the false charge. Having accomplished this, Beth might consider other avenues of relief.

CHAPTER 9
Insurable Interest

OVERVIEW

Insurance is a contract by which the insurance company (insurer) promises to pay a sum of money or give something of value to another (either the insured or the beneficiary) in the event that the insured is injured or sustains damage as the result of particular stated contingencies. Basically, insurance is an arrangement for transferring and allocating risk. All types of insurers use the principle of pooling of risk; that is, they spread the risk among a large number of people to make the premiums small compared to the coverage offered.

An insurance contract is called a *policy*. The consideration paid to the insurer is called a *premium,* and the insurance company is sometimes called an *underwriter*.

The high costs of living and the unpredictability of life make insurance a necessity for virtually every person and business in modern society. The availability of insurance and, in some circumstances, the right to collect under an insurance policy, however, are governed by the legal requirement that there be an insurable interest. This chapter explores that concept.

DEFINITION OF TERMS

BENEFICIARY. The party who is entitled to collect from the insurer in the event of an insured loss.

INSURABLE INTEREST. A legally recognized interest in the life of another person or in property. To be insurable, the interest must be such that a loss is experienced in the event the insured dies or the insured property is destroyed.

INSURED. One who purchases insurance or one whose life is insured.

INSURER. The party who provides insurance.

POLICY. The written contract of insurance.

PREMIUM. The payment to which the insurer is entitled in return for providing insurance.

A. Purpose of the Insurable Interest Requirement

1. *Limitations on Purchase of Insurance:* The law does not allow a party to obtain insurance on everyone or everything the party may wish to insure. The limitation that is placed on the purchase of insurance is the legal requirement that the purchaser have an insurable interest. The purpose of the insurable interest requirement is to prevent both gambling and the possibility that one would gain by the death of the insured person or the destruction of the insured property without suffering a loss.

2. *Prevention of Gambling:* The insurable interest requirement prevents insurance from being used as a gambling device. If the purchaser suffers no loss in the event the insured property is destroyed, the purchaser is simply gambling that it will be destroyed.

    EXAMPLE: Fred wanted to purchase flood insurance on Jan's house. Fred and Jan are not related in any way. If Fred is allowed to purchase such insurance, he stands to gain in the event Jan's house is flooded. Fred would, in effect, be gambling that a flood would occur. Thus, Fred is not allowed to purchase the insurance. He lacks an insurable interest.

3. *Reduction of Incentive for Wrongdoing:* The requirement of an insurable interest reduces the possibility that a party will be tempted to act illegally in order to collect on an insurance policy.

    EXAMPLE: Henry wishes to purchase $50,000 of fire insurance on Susan's house. Susan is a mere acquaintance of Henry. If Susan's house burns, Henry would collect $50,000 without suffering any loss. If Henry were allowed to purchase such insurance, he would have an added incentive to act illegally.

B. Insurable Interest in the Life of Another Person

1. *Financial Dependence or Close Relationship Required:* The law requires

a party to be financially dependent on or closely related to another person before that party can purchase insurance on the other person's life. This requirement removes the incentive for wrongdoing. If the insured person dies, the purchaser of the insurance has lost someone on whom he or she depended financially or to whom he or she was closely related. Thus, a loss is suffered.

2. *Relationship Requirement:* The degree of relationship which the purchaser of the insurance must bear to the insured is subject to state law. Insurance companies have also adopted guidelines. The relationship must be such that there is a financial or personal interest in the continued life of the insured.

EXAMPLE: Nancy is married to Sam. Nancy could reasonably be expected to suffer a financial or personal loss if Sam dies. She has an insurable interest in his life.

EXAMPLE: Steve purchased insurance on the life of his son Joe. It is presumed that Steve would suffer a great personal loss if Joe dies. Therefore, Steve has an insurable interest in Joe's life.

3. *Business Associates' Insurable Interest:* Business associates may have an insurable interest in each other's lives. If the associates depend upon each other's skill, judgment, or financial support, they may purchase insurance to cover the loss that would be realized upon the death of an associate.

EXAMPLE: Mike and Tom are partners in the retail shoe business. Each is responsible for exercising judgment and skill in the operation of the business. Each is dependent upon the contribution of the other. Therefore, an insurable interest in the life of the other partner exists.

4. *Employer's Insurable Interest:* An employer may have an insurable interest in the life of an employee. If the employer is dependent on the services of an employee and would suffer a loss upon the employee's death, an insurable interest exists.

5. *Creditor's Insurable Interest:* A creditor may have an insurable interest in the life of a debtor. One who extends credit to another has a direct interest in the continued life of that person. If death occurs before the debt is paid, the creditor might not receive full payment from the estate of the deceased debtor.

EXAMPLE: Sandra loans $5,000 to Joan. The loan is unsecured. Joan plans to make payments from her paychecks. If Joan dies before repayment, it is unlikely that Sandra would succeed in recovering the balance of the loan. Sandra has an insurable interest in Joan's life.

EXAMPLE: Paul enters into a $50,000 mortgage loan agreement with the National Bank. The bank, as a creditor of Paul, has an insurable interest in Paul's life.

6. *When Insurable Interest Must Exist:* An insurable interest in the life of another person must exist at the time the insurance is obtained. It need not exist at the time the insured person dies.

    EXAMPLE: Don purchased insurance on the life of his wife Debbie. Later they were divorced. Assuming that the policy is still in effect at the time of Debbie's death, Don is entitled to the proceeds from the policy even though he no longer has an insurable interest in her life. The insurable interest existed at the time the insurance was purchased.

7. *Beneficiary Need Not Have Insurable Interest:* A person can purchase insurance on his or her own life and designate as the beneficiary one who has no insurable interest in the life of the insured.

    EXAMPLE: George purchased insurance on his own life. He named Bruce as the beneficiary of the policy. Bruce is merely a friend of George. Because the insured party himself has named the beneficiary, there is no requirement that the beneficiary have an insurable interest. Bruce, however, could not purchase insurance on George's life because Bruce has no insurable interest.

C. **Insurable Interest in Property**

1. *Financial Interest:* The purchaser of property insurance must have a financial interest in the property insured. The requirement lessens the possibility that the purchaser would enjoy a gain if the property were destroyed.

    EXAMPLE: Brad would not be permitted to purchase insurance on Sally's car because he has no financial interest in it. If it were damaged or destroyed, Brad would suffer no loss. Insurance payments would be profit to Brad. He has no insurable interest in the car.

    a. *Ownership of property:* Ownership provides the financial interest required for an insurable interest. Whether the ownership is joint or solely in the name of the purchaser, it serves as the basis for an insurable interest. A purchaser of goods which have not yet been received may acquire an insurable interest if the goods are specifically identified.

    b. *Renter of property:* One who rents property has an insurable interest in it. Damage or destruction of the property would interfere with the tenant's right to possess and use the property during the term of the lease. Because the tenant would, therefore, suffer a loss, the law recognizes the existence of an insurable interest in the property.

    c. *Holder of security interest in property:* One who holds a security interest in property has an insurable interest in it. Because the property secures a loan, destruction of the property jeopardizes the financial interest of the lender.

    EXAMPLE: The Savings and Loan Association lends Dick $150,000 for the purchase of a house. To secure the loan, the Savings and Loan requires a mortgage interest in the property. If Dick fails to make the scheduled payments, the Savings and Loan can foreclose on the mortgage and have the property sold. If the property is damaged or destroyed, the Savings and Loan's financial interest in the property is affected. The law recognizes that a lender has an insurable interest with respect to the property that serves as security for the loan.

2. *When Insurable Interest Must Exist:* The insurable interest in property must exist at the time the loss occurs. This differs from the requirement that the insurable interest in the life of another person must exist at the time the insurance is purchased (see Section B-6 in this chapter).

    EXAMPLE: Richard purchased insurance on his home. Later he sold his home to Karen. After the sale to Karen, the home was destroyed by fire. Richard cannot recover on his insurance policy because he did not have an insurable interest at the time of the loss.

3. *Assignability:* Insurance policies relating to property are assignable after the loss occurs. Property insurance cannot be assigned before the loss.

    EXAMPLE: Mary has fire insurance on her home. While she is attending a job interview in another city, her home is destroyed by fire. Mary decides to take the job and move. She may assign the fire insurance policy to someone else. She could not, however, have assigned the policy prior to the loss.

Chapter 9: Review Questions

PART A: Multiple-Choice Questions

DIRECTIONS: Select the best answer from the four alternatives. Write your answer in the blank to the left of the number.

_____

1. Which of the following parties would have an insurable interest in David's life?

    a. David's wife
    b. David's employer
    c. David's creditor
    d. All of the above

_____

2. Which of the following parties would have an insurable interest in the car Mary just purchased?

    a. Mary's boyfriend
    b. The bank that holds title to the car as security for the $15,000 loan
    c. Mary's parents
    d. None of the above

_____

3. Which of the following could be named by Sheila as beneficiary in a policy on Sheila's life?

    a. Sheila's husband
    b. A neighbor
    c. Both (a) and (b)
    d. Neither (a) nor (b)

_____

4. Ann bought a $10,000 insurance policy on her husband's life and named herself as the beneficiary. Ann obtained a divorce from her husband. Her former husband died. Which of the following statements is true?

    a. Ann would be able to recover the $10,000.
    b. Ann would not be able to recover the $10,000 because she no longer had an insurable interest.
    c. Public policy prevents Ann from recovering the money.
    d. The insurance policy is no longer in effect.

Insurable Interest

_____ 5. Bob has a $5,000 accident property insurance policy on his grand piano. Which of the following statements is true?

    a. Bob can assign this property policy to anyone he chooses even though the grand piano is unharmed.
    b. Bob can only assign this policy to a close relative or to a creditor while the piano is unharmed.
    c. In the event the grand piano is destroyed, Bob can then assign the policy to anyone he chooses.
    d. In the event the grand piano is destroyed, Bob can only assign the policy to someone who has an insurable interest in the piano.

PART B: Matching Sets

Matching Set 1

Match each definition (6-9) with the appropriate insurance term (A-D). Write the letter of your answer in the blank next to the number of the statement.

INSURANCE TERMS

    A. Premium
    B. Beneficiary
    C. Insured
    D. Insurer

DEFINITIONS

_____ 6. One who is entitled to collect in the event of an insured loss.

_____ 7. Party who provides insurance.

_____ 8. Payment in return for insurance coverage.

_____ 9. Purchaser of insurance or one who is covered by insurance.

Matching Set 2

Match the statement concerning when the insurable interest must exist (A-B) with the appropriate insurance situation (10-13). Write the letter of your answer in the blank to the left of the statement.

EXISTENCE OF INSURABLE INTEREST

A. Insurable interest must exist at the time insurance is purchased in order to allow recovery in the event of loss.
B. Insurable interest must exist at the time loss occurs in order to allow recovery.

INSURANCE SITUATIONS

_____ 10. A spouse's life insurance policy.

_____ 11. Home insurance.

_____ 12. Employer's insurance on life of a key employee.

_____ 13. Lender's insurance on property securing a loan.

Insurable Interest

PART C: Case Problems

DIRECTIONS: For each of the questions relating to the following case problems, select the best answer from the four alternatives. Write the letter of your answer in the blank to the left of the number.

Case 1
Max is a co-owner of an advertising agency with Cindy. On behalf of the business, he wishes to purchase life insurance on the life of Cindy and on the life of George who is a key employee. Max also wishes to purchase life insurance on the life of Gene who is a potential client whose account would be crucial to the success of Max's business.

_____ 14. Which of the following statements is correct?

   a. There is an insurable interest only on the life of Cindy.
   b. There is an insurable interest only on the lives of Cindy and George.
   c. There is an insurable interest on the lives of Cindy, George, and Gene.
   d. There is not an insurable interest on the lives of any of the named parties.

Case 2
Max also wishes to insure, on behalf of the business, a building owned by the business, a building which the business rents from Ace Manufacturing Co., and a fleet of cars which the business leases from ABC Motors.

_____ 15. Which of the following statements is correct?

   a. There is an insurable interest in the building owned by the business, but not in the rented building.
   b. There is an insurable interest in both buildings but not in the cars.
   c. There is an insurable interest in both buildings and in the cars.
   d. There is no insurable interest in either the buildings or in the cars.

Case 3
Alice purchased a life insurance policy on the life of her husband Norm. She also purchased insurance on the house in which she lived and on her summer home in Michigan. Over the next year Alice divorced Norm, sold her home, and assigned her insurance policy on the Michigan summer home to Cal. Over the next year Norm died and both houses burned down. Alice attempts to collect on the two insurance policies she still holds.

_____ 16. Which result is correct?

   a. She will collect on the life insurance policy (assuming no foul play is established).
   b. She will collect on both policies.
   c. She will collect on the home insurance policy only.
   d. She will not collect on any policy.

17. Cal attempts to collect on the insurance policy that was assigned to him on the Michigan property.

   a. He will collect since insurance policies are assignable.
   b. He will collect if there is no foul play.
   c. He will not collect because insurance policies on property cannot be assigned.
   d. He will not collect because insurance policies on property can only be assigned after the loss occurs.

Chapter 9: Solutions

PART A: Multiple-Choice Questions

	Answer	Refer to Chapter Section
1.	(d)	[B] Answers (a), (b), and (c) are all correct. Answer (a) is correct because David's wife has a personal and financial interest in his life. Answers (b) and (c) are correct because both the employer and the creditor have an interest in David's life.
2.	(b)	[C-1-c] This is the correct answer because the bank has a financial interest in the car. Neither Mary's boyfriend nor her parents have a financial interest in her car.
3.	(c)	[B-7] Answers (a) and (b) are correct because anyone can be named as a beneficiary.
4.	(a)	[B-6] One needs to have an insurable interest in the insured's life only at the time the policy was obtained.
5.	(c)	[C-3] After a loss occurs, the insurance owner can assign the policy to anyone.

PART B: Matching Sets

Matching Set 1

6.	(B)	[Overview, Definitions]
7.	(D)	[Overview, Definitions]
8.	(A)	[Overview, Definitions]
9.	(C)	[Overview, Definitions]

Matching Set 2

10.	(A)	[B-6]
11.	(B)	[C-2]
12.	(A)	[B-6]
13.	(B)	[C-2]

PART C: Case Problems

14. (b) [B-3 and B-4] There is an insurable interest in key business associates and key employees. An insurable interest does not exist, however, as to a potential client.

15. (c) [C-1-a and C-1-b] There is an insurable interest in property which is owned or rented.

16. (a) [B-6 and C-2] Alice's insurable interest in the life of Norm existed at the time the insurance was obtained. However, the insurable interest in property must exist at the time the loss occurs in order for there to be recovery. Since Alice no longer had an insurable interest in the property, she cannot collect.

17. (d) [C-3] At the time Alice assigned the policy to Cal, Cal had no insurable interest in the property and no loss had yet occurred. Such an assignment can occur after the loss is experienced.

CHAPTER 10
Agency

OVERVIEW

Agents make it possible for a party to expand its business dealings. Corporations could not act without agents, and partnerships would be greatly impaired by such a limitation. Without agents, an individual party could only transact business in person. Yet with the advantages of agency come complications. What is the relationship between the principal and agent? What is the nature of the relationship between the agent and third parties with whom the agent deals on behalf of the principal? Moreover, when does an agency relationship exist, and how is it terminated? The answers to these questions are to be found in the law of agency. This chapter presents the major rules of agency law.

In studying agency, the candidate should become aware of the different types of authority that an agent may possess. The candidate should know the types of agency relationships and the legal consequences of each. The details of agency law are better understood when viewed in the context of the agency relationship itself and the purposes it is designed to achieve. Accordingly, this chapter begins with a look at the creation of the agency relationship.

DEFINITION OF TERMS

AGENCY. A relationship in which one party acts for and on behalf of another party.
AGENT. One who has authority to act for and on behalf of another party (the principal).

APPARENT AUTHORITY. Authority that a third party reasonably believes an agent possesses based upon circumstances which the principal has allowed to exist, even though the agent in fact does not have the express or implied authority.

AUTHORITY. The power granted to an agent by a principal to enter into contracts.

CONFLICT OF INTEREST. A conflict between personal interest and the official responsibilities of a person in a position of trust, such as an agent.

DISCLOSED PRINCIPAL. A principal whose identity is known to the third party with whom the principal's agent deals.

EMERGENCY AUTHORITY. A type of implied authority that exists during a sudden, unexpected happening or unforeseen combination of circumstances that requires immediate action.

EMPLOYEE. One who works for another and is subject to the other person's right to control his or her physical conduct. An agent may be, but need not be, an employee.

EXPRESS AUTHORITY. Authority granted by the principal in words, whether they be written or oral.

FRAUD. A misstatement or misrepresentation of a material fact made with knowledge of its falsity.

GENERAL AGENT. One who is authorized to represent a principal in a number of transactions over a period of time.

GRATUITOUS AGENT. One who agrees to represent a principal without being compensated for services.

IMPLIED AUTHORITY. Authority to do those things that are reasonably necessary to the exercise of express authority and to the achievement of the objectives of the agency.

INDEPENDENT CONTRACTOR. One who is retained to achieve a desired result and who is given substantial freedom in deciding the manner to be used to accomplish the objective. An agent may be, but need not be, an independent contractor.

NEGLIGENT CONDUCT. Careless behavior that results in injury to another person or organization.

PARTIALLY DISCLOSED PRINCIPAL. A principal whose existence is known but whose identity is unknown to the third party with whom the principal's agent deals.

POWER OF ATTORNEY. A document that formally authorizes one person to act on behalf of another person as to matters stated in the document.

PRINCIPAL. One who acts through an agent.

SPECIAL AGENT. One who is authorized by a principal to perform a single task or to achieve a narrow goal on behalf of the principal.

THIRD PARTY. One who deals with an agent who is representing a principal.

UNDISCLOSED PRINCIPAL. A principal whose existence is unknown to the third party with whom the principal's agent deals.

Agency

A. Creation

An agency relationship exists when it is agreed among parties that one will act for and on behalf of the other. The party acting on behalf of the other is known as the *agent*. The one on whose behalf the agent is acting is known as the *principal*.

1. *Consideration Not Required:* Consideration is not required for the creation of an agency.

    EXAMPLE: *Frank says to Bruno, "Do me a favor and take my wagon to town and sell it for the highest price that you can negotiate." Bruno agrees. There is a valid agency relationship. No consideration is required.*

2. *No General Requirement for Writing:* Only certain agency agreements must be in writing.

    a. *Agency agreements that must be in writing:* If the contract which an agent is authorized to enter on behalf of the principal is legally required to be in writing, then the agency agreement itself must be in writing.

    (1) *General statutes:* The statute of frauds and the Uniform Commercial Code dictate which contracts must be in writing (see Chapter 3: Contracts).

    EXAMPLE 1: *Al agrees to act as Paul's agent for the purpose of selling Paul's house. The agreement must be in writing. Because a contract for the sale of land must be in writing, an agreement authorizing an agency to buy or sell land must likewise be in writing.*

    EXAMPLE 2: *Paul authorizes Al to sell Paul's car for $1,000. The agency agreement must be in writing. A contract for the sale of goods for $500 or more must be in writing. Therefore, an agreement authorizing an agent to sell such goods must be in writing.*

    EXAMPLE 3: *Paul authorizes Al to hire a sales representative for Al's company to serve for a three-year period. The agency agreement between Paul and Al must be in writing because the contract that Al is authorized to enter on behalf of Paul cannot be completed within one year and therefore must be in writing.*

    (2) *Special statutes:* Other specific state statutes may require that certain kinds of agency agreements be in writing. For

example, the law in most states requires that powers of attorney, whereby one party is formally authorized to represent another in certain matters, be in writing.

- **b.** *Agency agreements not in writing:* Unless the contract the agent is authorized to enter on behalf of the principal is legally required to be in writing or a specific state statute requires that the agency agreement be in writing, the agency agreement need not be in writing.

    EXAMPLE: Patricia hires Alice to work as Patricia's agent for purposes of selling suntan oil at the local beach. The agreement is subject to the general rule that agency agreements need not be in writing.

3. *Capacity of Principal:* A principal can only accomplish through an agency those things that the principal personally has the capacity to do. A corporation or a partnership may serve as a principal. (For a review of capacity, see Chapter 3: Contracts.)

    - **a.** *Effect on contracts entered by agent:* It is the capacity of the principal, not that of the agent, that affects the contracts entered by the agent on behalf of the principal.

        EXAMPLE: John, who is 16 years old, hired Bob, a 25-year-old, to act as John's agent for the purpose of purchasing an antique vase. Because John, the principal, is a minor, the contract Bob enters on John's behalf can be disaffirmed by John. (See Chapter 3: Contracts.)

    - **b.** *Voidance of agency agreement:* A principal who lacks capacity may void the agency agreement itself.

        EXAMPLE: Cliff, a minor, hires Brad, an adult, to serve as Cliff's agent for a term of six months. Cliff may disaffirm the agreement, due to his minority, and end the agency.

4. *Capacity of Agent:* Any party capable of understanding the nature of the task to be performed may serve as an agent. A corporation or a partnership may serve as an agent.

    - **a.** *Binding contract:* Even though the agent may lack contractual capacity because of minority or mental incapacity, the agent can nevertheless enter into a binding contract on behalf of the principal.

        EXAMPLE: Bonnie, an adult, hires Angie, a minor, to serve as Bonnie's agent for the purpose of purchasing certain stereo equipment. *The contract that Angie enters on Bonnie's behalf is not voidable. It is Bonnie's capacity as the principal that is relevant. (See Section A-3 in this chapter.)*

b. *Disaffirming agency agreement:* An agent who lacks capacity may disaffirm the agency agreement.

EXAMPLE: Bruce, an adult, hires William, a minor, to serve as Bruce's agent for a term of nine months. William may disaffirm the agreement due to his minority. Thus, although William's actions as Bruce's agent can result in binding contracts, William may assert his minority to end the agency relationship prematurely between himself and Bruce.

B. Types of Agencies

There are three basic types of agencies. Under some circumstances, the type of agency affects the rights and liabilities of the parties. It is therefore important to be able to recognize the various types.

1. *Disclosed Principal:* If the identity of the principal is known to the third party with whom the agent deals, the agency is one with a *disclosed principal.*

    EXAMPLE: Ann acts as Peter's agent in dealing with Thomas. Thomas knows Peter's identity and knows that Ann is acting as Peter's agent. Peter is a disclosed principal.

2. *Partially Disclosed Principal:* If only the existence of the principal is known to the third party with whom the agent deals, the agency is one with a *partially disclosed principal.* The third party knows there is a principal but does not know who it is.

    EXAMPLE: Ann acts as Peter's agent in dealing with Thomas. Thomas knows that Ann is acting on behalf of a principal but does not know who the principal is. Peter is a partially disclosed principal.

3. *Undisclosed Principal:* If the third party is unaware that the agent is representing anyone, the agency is one with an undisclosed principal.

    EXAMPLE: Ann acts as Peter's agent in dealing with Thomas. Thomas thinks Ann is acting on Ann's own behalf. Peter is an undisclosed principal.

C. **Types of Agents**

The law recognizes various types of agents: gratuitous agent, general agent, special agent, independent contractor, and employee.

1. *Gratuitous Agent:* A gratuitous agent is one who agrees to represent the principal without being compensated for services.

    EXAMPLE: As a favor to Mary, Doris agrees to sell Mary's vacuum cleaner at Doris's garage sale. Doris has agreed to serve as Mary's agent without receiving anything in return for her services, so Doris is a gratuitous agent.

2. *General Agent:* A general agent is authorized to represent the principal in a number of transactions over a period of time.

    EXAMPLE: The Brown Company, a shoe manufacturer, hires Tony to serve as its agent for the purpose of selling shoes to retail stores in a three-state area for a period of one year. Tony is a general agent.

3. *Special Agent:* A special agent is authorized to perform a single task or to achieve a single goal.

    EXAMPLE: Esther hires Sarah to serve as Esther's agent for the purpose of selling Esther's boat. Sarah is a special agent.

4. *Independent Contractor:* An agent who is retained by the principal to achieve desired results and who has substantial freedom in the manner used to accomplish these goals is an *independent contractor*. The principal does not have the right to control the physical conduct of the independent contractor.

    EXAMPLE: George hires Brenda, a lawyer, to represent him in a lawsuit that is going to trial. Because the lawyer is expected to use her own skills and judgment in trying a case, Brenda is an independent contractor.

5. *Employee:* If the agency agreement gives the principal the right to control the agent's physical conduct, the agent is an employee.

    EXAMPLE: Midwest Promotions, Incorporated, operates a large auditorium, in which various events are staged during the year. Midwest hires Lance as a ticket agent. His job is to promote and sell tickets to the events. According to the terms of the agreement, Lance is to work at Midwest's office from 8:30 A.M. to 4:30 P.M. He is to sell tickets at the listed prices only. Midwest also requires Lance to wear a uniform. Lance is an employee.

D. Types of Authority

An agent may possess four types of authority: express authority, implied authority, emergency authority, and apparent authority.

1. *Express Authority:* A principal's written or oral instructions to an agent constitute express authority.

2. *Implied Authority:* An agent may have implied authority to do those things that are reasonably necessary to exercise the express authority of an agent and to achieve the objectives of the agency. Although authority to do such things is not expressly stated, the agent reasonably believes that the principal intended the agent to have such authority.

   EXAMPLE: The Chemex Company hires Jack as its agent for purposes of selling the company's new industrial-strength cleaning fluid. Jack's contract states that he has authority to sell the product to factories in a three-state area at a stated price. In order to accomplish the objective of the agency, Jack mails letters to hundreds of factories in the stated area, phones the factories, and makes trips to visit interested factories so he can demonstrate the product. Jack makes a number of sales at the established price. Jack has express authority to make the sales. He has implied authority to mail letters, phone potential customers, and make personal visits for the purpose of promoting sales.

3. *Emergency Authority:* A type of implied authority, emergency authority, exists during a sudden, unexpected happening or unforeseen combination of circumstances that requires immediate action. Emergency authority permits an agent to take reasonably necessary steps to carry out tasks that are within the scope of the agent's actual authority.

   EXAMPLE: Vince was employed as a sales agent for ACE Copy Machines, Inc. He was scheduled to make a critical sales presentation to WorldWide Communicators, Inc. at 8:00 A.M. WorldWide was an extremely important potential client. Vince injured his back while getting out of bed on the morning of the presentation. Because of the injury, he was unable to lift the copy machine that was an essential part of the sales presentation. Vince hired Arnold, the only available person, to carry the machine for him to WorldWide's office. Vince had emergency authority to obtain assistance.

4. *Apparent Authority:* Apparent authority stems from the circumstances that the principal allows to exist. If, based on these circumstances, a third party who deals with the agent reasonably believes that the agent has certain authority, the law permits the third party to rely on that reasonable belief. In other words, the law allows the third party to rely on the appearance of things, even though there may not be express or implied authority on the part of the agent. The authority that derives not

from the words or intentions of the principal, but from the circumstances the principal allows to exist, is known as apparent authority.

EXAMPLE: Mike owns a furniture store. He hires Joe to work as a janitor. One day Mike has to make a short trip to the local bank to make a deposit. Instead of closing the store, Mike simply asks Joe to watch the store and tell any customers who enter that Mike will return within a half hour. Freda enters the store for the first time. She sees Joe standing behind the cash register. Assuming that Joe is a salesclerk, she asks him how much a certain chair costs. Joe responds by stating that the chair is on sale for $100. In fact, the chair is priced at $300. Freda purchases the chair and takes it home. Upon discovering what happened, Mike seeks to recover the chair or the $200 difference between the actual price and what Freda paid. Mike will not succeed. Joe had apparent authority. Mike knowingly allowed the circumstances to exist under which Freda could reasonably believe that Joe had authority to sell the chair.

E. Obligations of Agent to Principal

The agent owes the highest duty of loyalty to the principal.

1. *Duty to Act within Authority:* The agent has a duty to act within his/her actual authority, that is, not to exceed power to the detriment of the principal.

   a. *Actual authority:* The actual authority may be express or implied (see Sections D-1 and D-2 in this chapter).

   EXAMPLE: Sharon leaves her bicycle with Lisa. Sharon tells Lisa, "Rent my bicycle if you can to someone for $3 per day, but do not sell it." Lisa sells the bicycle to Clyde. Lisa has breached her duty to Sharon by not acting within her actual authority. Lisa is liable to Sharon for the value of the bicycle.

   b. *Principal's instructions:* The agent is required to follow only legal instructions from the principal.

   EXAMPLE: Dick works as a salesclerk in Morry's hardware store. Morry instructs Dick not to register cash sales on the cash register so that no tax need be paid. Dick cannot be required to follow instructions that constitute violations of the law.

2. *Duty to Perform:* The agent has a duty to personally perform the duties undertaken in the agency agreement. The law permits the agent to delegate his/her duties only in certain limited circumstances.

a. *Delegation of performance:* If the task is extremely simple, requiring no skill or expertise, it may be delegated.

b. *Customary delegation:* If it is customary for such tasks to be delegated, the agent may delegate unless the agent has specifically agreed to perform personally.

c. *Impracticality of agent to perform:* If the principal knows it is highly impractical for the agent to perform personally and has not specifically forbidden delegation, the agent may delegate his/her duties.

d. *Delegation at own risk:* If an unforeseeable situation develops and the agent cannot reach the principal to inform the principal that the agent cannot perform, the agent may delegate the duties at his/her own risk.

e. *Principal agreement to delegation:* Of course, if the principal agrees to a delegation, the agent may delegate (see Chapter 3: Contracts).

3. *Duty to Exercise Care and Skill:* The agent has a duty to exercise reasonable care and skill in performing services for the principal. The agent is liable for any damages that failure to exercise reasonable care and skill causes the principal to suffer.

EXAMPLE: Tom hires Warren to serve as his agent for the purpose of purchasing milking cows to be used on Tom's dairy farm. Warren is an experienced purchaser of milking cows. Warren nevertheless fails to inspect a dozen cows he purchases on Tom's behalf. The cows are obviously diseased and unfit for use as milking cows. Warren has breached his duty of exercising reasonable care and skill in serving as Tom's agent. Warren is liable to Tom for the damage his breach of duty caused.

4. *Duty to Account to Principal:* The agent has a duty to account to the principal for all money or other property which the agent has handled on behalf of the principal.

5. *Duty Not to Commingle Property:* The agent has a duty not to commingle personal funds or other property with that of the principal.

EXAMPLE: Bill serves as Walter's agent for purposes of renting apartments owned by Walter. Bill receives security deposits from tenants and places the money in his personal bank account along with his personal funds. Bill has breached his duty to Walter because Bill did not keep his principal's funds separate from his own.

6. *Duty to Inform Principal:* The agent has a duty to inform the principal of relevant information that comes to the attention of the agent.

   EXAMPLE: Wendy is employed as a sales agent by Modern Fashions, Inc., a corporation that manufactures and sells clothing. She discovers that Mirror Image, Inc., a competitor of Modern Fashions, had manufactured a line of clothing practically identical to Modern Fashions' latest line. Wendy is obligated to pass this information on to her employer. Wendy also learns that the stock of the Johnson Company, a corporation engaged in uranium mining, is likely to double in the next two days. She is not obligated to relate this information to her employer because it does not relate to the business of her employer.

7. *Duty to Avoid Conflicts of Interest:* The agent has a duty to avoid conflicts of interest.

   a. *Competition with principal:* The agent must not compete against the principal or work for a competitor of the principal.

   b. *Conflict of interest:* If a conflict of interest does develop, the agent must promptly inform the principal of the conflict. Only if the principal, with full knowledge of the conflict, consents to the agent's continued service can the agent maintain this position.

   EXAMPLE: Bob works as a purchasing agent for Ajax Used Auto Parts, Inc., a corporation that buys used auto parts. Bob takes a part-time job as a purchasing agent for Baxter, Inc., a competitor of Ajax. Bob has breached his duty to Ajax because he has undertaken a job that conflicts with his duty of loyalty to Ajax. Only if Bob fully discloses the conflict to Ajax and obtains Ajax's approval can he continue to work for Baxter.

8. *Duty to Make No Secret Profit:* The agent has a duty not to make a secret profit. Any money or other property obtained by the agent must be reported to the principal.

   EXAMPLE: Andrew serves as a purchasing agent for Rainbow Industries, Inc., a company that purchases 20 new cars each year for use by company executives. Andrew received a secret payment of $10,000 in return for purchasing 20 cars from Smiley Motors, a local car dealer, on behalf of the company. Andrew has breached his duty of loyalty to Rainbow by receiving this secret profit.

9. *Duty Not to Use Agency-Related Information for Personal Gain:* The agent has a duty not to use information obtained through the agency for personal gain at the expense of the principal.

   a. *Seizing principal's opportunity:* The agent must not seize the

Agency 217

principal's opportunity.

EXAMPLE: Alice serves as a sales representative for Lowell Industries, a rapidly growing company that is looking for an attractive site for a new corporate headquarters. In the course of her work for Lowell Industries, Alice has a conversation with Rick, who informs her of the availability of an ideal site for such a building. Alice acts to buy the land for herself. She has breached the duty of loyalty to her principal by taking advantage of the principal's opportunity.

(1) *Notification of opportunity to principal:* If the agent notifies the principal of the opportunity, and it is clear that the principal will not act to take advantage of the opportunity, the agent may then proceed.

EXAMPLE: Pat, an agent of Index Industries, learns of a promising business opportunity. He notifies Index's board of directors. At a formal meeting the board votes not to act on the opportunity. Pat is free to pursue the opportunity on his own.

(2) *Principal's inability to act on opportunity:* If the principal is obviously unable to take advantage of the opportunity, the agent may act on his or her own behalf.

EXAMPLE: Ben is an agent of the Western Lumber Company. Ben learns of the availability of 20,000 acres of richly wooded land. Western has filed for bankruptcy, listing $8 million in unpaid debts and no assets. Although Ben should notify Western of the opportunity, he may pursue it on his own behalf because the principal is obviously unable to act on the opportunity.

b. *Divulging confidential information of principal:* The agent must not divulge confidential information of the principal.

EXAMPLE: Jane is employed as a paralegal by Shirley, who is a lawyer. Jane releases information from a confidential file to Mary, who is suing one of Shirley's clients. Jane divulged the information in the hope of obtaining a higher-paying job with Mary. Jane has breached her duty of loyalty to Shirley.

F. Obligations of Agent to Third Party

The obligation of an agent to a third party often depends upon the type of agency involved (see Sections B-1, B-2, and B-3 in this chapter).

1. *Contract on Behalf of Disclosed Principal:* An agent who enters a contract on behalf of a disclosed principal incurs no liability on the contract.

   EXAMPLE: Alan, acting within his actual authority, enters a contract with Tom, who knows that Alan is acting merely as Paul's agent. Alan is not personally liable on the contract. If Paul breaches the contract, Tom can recover damages from Paul only.

2. *Contract on Behalf of Partially Disclosed Principal:* An agent who enters a contract on behalf of a partially disclosed principal can be held liable to the third party.

   EXAMPLE: Amy, acting within her actual authority, enters a contract with Theresa, who knows that Amy is acting as an agent but does not know the identity of Amy's principal, Phyllis. If the contract is breached, Theresa can recover damages from Amy. Because Theresa did not know of Phyllis's identity, she relied on Amy's background and reputation in contracting with Amy. Thus, Theresa is allowed to hold Amy responsible in the event the contract is breached.

   Note: If the third party determines the identity of the principal, that party may enforce or pursue either the principal or the agent.

3. *Contract on Behalf of Undisclosed Principal:* An agent who enters a contract on behalf of an undisclosed principal can be held liable to the third party.

   EXAMPLE: Alex, acting within his actual authority, enters a contract with Terry, who does not know that Alex is acting as an agent for Paulette. Terry reasonably believes that Alex is acting on Alex's own behalf. If the contract is breached, Terry can recover damages from Alex. Because Terry reasonably believed that Alex was acting for himself, Terry relied on Alex's background and reputation in contracting with Alex. Terry is, therefore, allowed to hold Alex responsible in the event the contract is breached.

4. *Recovery of Losses Resulting from Fraud:* The third party may recover from the agent for losses suffered as a result of the agent's fraud or deceit.

   EXAMPLE: Andrew is Phil's agent for purposes of selling Phil's products. Andrew falsely represents to Tim that Andrew is authorized to sell Phil's building. Relying upon this representation, Tim pays Andrew $5,000 as a down payment on the building. Tim may recover the money from Andrew due to Andrew's misrepresentation.

Agency

EXAMPLE: Polly employs Ann as an agent for purposes of selling the shoes Polly manufactures to retailers. Ann is not authorized by Polly to make any false representations about the place where the shoes were manufactured. Ann tells Thomas, a purchaser, that the shoes are imported from Rome. The statement is false. Thomas can recover damages resulting from the misrepresentation from Ann.

5. *Liability for Injury Resulting from Negligence:* An agent is liable to a third party who is injured as a result of the agent's negligent conduct.

EXAMPLE: Al, while acting on Pat's behalf, is driving to Texas to conduct a business transaction. Al negligently fails to stop at an intersection and injures Toby, who had the right of way. Toby can recover damages from Al.

G. **Obligations of Principal to Agent**

The principal's duties to the agent may be divided into five categories: duty to compensate, duty to honor contract terms, duty to reimburse expenses, duty to indemnify, and duty to compensate injured employees.

1. *Duty to Compensate:* Unless it is agreed that the agent will serve as a gratuitous agent (see Section C-1 in this chapter), the principal is obligated to pay the agent for the services rendered.

    a. *Payment of reasonable value for services:* If the amount of compensation was not specifically agreed upon, the principal is under a duty to pay the agent the reasonable value of services.

    b. *Accounting records:* The principal is obligated to keep a record of all money or other property owed to the agent. This record must be made available to the agent upon request (that is, when the agent demands an accounting).

2. *Duty to Honor Contract Terms:* In addition to the duty to compensate the agent in the absence of a contrary agreement, a principal who has contracted with an agent must abide by the terms of the contract.

    a. *Express or implied terms:* The terms of the contract may be express or implied (see Chapter 3: Contracts). The circumstances are important in determining implied terms.

    b. *Implied promise not to interfere:* The principal is deemed to have made an implied promise not to interfere with the agent's efforts.

    EXAMPLE: Arnold agreed to serve as Paul's agent for the purpose of selling Paul's race horse, Molasses. When Arnold attempted to show the horse to a prospective buyer, Paul would not give Arnold the keys to the stable. When Arnold attempted to make other arrangements to show the horse, Paul refused. Paul has breached his implied promise not to interfere unreasonably with Arnold's efforts to sell the horse.

3. *Duty to Reimburse Expenses:* The principal is obligated to reimburse the agent for authorized expenditures the agent has made.

    EXAMPLE: Pam hires Ann to serve as her agent in managing Pam's clothing store. In order to prevent the electricity from being turned off while Pam was vacationing in Europe, Ann paid the store's electricity bill. Pam is obligated to reimburse Ann for the payment.

4. *Duty to Indemnify:* The principal is obligated to indemnify the agent for losses suffered by the agent in the course of the agent's duties.

    EXAMPLE: Peter hires Andy to serve as his agent for the purpose of purchasing a yacht from Tom. Peter directs Andy to make no mention of the agency relationship and to act as if Andy is purchasing the boat for himself. Andy follows these instructions and enters into a contract with Tom for the purchase of the yacht on the terms that Peter had indicated he would find acceptable. Peter forwards the down payment to Andy. After Peter takes possession of the boat, however, he fails to make any further payments. Tom sues Andy and wins a judgment, which Andy pays. Andy is entitled to reimbursement from Peter.

5. *Duty to Compensate Injured Employees:* The principal has a duty to compensate employee agents for injuries suffered in the course of employment. The distinction between employees and independent contractors becomes important in this context (see Sections C-4 and C-5 in this chapter).

    EXAMPLE 1: George employs 30 salespersons in his furniture store. Each salesperson is required to work certain hours and to wear a jacket supplied by the company. The salespersons are paid an hourly wage in addition to commissions on sales made. Ted, a salesperson, was injured when a large dresser fell on his foot while he was showing the dresser to customers. George is obligated to compensate Ted for his injury because Ted is an employee.

    EXAMPLE 2: George agrees to have Greg serve as his agent for the purpose of negotiating the purchase of certain land on which George would like to build a new furniture store. Greg is an experienced negotiator and is not given detailed instructions by George. Greg's compensation will be a commission if the sale is completed. While driving to a meeting with the land owner, Greg's car is struck by one driven by a negligent motorist. George is not obligated to compensate

Greg for his injuries because Greg is an independent contractor.

H. Obligations of Principal to Third Parties

The principal's liability to third parties may result from contracts entered into by an agent on the principal's behalf or from injuries caused by the agent's conduct within the scope of the agent's employment.

1. *Principal's Duty to Perform Contract:* The principal has a duty to perform on contracts entered into on the principal's behalf by an agent who acted with authority.

    a. *Authorized acts of principal:* Whether the agent's authority is express, implied, or only apparent, the principal is bound by his/her authorized acts (see Section D in this chapter).

    b. *Authorized acts of agent:* The principal is bound by the authorized acts of his/her agent whether the principal is disclosed, partially disclosed, or undisclosed (see Section B in this chapter).

      (1) Even though the third party did not know the identity of a partially disclosed principal, the party may nevertheless hold the principal liable on contracts entered on behalf of the principal by an authorized agent.

      (2) Even though the third party did not know of the existence of a principal at the time of entering into the contract, the party may, upon learning of the principal, hold the principal liable.

        EXAMPLE: Alex acted as Patrick's agent in dealing with Terrence. Terrence thought that Alex was acting on Alex's own behalf. Terrence entered into a contract with Alex. Later, upon learning that Alex was acting on behalf of Patrick, Terrence elects to hold Patrick responsible for performing the contract. Patrick is responsible to Terrence.

    c. *Ratification of agent's acts:* If the agent acted without authority, the principal may still be bound if he/she ratifies the acts of the agent.

      (1) Ratification occurs when the principal adopts the unauthorized acts of the agent.

      (2) Ratification need not be stated in words. If the principal accepts the benefits of the agent's unauthorized acts with the intent of ratifying those acts, the principal has ratified.

(3) The principal can ratify only if he/she has knowledge of all relevant facts.

EXAMPLE: Alex, while serving as Patrick's agent, acted beyond his authority and entered into a contract with Terrence. Upon learning of the unauthorized act and the resulting contract, Patrick accepted the benefits of the contract with the intent of being bound by its terms. Patrick has ratified Alex's unauthorized act.

2. *Principal's Liability for Injuries to Third Parties:* The principal is liable to third parties for injuries caused by negligent or intentional acts of an employee acting within the scope of employment. This legal doctrine is known as *respondent superior.*

   a. *Injuries by independent contractor:* A principal is not ordinarily liable for injuries caused by an independent contractor (see Section C-4 in this chapter).

   b. *Interests served by employees:* In determining whether an employee is acting within the scope of the employee's authority, courts consider the interest the employee was serving at the time the employee caused the injury.

      (1) If the agent was serving only the principal's interest, the agent will probably be found to have been acting within the scope of employment.

      (2) If the agent was serving both the agent's and the principal's interest, the agent will probably be found to have been acting within the scope of employment.

      (3) If the agent was serving only the agent's interest, the agent will probably be found to have been acting outside the scope of the agent's authority.

      EXAMPLE: Ralph employs Jim to travel from store to store in Central City to solicit sales for Ralph's awning business. While driving between stores, Jim negligently injures Mike. Ralph is liable to Mike.

      EXAMPLE: Assume that, at the time he negligently injured Mike, Jim had decided to take the rest of the day off and was 20 miles outside of Central City on his way to a lake. Ralph, Jim's employer, is not liable to Mike. Jim was serving only his own purpose. He had abandoned his duties to Ralph and was outside the scope of his employment.

Agency

I. **Obligations of Third Parties to Principals and Agents**

Third parties are bound to perform on contracts they enter into with agents.

1. *Contract with Agent for Disclosed Principal:* A third party who contracts with an agent who is acting on behalf of a disclosed principal owes a duty to the principal to perform contractual obligations.

2. *Contract with Agent for Partially Disclosed Principal:* A third party who contracts with an agent acting on behalf of a partially disclosed principal owes a duty to the principal and to the agent to perform contractual obligations.

   EXAMPLE: Tess contracts with Annette, who is acting for Pam, a partially disclosed principal. If Tess fails to perform under the contract, either Annette or Pam may sue Tess for breach of contract.

3. *Contract with Agent for Undisclosed Principal:* A third party who contracts with an agent who is acting on behalf of an undisclosed principal owes a duty of performance to the agent and, in most cases, to the principal.

   a. *Duty of performance to agent:* The third party owes a duty of performance to the agent because he or she contracted with the agent, thinking that the agent was acting on the agent's behalf.

   b. *Duty of performance to undisclosed principal:* The third party owes a duty of performance to the undisclosed principal unless one of the following situations exists.

      (1) If the contract requires the agent to perform contractual duties personally, the undisclosed principal cannot hold the third party liable for breach of contract.

      (2) If the agent lies to the third party by denying that he or she is acting as an agent, the undisclosed principal cannot hold the third party liable for breach of contract.

      (3) If the agent or undisclosed principal knows, or should know, that the third party would not agree to do business with the principal, the undisclosed principal cannot hold the third party liable for breach of contract.

4. *Third-Party Performance on Contract:* Under no circumstances can the third party be required to perform contractual duties twice. Even where both the agent and the principal can hold the third party responsible for performance, once performance is rendered or once damages are paid, the third party is relieved of further obligation.

J. **Termination of Agency Relationship**

An agency may be terminated in the following ways:

1. *Mutual Agreement:* The principal and agent can terminate the agency by mutual agreement.

2. *Agency Agreement:* The agency agreement itself may provide for termination of the agency.

   a. *Accomplishment of agency purpose:* If the purpose of the agency, as specified in the agreement, is accomplished, the agency terminates.

   b. *Expiration of time:* The agreement may specify that the agency is to last only for a specified time. The agency terminates when that time expires.

3. *Notification of Intent to Terminate Agency:* Either the principal or the agent may terminate the agency by notifying the other party of his/her intent to terminate.

   a. *Limited right to terminate:* While either party has the *power* to terminate the agency, the right to terminate may be limited by the agency agreement.

   b. *Liability for damages:* If a party exercises his or her power to terminate without having the right to terminate, he/she is liable to the other party for any damages the termination caused.

      EXAMPLE: Patricia and Anthony agree that their agency relationship will last for one year. After only two months, Patricia acts to terminate the agency. Patricia is liable for any damages the termination has caused Anthony to suffer.

4. *Death:* The death of either the principal or agent terminates the agency.

5. *Insanity:* The insanity of either the principal or agent terminates the agency.

6. *Impossibility of Performance:* When the objective of the agency becomes impossible to accomplish, the agency is terminated.

   EXAMPLE: Rick agrees to serve as Bob's agent for the purpose of selling Bob's motorcycle. When the motorcycle is destroyed by fire, the agency is terminated.

7. *Illegality of Agency Agreement:* When the agency agreement becomes

Agency

illegal because of a change in the law, the agency is terminated.

EXAMPLE: Sam hires Bill to serve as his agent for the purpose of purchasing a certain type of hunting rifle. After Sam and Bill enter into an agency relationship, the legislature of their state enacts a law making the purchase of such a gun illegal. The agency is terminated when the law becomes effective.

8. *Change in Circumstances:* The agency terminates when the agent should know from the change in circumstances that the principal no longer desires the agent to perform under the agency agreement.

EXAMPLE: Dick agrees to serve as Hal's agent for the purpose of purchasing auto parts for Hal's 1932 Ford automobile. When Dick learns that Hal has sold the car, the agency terminates. Dick should know that Hal no longer desires him to acquire parts for the vehicle.

K. **Notification of Termination of Agency Relationship**

When the agency is terminated, the principal should notify all parties who had knowledge of the agency. Such notice will eliminate apparent authority. In the absence of such notice, the principal may be bound by an agent acting with apparent authority.

1. *Oral or Written Notice:* Parties who previously dealt with the agent must be notified orally or in writing.

2. *Notice Published in Newspaper:* Other parties can be notified by a notice published in a newspaper of general circulation in the area where the agent was operating.

3. *No Formal Notification Needed:* If the agency was terminated by death, illegality, or insanity, it may not be necessary for the principal to notify others of the termination.

Agency

Chapter 10: Review Questions

PART A: Multiple-Choice Questions

DIRECTIONS: Select the best answer from the four alternatives. Write your answer in the blank to the left of the number.

_____ 1. Wally agrees to offer Ernie's snow blower for sale for $150 at Wally's garage sale. Their agreement is oral. Wally is not entitled to any compensation under the terms of the agreement. Is there an agency relationship between Wally and Ernie?

   a. No, because the agreement is not in writing.
   b. No, because there was no consideration.
   c. Both (a) and (b) are correct.
   d. Yes, there is an agency relationship.

_____ 2. Connie, a 16-year-old, hired Ann, a 22-year-old, to act as Connie's agent for the purpose of purchasing some fishing equipment. Ann contracted to purchase the designated equipment as Connie's agent. Connie, however, wishes to disaffirm the purchase contract. May Connie legally disaffirm the purchase contract?

   a. Yes, because she is a minor.
   b. No, because the capacity of the agent governs.
   c. No, because she did not disaffirm the agency agreement before the purchase contract was entered into by the agent.
   d. Connie can only disaffirm if the sale price of the equipment exceeded $500.

_____ 3. Al acts as Paul's agent in dealing with Tom. Tom knows that Al is acting on behalf of a principal, but Tom does not know who the principal is. Paul is

   a. a disclosed principal.
   b. a partially disclosed principal.
   c. an undisclosed principal.
   d. none of the above.

4. Gina works as a salesperson for her mother's sign company. Gina travels to various businesses in the city attempting to sell signs. Gina has agreed to work for her mother's company without any compensation for a period of one year. What kind of agent is Gina?

    a. Gratuitous agent
    b. General agent
    c. Special agent
    d. Gratuitous, general agent

5. St. Peter's Church hired Mike to paint a detailed religious scene on the ceiling of its new church. Mike was authorized to select the colors and materials to be used. He was recognized as an expert in his field. Mike became very busy and delegated his duties to Angelo, a young unknown and inexperienced artist. The church claims that Mike is not legally permitted to delegate his duties. Is the church correct?

    a. No, because the law permits an agent to delegate duties in all cases.
    b. No, because Mike didn't know he would become very busy.
    c. Yes, because Mike's duties required special skill and expertise.
    d. Yes, because an agent may never delegate duties.

6. Jennifer is employed as a purchasing agent by Alpha, Inc., a company that purchases many chemicals. Jennifer owns a significant amount of stock in the Beta Chemical Company. Jennifer contracted on behalf of Alpha to purchase chemicals from Beta. Has Jennifer breached the duty she owes to Alpha?

    a. Yes, unless Jennifer notified Alpha of her conflict of interest and received Alpha's authorization to contract with Beta despite her conflict of interest.
    b. No, there is no evidence that the purchase from Beta was a poor deal.
    c. Yes, there is no way that an agent can contract with another party on behalf of the principal when a conflict of interest exists.
    d. No, the mere fact that Jennifer had an interest in Beta is irrelevant.

7. Which of the following kinds of authority must an agent have in order to bind the principal to a contract?

    a. Express authority
    b. Implied authority
    c. Apparent authority
    d. Any one of the above

Agency   229

_____ 8. An agent who enters into an authorized contract on behalf of the principal is *not* liable on the contract in which of the following circumstances?

   a. If the agent acted for a disclosed principal.
   b. If the agent acted for a partially disclosed principal.
   c. If the agent acted for an undisclosed principal.
   d. None of the above.

_____ 9. Paula hired Alice as her agent for the purpose of selling Paula's ring. The ring has an imitation diamond. Alice falsely represented to Tanya that the diamond was genuine. Based on that representation, Tanya paid $3,000 for the ring. May Tanya recover the money from Alice?

   a. Yes, an agent is liable for losses caused by the agent's fraud or deceit.
   b. Yes, an agent is always liable under contracts entered into on behalf of the principal.
   c. No, an agent cannot be held liable under a contract entered into on behalf of a principal.
   d. No, only the principal, Paula, is liable.

_____ 10. Which of the following is *not* an obligation of the principal?

   a. Duty to reimburse the agent for authorized expenditures.
   b. Duty to indemnify the agent for losses suffered by the agent as a result of the principal's failure to honor an authorized contract which the agent entered on the principal's behalf.
   c. Duty to compensate an injured independent contractor agent.
   d. All of the above.

_____ 11. A principal has a duty to perform on contracts entered into on the principal's behalf by an agent who acted without authority if

   a. the agent is indemnified.
   b. the contract is ratified.
   c. the contract is fair.
   d. none of the above.

_____ 12. Andy is employed as a salesperson in Paula's hardware store. Andy negligently dropped a heavy box on the toe of Sam, a customer. Against whom may Sam recover for his injury?

   a. Paula, the principal.
   b. Andy, the agent.
   c. Sam may recover against Paula or Andy.
   d. Sam cannot recover against Andy or Paula.

13. A third party who contracts with an agent owes a duty of performance to the principal

    a. if the principal is disclosed.
    b. if the principal is partially disclosed.
    c. in most cases in which the principal is undisclosed.
    d. all of the above.

14. Pete and Dick entered into an agency agreement that, by its terms, was to run for two years. Pete was to serve as Dick's agent. Pete notified Dick that he was terminating the agency after only two weeks had passed. Dick claims that Pete cannot terminate the agency. Which of the following is true?

    a. Pete has the power to terminate, but not the right.
    b. Pete has the right to terminate, but not the power.
    c. Pete cannot terminate the agency.
    d. Pete has both the power and the right to terminate the agency.

15. Kate was employed as Wanda's agent for the purpose of selling encyclopedias. Claude had previously dealt with Kate while she was acting as Wanda's agent. Wanda fired Kate. After being fired, Kate, representing herself as Wanda's agent, contracted to sell encyclopedias to Claude. Claude paid Kate $100 as a down payment. Kate then left town. Can Claude enforce the contract against Wanda?

    a. No, because the agency had been terminated.
    b. No, because Claude was not entitled to actual notice of the termination.
    c. Yes, because Kate had apparent authority.
    d. Yes, because Kate need not have authority in order to bind Wanda.

Agency

PART B: Matching Sets

Matching Set 1

Match the type of principal (A-C) with the correct fact statement (16-19). Write the letter of your answer in the blank to the left of the number.

TYPES OF PRINCIPALS

A. Disclosed Principal
B. Partially Disclosed Principal
C. Undisclosed Principal

FACT STATEMENTS

_____ 16. The third party with whom the agent is dealing believes the agent is acting in the agent's own behalf.

_____ 17. The third party knows only that the agent is acting on behalf of someone else.

_____ 18. The third party knows on whose behalf the agent is acting.

_____ 19. The agent has no liability on a contract entered on behalf of this type of principal.

Matching Set 2

Match the type of authority (A-C) with the appropriate statement (20-23). Write the letter of your answer in the blank to the left of the number.

TYPES OF AUTHORITY

A. Express Authority
B. Implied Authority
C. Apparent Authority

FACT STATEMENTS

_____ 20. Authority that is based upon the reasonable belief of a third party.

_____ 21. Authority that is based upon written or oral instructions.

_____ 22. Authority that is based upon reasonable necessity.

_____ 23. Authority that is beyond actual authority.

Matching Set 3

Match the type of agent (A-D) with the appropriate fact statement (24-27). Write the letter of your answer in the space to the left of the number.

TYPES OF AGENTS

A. Gratuitous Agent
B. General Agent
C. Special Agent
D. Independent Contractor

FACT STATEMENTS

_____ 24. Agent who is authorized to perform a single task.

_____ 25. Agent whose physical conduct is free of principal's right to control.

_____ 26. Agent who agrees to serve without compensation.

_____ 27. Agent who is authorized to represent principal in a number of transactions over a period of time.

Matching Set 4

Match the statement describing the agent's liability (A-B) with the correct fact statement (28-31). Write the letter of your answer in the blank to the left of the number.

AGENT'S LIABILITY

A. Agent incurs no liability.
B. Agent can be held liable to third party.

FACT STATEMENTS

_____ 28. Agent enters contract on behalf of a partially disclosed principal.

_____ 29. Agent enters contract on behalf of a disclosed principal.

_____ 30. Agent enters contract on behalf of an undisclosed principal.

_____ 31. Agent acting on behalf of a disclosed principal negligently injures a third party.

Agency   235

PART C: Case Problems

DIRECTIONS: For each of the questions relating to the following case problems, select the best answer from the four alternatives. Write your answer in the blank to the left of the number.

Case 1

Susan, president of a small advertising firm, obtained approval from the board of directors to purchase all new office furniture and to sell the used furniture. She placed an ad in the local paper announcing that used furniture would be sold on a particular Saturday. On the designated day Susan left Gil in charge of the sale. She told him, however, not to sell any lamps because the board had decided to keep all lamps and light fixtures.

Gil sold all of the furniture, including seven lamps, to parties who responded to the ad. He placed the money obtained from the sale in his personal bank account without writing down the exact amount of the sale proceeds. He cannot remember how much of the deposit was from sale proceeds and how much was from his winnings at the race track that afternoon.

_____ 32. Upon learning of these events, Susan's firm seeks to recover the lamps from the purchaser who has now been identified as Sandy. Which of the following statements is true?

   a. The firm will recover the lamps from Sandy because Gil had no actual authority to sell them.
   b. The firm will recover the lamps from Sandy because Gil had been specifically instructed by his principal not to sell them.
   c. Sandy will be permitted to keep the lamps because Gil possessed emergency authority to sell them.
   d. Sandy will be permitted to keep the lamps because Gil had apparent authority to sell them.

_____ 33. Which of the following duties of an agent did Gil *not* violate?

   a. Duty to use care and skill.
   b. Duty not to commingle.
   c. Duty not to use agency-related information for personal gain.
   d. Duty to account to principal.

Case 2

Pat owns and operates a business known as Computer Solutions. Pat employs Bill as a word processor. Bill agrees to work from 9:00 a.m. to 5:00 p.m., with one hour off for lunch. He is provided a work station and is given work to perform by Pat. Bill is paid an hourly wage.

Pat also employs Judy as a program originator. Judy picks up assignments, meets with clients, and meets with Pat at various times. Judy has office space at the business but does much of her work at home or at the lake or anywhere a good idea comes to mind. Judy is paid a commission on jobs that she performs. Last year she earned commissions in seven of the 12 months.

Bill was injured at his work station when a ceiling tile fell on his head. Judy was injured by a negligent driver one night while driving to the library to obtain a book containing new ideas for computer programs.

_____ 34. Which of the following best describes the liability of Computer Solutions?

   a. Both Bill and Judy are entitled to compensation from the business.
   b. Bill is entitled to compensation from the business, but Judy is not.
   c. Judy is entitled to compensation from the business, but Bill is not.
   d. Neither Bill nor Judy is entitled to compensation.

_____ 35. Judy contracted with Bruce to provide a certain computer program to him by November 1 for $250. Bruce knew that Judy was acting on behalf of a business, but he did not know which business. The program was delivered on time, but Bruce failed to pay the agreed-upon amount. Which of the following best describes Bruce's liability?

   a. Only Judy may collect the $250 from Bruce.
   b. Only the business, Computer Solutions, may collect $250 from Bruce.
   c. Either Judy or Computer Solutions may collect $250 from Bruce.
   d. Neither Judy nor Computer Solutions may collect $250 from Bruce.

Agency

Case 3

George started a pharmaceutical firm to market a new drug known as Tridol. He hired Al, Barb, and Connie as sales agents. Each signed an agency agreement for one year. Each was given a certain sales territory. One month later Al notified George that he was terminating his agency relationship. The next month Barb died after using Tridol. The next month the federal Food and Drug Administration declared the sale of Tridol illegal.

36. Which statement concerning Al's agency relationship is correct?

   a. The agency terminated upon Al's notification of George.
   b. The agency terminated when the sale of Tridol was made illegal.
   c. The agency will terminate at the end of the one-year period.
   d. The agency will remain in effect until it is mutually terminated.

37. Which of the following statements is correct?

   a. The agency relationship of both Barb and Connie terminated upon Al's notification of George.
   b. The agency relationship of both Barb and Connie terminated upon the death of Barb.
   c. The agency relationship of both Barb and Connie terminated when the sale of Tridol was made illegal.
   d. Barb's agency relationship terminated upon her death, but Connie's did not terminate until the sale of Tridol was made illegal.

Case 4

Warner is employed by Mediocre Foods as a sales and delivery person. He drives a company truck along a specified route and fills orders from his truck. While unloading some frozen meat, Warner bumped Ann causing her to fall, injuring her arm. While driving to the next store on the route, Warner bumped into the back of a garbage truck and injured Bill who was loading garbage into the truck. Warner decided to take the remainder of the day off and visit his grandmother at a nursing home. After driving ten miles off his route, Warner crashed into a vehicle stopped at a red light, causing injury to Cal, its driver.

38. Which of the following statements is true?

   a. Mediocre Foods is liable to Ann, Bill, and Cal.
   b. Warner is liable to Ann, Bill, and Cal.
   c. Mediocre Foods is liable only to Ann.
   d. Warner is liable only to Cal.

39. Mediocre Foods notified Warner of his termination. Nevertheless, he later went to Able's Foods, a customer he had sold to for seven years and took advance payment for a large order. Able's Foods now seeks to collect from Mediocre Foods because the delivery of its order was never made. Which of the following statements is accurate?

   a. Able has no right to recover because Warner's agency had already been terminated.
   b. Able can recover unless Mediocre published a notice of termination in a newspaper of general circulation in the area where Able does business.
   c. Able can recover if it was notified both orally and in writing of the termination.
   d. Able can recover unless it was notified either orally or in writing of the termination.

40. Two weeks after being terminated, Warner introduced himself at Bentley's Grocery as an agent for Mediocre Foods. Warner had never been to Bentley's before. He took advance payment for a large order. Which of the following statements is true concerning Bentley's right to recover its payment from Mediocre?

   a. Bentley's cannot recover because the agency had already been terminated.
   b. Bentley's cannot recover because it was not notified orally or in writing of the termination.
   c. Bentley's can probably recover unless notice of Warner's termination was published in a newspaper of general circulation in the area where Bentley was operating.
   d. Bentley's cannot recover because no notice to third parties is required when an agent is fired.

Chapter 10: Solutions

PART A: Multiple-Choice Questions

	Answer	Refer to Chapter Section
1.	(d)	[A-1, A-2-b] There is an agency relationship between the parties. As a general rule, agency agreements need not be in writing. Only if the contract which the agent is authorized to enter on behalf of the principal is legally required to be in writing must the agency agreement be in writing. In this case Wally is authorized to enter into a contract to sell a snow blower (goods) for Ernie for $150. Because this is under $500, the contract would not have to be in writing.
2.	(a)	[A-3-a, A-3-b] It is the capacity of the principal that is important in determining whether a contract entered into by an authorized agent can be disaffirmed. Because Connie, the principal, is a minor, she is permitted to disaffirm. It is not necessary that the minor principal have disaffirmed the agency agreement before disaffirming the contract entered into by the agent.
3.	(b)	[B-2] The third party (Tom) knows of the existence of the principal but does not know the principal's identity, so Paul is therefore a partially disclosed principal. If Tom had known of Paul's identity, Paul would be a disclosed principal. If Tom had reasonably believed that Al was acting on his own behalf without any principal being involved, Paul would be an undisclosed principal.
4.	(d)	[C-1, C-2] Under the terms of the agency agreement, Gina is not entitled to compensation for her services; she is therefore a gratuitous agent. Because she is authorized to represent the company in a series of transactions over a period of time, she is a general agent.
5.	(c)	[E-2-a] An agent may delegate duties only in certain limited circumstances. In this case Mike's duties require special skill and therefore cannot be delegated. The mere fact that Mike became very busy does not allow him to delegate his duties.

6. (a) [E-7-b] An agent has a duty to avoid conflicts of interest. Jennifer owned stock in Beta, and a conflict of interest therefore existed. Jennifer was obligated to notify Alpha of the conflict. Unless Alpha, with full knowledge of the conflict, approved of the transaction with Beta, Jennifer would be in breach of her duty of loyalty.

7. (d) [D-1, D-2, and D-4] An agent who possesses express, implied, or apparent authority can bind the principal to a contract.

8. (a) [F-1] An agent who enters into a contract on behalf of an undisclosed or partially disclosed principal is liable on the contract. Only the agent who acts for the disclosed principal can avoid liability on the contracts entered into on behalf of the principal.

9. (a) [F-4] An agent is liable for losses caused by the agent's fraud or deceit.

10. (c) [G-5] The principal is obligated to compensate injured agents who are employees for injuries sustained in the course of their employment, but independent contractors are not entitled to such compensation. Answers (a) and (b) are obligations of the principal.

11. (b) [H-1-c] A principal may ratify an unauthorized contract and thereby become bound by its terms. Ratification requires that the principal have knowledge of all relevant facts and that the principal accept the benefits of the contract with the intent of being bound by its terms. Without ratification, a principal is not bound by an unauthorized contract.

12. (c) [F-5, H-2-b] Because Andy was negligent, he is liable for the injury he caused. Because the negligent act occurred in the course of the agent's employment, the principal is also liable. Andy was an employee, not an independent contractor.

13. (d) [I-1, I-2, and I-3] The principal can enforce the contract against the third party if the principal was disclosed or partially disclosed. In addition, an undisclosed principal can enforce the contract in most cases. Only if the contract required the agent to perform personally, or if the agent denied to the third party that he or she was acting as an agent, or if the agent should have known that the third party would not agree with the principal, can the third party refuse to perform the contract for the principal.

Agency

14. (a) [J-3-a] Either the principal or the agent has the power to terminate the agency at any time. In this case the parties have limited their right to terminate. Pete had no right to terminate for two years. Pete therefore can terminate the agency, but he is liable for any damages that his termination causes because he exercised his power to terminate without possessing the right to terminate.

15. (c) [K-1] Because Claude had previously dealt with Kate acting as Wanda's agent, he was entitled to actual notice. No notice of termination was given. Kate had apparent authority to bind her principal. Kate, of course, is liable to Wanda for her wrongdoing.

PART B: Matching Sets

Matching Set 1

16. (C) [B-3]

17. (B) [B-2]

18. (A) [B-1]

19. (A) [F-1]

Matching Set 2

20. (C) [D-4]

21. (A) [D-1]

22. (B) [D-2]

23. (C) [E-1-a]

Matching Set 3

24. (C) [C-3]

25. (D) [C-4]

26. (A) [C-1]

27. (B) [C-2]

Matching Set 4

28.	(B)	[F-2]
29.	(A)	[F-1]
30.	(B)	[F-3]
31.	(B)	[F-5]

PART C: Case Problems

32. (d)   [D-4] By leaving Gil in charge of the sale after advertising it as a furniture sale, the firm allowed circumstances to exist that would lead a reasonable person to conclude that Gil had authority to sell the lamps. Sandy was allowed to rely on the appearance of things, even though Gil lacked actual authority to sell the lamps.

33. (c)   [E] Gil breached each of the listed duties except using agency-related information for personal gain.

34. (b)   [G-5] Bill, as an employee injured during the course of his employment, is entitled to collect damages from his employer. Judy is an independent contractor and, as such, is not entitled to recover damages from the business.

35. (c)   [I-2] One who contracts with an agent acting on behalf of a partially disclosed principal may be required to pay the agent or the principal. Bruce could not, however, be required to pay twice.

36. (a)   [J-3] Although Al lacked the right to terminate the agency after one month, he had the power to do so.

37. (d)   [J] Both death and illegality cause termination of an agency. Barb's agency was terminated when she died. Connie's remained, but was terminated by the FDA's action when the sale of Tridol became illegal.

38. (b)   [F-5] An agent is always liable for his own negligence, whether or not the principal can also be held liable. Mediocre Foods can also be held liable for injuries to Ann and Bill which occurred in the scope of Warner's employment.

39. (d)   [K-1] Since Able had previously dealt with Warner in his capacity as an agent of Mediocre Foods, Able was entitled to either oral or written notification of the termination.

40. (c)   [K-2] Since Bentley's had not dealt with Warner before, it was entitled only to notice by publication. Had the agency been terminated by death, illegality, or insanity, no notice would have been required.

CHAPTER 11
Business Entities

OVERVIEW

This chapter reviews the laws governing the formation, creation, and termination of sole entrepreneurships, partnerships, and corporations. A candidate should be able to visualize the life cycle of a business entity: the manner of formation, business operation, and the termination.

The agency-law concepts learned earlier may be applied to the study of business entities. For example, a partner, when acting on behalf of the partnership, always acts as an agent, not a principal. Therefore, a partner will have the authority to act that a general agent would normally possess (actual plus implied authority). In contrast, a shareholder of a corporation has no agency authority to bind the corporation. Shareholders are considered investors with very limited decision-making input. Directors determine policy, and officers, who are the agents of the corporation, implement policy and handle day-to-day transactions.

The candidate should attempt to understand the basic similarities and distinctions between partnerships and corporations.

DEFINITION OF TERMS

ARTICLES OF INCORPORATION. The legal framework in which a corporation operates. It is filed with the state at the time of incorporation.

AUTHORIZED SHARES. The number of shares established in the articles of incorporation.

BYLAWS. Regulations of the corporation that govern internal management and day-to-day operational structure.

COMMON STOCK. Stock that represents ownership in a corporation. Each share of stock may earn a dividend only after all corporate obligations, including those to owners of preferred stock, are satisfied.

CONVERTIBLE STOCK. Stock that can be exchanged for shares of another class (such as preferred to common) at the option of the holder of the stock.

DISSOLUTION. The change in the relationship of the partners caused by any partner ceasing to be associated with carrying on the business.

DOMESTIC CORPORATION. A corporation doing business in the state in which it is incorporated.

ESTOPPEL. A party to a lawsuit will be precluded (stopped) from raising a defense.

FIDUCIARY DUTY. A duty of trust, loyalty, and full disclosure owed by one person to another.

FOREIGN CORPORATION. A corporation doing business in a state other than the one in which it is incorporated.

ISSUED STOCK. Authorized stock actually sold by the corporation.

JOINT LIABILITY. In partnership law, a party suing the partnership on a contract claim must sue all partners individually if any partner(s) is (are) included in the suit; responsibility as a group.

JOINT AND SEVERAL LIABILITY. In partnership law, a party suing the partnership on a tort claim may include any number of partners in the suit; responsibility either as a group or individually.

LIMITED PARTNER. The partner is treated as an investor only and may not engage in active day-to-day management of the business or lend his/her name to the partnership name. A limited partner is potentially liable on partnership debts only to the extent of capital contribution.

OUTSTANDING STOCK. Stock sold by the corporation and not reacquired.

PARTNERSHIP. An association of two or more persons to carry on a business for profit as co-owners.

PREEMPTIVE RIGHTS. The right of a shareholder to retain his/her percentage of corporate ownership by being able to purchase that percentage of a new stock issue.

PREFERRED STOCK. Stock that represents ownership in a corporation entitling the stockholder to certain advantages not available to owners of common stock.

PROMOTER. The person(s) who organizes (creates) a new corporation and solicits stock subscriptions.

PROXY. Written authorization by a shareholder to another person granting the power to vote the shareholder's stock.

REDEEMABLE STOCK. Stock that can be reacquired at the option of the corporation (generally preferred stock).

TRADING PARTNERSHIP. A partnership engaged in the buying and/or selling of goods.

TREASURY STOCK. Stock sold by the corporation but subsequently reacquired.

A. Sole Entrepreneurship

A sole entrepreneurship, sometimes called a sole proprietorship, is a business owned and operated by only one person.

1. *Formation of Sole Entrepreneurship:*

    a. *Single owner:* This type of business has only one owner and is *not* incorporated (not a corporation).

    b. *Variable size:* Although there is a single owner, there can be any number of employees. A business may be large or small and still be in the form of a sole entrepreneurship.

    c. *Unlimited liability:* As the only owner, a sole proprietor can potentially be liable for all of the debts of the business (plus the owner's personal debts).

2. *Creation of Sole Entrepreneurship:* A sole entrepreneurship is created subject to state law. Generally, no detailed procedures are required for the creation of a sole entrepreneurship. Generally, the true owner's name must be registered in the local courthouse, along with the trade and/or business name if the name of the business is not to be the owner's name.

    EXAMPLE: If John Doe begins a business called Lucky Pizza, he would have to register the business name (Lucky Pizza) along with his name as the sole owner. This is a sole entrepreneurship.

3. *Operation:*

    a. *Government regulation:* The sole entrepreneurship is generally subject to governmental regulations, just as any partnership or corporation might be. Small businesses (regardless of the business form), however, are often exempt from laws and/or regulations for reasons such as these:

        (1) The business has little impact, if any, upon interstate commerce.

        (2) The size of the business is small (few employees or small gross sales).

        EXAMPLE: Title VII of the Civil Rights Act of 1964, the basic law concerning employment discrimination, applies only to businesses having 15 or more employees.

b. *Income tax applicable:* The sole entrepreneurship, as an entity, pays no income tax. (Profits or losses are reflected on the owner's personal income tax return.)

c. *Employee benefits provided:* Workmen's compensation, unemployment compensation, and FICA payments are all required of the sole entrepreneurship, just as they are required of a partnership or a corporation.

d. *Agency:* The laws of agency apply to the sole entrepreneurship.

  (1) The owner is the principal.

  (2) Any agents have whatever express authority is given by the principal plus that authority resulting from their agency position and/or standard trade practices.

e. *Termination:* No formal procedure exists for the sole owner to terminate the business. So long as no fraud results as to creditors, the owner may simply cease doing business.

B. Partnership

A partnership is a business entity owned and operated by two or more persons (called partners). The formal definition of a partnership is an association of two or more persons to carry on as co-owners of a business for profit.

1. *Formation of Partnerships:* Partnerships are governed by state laws (statutes). Many states have adopted the Uniform Partnership Act (UPA), a model act, as the state's partnership law. The purpose of the UPA is to achieve uniformity among states concerning partnership laws.

2. *Creation of Partnerships:* Partnerships may be created by an express partnership agreement, by determination of the courts, and by estoppel.

a. *Express partnership agreement:* A written partnership agreement (articles of partnership) is always advisable to assure clarity and understanding of the intent of the partners. However, an oral partnership agreement is legally enforceable, so long as a writing is not required under the statute of frauds.

EXAMPLE: Andrew, Betty, and Charles form the ABC Partnership

Business Entities   247

which is to exist for ten years. The agreement must be in writing because it will not be completed within one year.

b. *Determination of the courts:* Sometimes it is not clear whether a partnership exists or not. In these cases a court may be called upon to examine the overall facts and determine whether or not a partnership exists. Here are the more common tests courts utilize:

(1) *Sharing of profits:* No one test need be met, but courts place the most emphasis upon this one.

EXAMPLE: Al and Bob jointly open a record shop. They agree to share profits. A court would probably find a partnership.

Courts recognize three common situations where a sharing of profits may occur, but no partnership status will be found.

(a) *Rent:*

EXAMPLE: The Penny Company agrees to pay a portion of profits from its American Mall Store to the mall owners as part of the rent payment. This is not a partnership.

(b) *Loans:*

EXAMPLE: The First Bank lends money to J. T. Holmes, a farmer, for crops. The farmer's repayment is tied to farm profits, but this is not considered a partnership.

(c) *Employment:*

EXAMPLE: Al Whitman is to receive 10 percent of the profits at a partnership's store because he is the manager of the store. This alone does not make Al a partner.

(2) *Activity and duration:* The amount of activity involved and the planned duration.

(3) *Designation of business:* Designation of such existence by partners/parties.

(4) *Title:* Title to property used in business.

c. *Partnership by estoppel:* Partnership by estoppel is based on the same theory as agency by estoppel. *Estoppel* means that a party to a lawsuit will be precluded (stopped) from raising a defense. In partnership law, the fact that no partnership actually exists among persons who are involved will not be allowed as a defense by these persons. A court finds "partnership by estoppel" in order to avoid inequity to an innocent third party.

EXAMPLE: Andrew, Betty, and Charles represent to a bank that they are partners in a restaurant to facilitate the lending of moneys to Andrew, the actual owner. Andrew, Betty, and Charles will be considered a partnership as to the bank.

EXAMPLE: Assume Alice and Bob are not actual partners. In front of Alice, Bob tells Phyllis that Alice and Bob are partners. Alice would be liable as if, in fact, a partner for Phyllis's loan to the supposed partnership of Alice and Bob.

3. *Theories of Partnerships:* Two theories forming the basic foundation for partnerships are aggregate theory and entity theory.

   a. *Aggregate theory:* The partnership is the sum of the individuals.

      (1) The partnership is not viewed as a business entity in and of itself, but rather as the individual partners collectively.

      EXAMPLE: A partnership pays no federal income tax. Each partner reports his/her share of profits or losses on individual income tax returns.

      EXAMPLE: The partners must be collectively sued for a recovery against the partnership under the UPA.

      (2) The UPA basically follows the aggregate theory.

   b. *Entity theory:* The partnership is an entity in itself.

      (1) The partnership is not viewed as a business entity in and of itself, but as the individual partners collectively.

      (2) This theory is generally applied to the ownership of property.

      EXAMPLE: Andrew, Betty, and Charles form ABC Partnership. Partnership funds are used to buy a building in the partnership name. The building will be considered partnership property.

      (3) A joint venture may be formed for a single transaction or primarily for investment purposes without truly being an ongoing business in and of itself.

Business Entities 249

EXAMPLE: Three doctors buy a duplex to be rented for investment purposes.

EXAMPLE: Two oil corporations join to remove oil from a certain offshore oil field.

The basic rules of partnership law still apply in joint ventures. A joint venturer cannot achieve personal gain at the expense of the joint venture without the knowledge and consent of the other joint venturers.

4. *Types of Partnerships:* Partnerships may be general or limited, depending on the nature of the partnership formed.

   a. *General partnership:* This type of partnership is sometimes called an ordinary or regular partnership.

   b. *Limited partnership* (created specially by state statute): This type of partnership has been established in many states to allow persons to invest in the partnership business without fear of personal loss beyond the original investment. In this type of partnership, there must be at least one general (regular) partner and one limited partner. The general partner is similar to the partner in a general partnership.

   (1) Without specific state law authorizing a limited partnership, there cannot be one. A limited partnership agreement must be filed with the state (usually not required for a general partnership).

   (2) A limited partner is treated as the equivalent of a shareholder in a corporation:

   (a) A limited partner's potential liability for the partnership debt is limited to the limited partner's capital contribution.

   (b) A limited partner may not participate in the active, day-to-day management of the partnership.

   EXAMPLE: Ben is a limited partner in the ABC Partnership. Ben may not be actively involved in partnership business decisions.

   (c) A limited partner shares in profits according to the partnership agreement.

   (d) A limited partner may not lend his/her name to the

partnership name.

- (e) A limited partner has no inherent agency authority to bind the limited partnership.

    EXAMPLE: Using the same example, Ben has no authority to bind the partnership to any contracts with third parties.

- (f) A limited partner who acts as a general partner loses statutory protection and will be liable as any other general partner.

c. *Trading partnership:* A partnership involved in the buying or selling of goods is a trading partnership. If a partnership is classified as a trading partnership, the partners will have broader authority to bind the partnership.

d. *Nontrading partnership:* Any partnership not engaged in the buying or selling of goods is a nontrading partnership.

EXAMPLE: A law partnership is formed to provide legal services and is, therefore, a nontrading partnership.

5. *Partnership Operations:*

a. *Basic rules:* Five basic rules exist under the UPA in regard to the operation of a partnership:

(1) *Agency:* Every partner is an agent of the partnership.

EXAMPLE: Michael is a partner of XYZ Partnership. Therefore, he is an agent of the partnership. When Michael acts on behalf of the partnership, he is acting as an agent, not as a principal.

(2) *Profit/loss sharing:* Partners share profits and losses equally (unless otherwise stated in their partnership agreement).

EXAMPLE: The partnership agreement of Golden Company is silent as to the sharing of profits among the five partners. Accordingly, each partner will receive 20 percent of the profits even if one partner had put up 50 percent of the capital.

(3) *Partners' liability:* Every partner is potentially personally liable for all of the debts of the partnership.

EXAMPLE: Partner X and the XYZ Partnership become bankrupt. Partners Y and Z may be held individually liable for all of the remaining debts of the partnership (but not for partner X's personal debts).

(4) *Admission of new partners:* Unanimous consent is required to admit a new partner (unless a partnership agreement exists to the contrary).

(5) *Management of partnership:* The partners have equal management rights (unless there is a partnership agreement to the contrary). In essence, each partner has one vote in partnership matters.

b. *Partnership property:*

(1) *Individual partner's interest:* An individual partner's interest in partnership property is governed by the following rules:

(a) *Interest in partnership property:* Each partner's interest in the partnership property is considered personal property even if real property is owned by the partnership. (In essence, the interest is treated in the same manner as ownership of corporate stock.)

(b) *Right to use partnership property:* A partner has the right to use and possess partnership property only for partnership purposes.

EXAMPLE: Robert, a partner, may not take some partnership paintings home for his personal use.

(c) *Rights of deceased partner's estate:* If a partner dies, the partner's estate does not have any rights as to specific partnership property, but instead an overall interest equivalent to what the partner possessed—that is, a percentage figure.

EXAMPLE: Alex, a partner in ABC Partnership, dies. Alex's estate has a right to Alex's respective interest in the partnership but no right to specific partnership property. Alex's widow would like to claim the antique Windsor chairs from the partnership reception area, but her only right is to Alex's interest in the partnership, not to specific furniture owned by the partnership.

(d) *Assignment of partnership interest:* A partner may

assign but not sell his/her partnership interest without the consent of the other partners.

- The assignee, the party receiving the assignment, receives the rights to assignor-partner's interest (primarily rights to that partner's share of the income).

- The assignee gets no management rights within the partnership since the assignee is not a partner. (Remember, a new partner within the partnership can join a partnership only if unanimous agreement of the existing partners occurs.)

- An assignment generally does not cause dissolution of the partnership.

EXAMPLE: Ellen assigns her one-third partnership interest to The State Bank as collateral for a loan to build a vacation home. The State Bank is not a new partner.

(e) *Rights of personal creditors:* A partner's personal creditors have no rights to specific partnership property. A personal creditor may only get a court order establishing rights to distributions to the partner by the partnership.

(2) *Property ownership:* Tests to determine whether property belongs to the partnership or to an individual partner have been established to resolve ownership disputes. The tests include the following:

(a) *Title to the property:* The title reflects the legal title owner, but a court may still find that property belongs to the partnership even though title is in an individual partner's name.

(b) *Funds invested in property:* Ownership may be decided on the basis of funds invested by individuals to purchase and/or improve the questioned property.

(c) *Accounting for the partnership:* The manner in which the property is reflected in the partnership books may help to determine ownership (whether the property is treated as a partnership asset or not).

EXAMPLE: Partnership funds were used to purchase

Business Entities 253

> *a new pickup truck. The truck was licensed in the name of Sam, a partner, but carried as partnership property on the partnership books. The court would probably find the truck to be partnership property.*

  (3) *Conveyance of partnership property:* A partner normally does not have the apparent authority to convey partnership real property unless the partnership is regularly dealing in the sale of real property. A different result may occur if the partnership property is left in the individual name of a partner, and this partner conveys the property to a third party, who buys in good faith and without knowledge of the wrongful conveyance.

6. *Relationship of Partners to Third Persons:*

  a. *Authority to bind partnership:* A partner's authority to bind the partnership to third persons is determined by the following:

    (1) The laws of agency apply when a partner acts on behalf of the partnership.

    (2) A partner acts as an agent, not as a principal, when acting for or on behalf of a partnership.

    (3) A partner can bind the partnership as the result of using express, implied, or apparent authority, the usual types of agency authority. (See Chapter 10: Agency.)

> *EXAMPLE: Partner A visits a building for sale and signs a contract for the partnership to buy it. Unless the partnership deals in buildings in its ordinary course of business or unless specific partnership authority exists, the partnership will not be bound up to the seller.*

    (4) Secret instructions, as in agency law, are not binding if the partner would normally be considered by the third parties to have had the power to act, and the third party, acting in good faith, has no knowledge of any irregularity.

> *EXAMPLE: Partner B is told by the partnership members not to order Suds Beer for their bar. If Partner B, as manager, orders Suds Beer, the partnership would be liable. (A manager normally has the authority to determine which beer to order.)*

    (5) A partner has apparent authority to bind the partnership where the partnership has *knowledge* of unauthorized acts

and does nothing to prevent them.

(6) A partner of a trading partnership has the apparent authority to borrow money for the normal operations of the partnership.

EXAMPLE: The ABC Partnership operates a retail sporting goods store (this is a trading partnership). Partner A borrows $10,000 from First Bank purportedly for partnership purposes. The partnership would be liable to First Bank if A should abscond with the borrowed money immediately after A receives it.

(7) A partner does not normally possess the authority to

(a) submit a dispute to arbitration.

(b) dispose of goodwill or any other major asset.

(c) assign partnership property to creditors.

(d) admit partnership legal liability.

b. *Contract liability—joint liability:*

(1) *Joint liability:* Partners have joint liability for the contract obligations of the partnership. In essence, this means that, if a suit is brought against the partnership, all partners must be sued individually for partnership contract obligations.

EXAMPLE: ABC Partnership owes Patrick $5,000. Patrick must include A, B, and C if he includes any partner in conjunction with the suit against the partnership.

(2) *Release from personal liability:* The release of one partner from personal liability may release all partners from personal liability.

c. *Tort liability:*

(1) *Joint and several liability:* Partners have joint and several liability for tort actions of partners and/or employees occurring within the scope of employment. *Joint and several* means that the party bringing suit may sue the partnership and any combination of the partners.

EXAMPLE: Ellen brings a tort action against the ABC Partnership. Ellen may sue the partnership and any combi-

Business Entities   **255**

nation of the partners individually, such as ABC Partnership plus B.

(2) *Individual liability:* An individual partner is always liable for personal tortious actions even if acting for the partnership.

7. *Partnership Dissolution:* A partnership dissolution occurs when there is a change of partners. In essence, this means the old partnership terminates, and a new one is begun (if partnership continues after a partner's departure).

EXAMPLE: *Partner A of the ABC Partnership retires, but B and C wish to continue. The partnership of ABC will terminate, and the partnership of BC will exist thereafter.*

EXAMPLE: *In the same example, D becomes a new partner in place of A. The new partnership will be BCD.*

   a. *Order of termination:* The order of terminating a partner's interest or the partnership altogether is:

     (1) *Dissolution:* The old partnership is terminated.

     (2) *Winding-up* (process of termination): No new contracts may be agreed to except as necessary to end the business.

     (3) *Termination:* The partnership ceases operation.

   b. *Partner withdrawal:* In general, a partner always has the power to terminate his/her partnership relationship even though such a termination results in a breach of the partnership agreement.

EXAMPLE: *RST Partnership is a partnership formed with a ten-year life. In the third year R decides to quit the partnership to pursue a career in acting. R has the power but not the right to withdraw.*

There may be an improper or unauthorized termination by a partner. In this event

     (1) the withdrawing partner may be denied his/her share of the partnership goodwill. *Goodwill* is the value of the business above the value of the partnership assets overall.

     (2) remaining partners may decide to continue business after buying out the departing partner.

c. *Causes of dissolution:* Dissolution may be caused by acts of partners, operation of the law, or court discretion.

(1) *Acts of partners:*

  (a) *Unilateral action of a partner* (even though this causes a breach of partnership): A partner decides to leave the partnership.

  (b) *Agreement or assent:* The partners agree to dissolve the partnership.

   EXAMPLE: The ABC Partnership was created for a term of ten years. At the end of ten years the partnership will dissolve.

   EXAMPLE: In their third year, the partners of ABC decide to terminate the partnership business even though seven years remain.

  (c) *A partnership at will:* No set length of time is specified for the partnership to exist.

  (d) *Expulsion:* The partnership agreement specifically permits the expulsion of a partner.

(2) *Operation of the law:* Dissolution of the partnership occurs automatically without any partner action as a result of:

  (a) Bankruptcy of any partner or the partnership.

  (b) Illegality of business purpose.

  (c) Death of a partner.

(3) *Court discretion:* The court, through equitable discretion, determines that it would be best overall to dissolve the partnership because of the following:

  (a) *Willful and/or persistent breaches of partnership agreement:* A partner willfully breaches the partnership agreement, causing persistent problems for the other partners.

   EXAMPLE: Partner A continuously allows friends to drink at the partnership bar without charging or covering for the costs. The costs become excessive to the partnership.

Business Entities 257

(b) *Impossibility of success of the partnership:* Business can only be carried on at a loss.

EXAMPLE: The Ajax Partnership is engaged in a very competitive market in which it has shown three successive years of losses without the foreseeable likelihood of profits. The court could order partnership dissolution at the request of a partner even though others want to keep the business going.

(c) *Inability of partners to conduct business together:* The partners are unable to work together to conduct necessary business matters.

EXAMPLE: Alexander and Brad are partners of a profitable partnership business, but they are always engaged in extensive partnership bickering. Dissolution could be ordered even though Brad would like the partnership to continue.

(d) *Other factors:* The presence of other disrupting factors may make the carrying on of a partnership business impractical or impossible.

d. *Liabilities for departing partner:* Even though one partner leaves the partnership, that partner may still be liable to creditors if the partnership continues doing business.

(1) *Liability for past debts:*

(a) A departing partner is still potentially liable to existing creditors at the time of departure unless a *novation* is given by these creditors. A novation is an agreement to release the departing partner for another party.

EXAMPLE: A retires from the ABC Partnership. The partnership buys out A's share and agrees to assume A's potential liability to existing creditors. A would still have potential liability to these creditors without a novation.

(b) Where no novation occurs, a departing partner is still liable even though a new partner purchases the departing partner's interest.

EXAMPLE: A wishes to retire from the ABC Partnership. D purchases A's interest (with partnership consent) and agrees to assume A's potential share of liabilities. A is still *potentially liable to past creditors without a novation.*

(2) *Debt incurred by partnership after withdrawal:* The departed partner is liable unless proper legal notice was given to creditors. Actual notice must be given to past creditors of the partnership, and constructive notice must be given to all others (by a legal classified ad).

EXAMPLE: A retires from the ABC Partnership. A legal notice advertisement is run in the classified section of the newspaper telling of A's retirement. Such notice is not effective as to an actual creditor of the partnership. Thus, A could still bind the partnership, and/or the subsequent contracts of the partnership would be binding on A.

e. *Liabilities for new partner for past partnership debts:* A new partner is potentially liable for partnership debts prior to joining the partnership to the extent of his/her partnership contribution to the partnership.

8. *Settlement of Partnership Accounts at Termination:* At the termination of the partnership, a certain order of payment of partnership obligations must be followed:

a. *Outside creditors:* nonpartner creditors.

b. *Loans by partners:* inside creditors.

c. *Repayment of capital contribution by partners.*

d. *Payment of remaining profits* (if any).

C. **Corporation**

A corporation is considered distinct from the individuals who own it (the shareholders). A corporation is a legal entity, which means it can be sued or sue directly. A corporation must be formed according to procedures established by state law and must pay annual income taxes whereas a partnership does not.

1. *Organization of a Corporation:*

a. *Ownership and management of a corporation:* The owners of a corporation are the shareholders, while the directors are involved in establishing corporate policy and the officers of the corporation are involved in the management functions. Figure 11-1 shows how a corporation may be organized.

Figure 11-1
Corporation Organization

SHAREHOLDERS: OWNERS

ELECT
* Not agents of corporation
* Share in profits (dividends)
* No fiduciary duties unless majority shareholder
* Vote for changes to articles
* Approve merger, consolidation, or sale of assets not in the ordinary course of business
* Elect and remove directors

DIRECTORS: SET POLICY

ELECT
* Not agents of corporation
* Do have fiduciary duties to corporation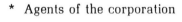
* Decide whether to authorize dividends
* Generally have power to amend bylaws
* Elect and remove officers

OFFICERS: CORPORATION AGENTS, IMPLEMENT POLICY

* Agents of the corporation
* Agency law principles apply
* Do have fiduciary duties to corporation

(1) *Shareholders:* Although shareholders are owners, they are neither managers nor agents. Shareholders are considered as investors with a corporate voice only in extraordinary policy matters. Only a majority shareholder may owe fiduciary duties to the corporation and to the minority shareholders.

EXAMPLE: Mary owns 50 shares of General Motors stock. Mary may also buy Ford shares. If Mary should invent a new type of battery, she would have no duty to provide it to General Motors (assuming that Mary is not otherwise affiliated with General Motors).

(2) *Directors:* The shareholders have the power to elect and remove the directors of the corporation. Directors have the responsibility to establish corporate policies. They are neither managers nor agents, but they do owe fiduciary duties to the corporation. Directors need not be shareholders or officers. The board of directors of the corporation is empowered to elect the officers of the corporation or, if necessary, to remove them from office.

EXAMPLE: A director of Ace Corporation discovers an excellent building lot location for Ace's expansion. The director has no inherent authority, as a director, to be able to obligate the corporation for the purchase of the lot. The director also cannot purchase the lot for personal gain and thereafter sell it to the corporation.

(3) *Officers:* Officers implement policy, manage, and serve as agents for the corporation. Officers owe fiduciary duties to the corporation.

EXAMPLE: Ace Corporation's board of directors votes to acquire a building for Ace's expansion. Corporate officers would be told to carry out the board's directive.

b. *Advantages of corporate form:* The primary advantages of the corporate form of business organization include the capital investment potential, limited liability for investors, perpetuity, and corporate control, among others.

(1) *Capital investment:* The corporation is designed to raise substantial capital from a large number of investors.

(2) *Limited liability for investors:* There is limited liability for investors, which means shareholders' personal liability for corporation losses is limited to the original purchase price paid for the stock (the original investment).

(3) *Perpetuity:* Perpetual business existence is possible.

(4) *Corporate control:* It is possible for effective control of the corporation to be vested in those with a minority of the investment (by using such techniques as nonvoting and/or preferred stock).

(5) *Employee benefits:* An investor-employee may be entitled to normal employee benefits (such as workers' compensation).

(6) *Favorable tax laws:* Tax laws have some provisions favor-

Business Entities 261

able to the corporate form.

(7) *Ability to resell:* Corporate stock is generally easier for the shareholder to sell than would be a partnership interest.

c. *Disadvantages of corporate form:* Some of the primary disadvantages of the corporate form of business organization include the higher cost of formation, corporate income taxes required, licensing, and government regulation affecting corporations.

(1) *High cost of formation:* The cost of formation and maintenance could be particularly significant for a small corporation because of

(a) *License fees.*

(b) *Franchise taxes.*

(c) *Attorney fees:* An attorney must be utilized in any corporate litigation.

(d) *State corporate rules and regulations:* Numerous rules and regulations may not practically apply to a small corporation but must still be complied with.

(2) *Income taxes:* The corporation pays income taxes on income earned, and shareholders later pay income taxes on dividends received (double taxation).

(3) *Licensing:* A corporation must be licensed and qualified to do business in each state in which it actually does business.

(4) *Government regulation:* A corporation is often subject to more overall regulation than other types of business entities.

d. *Classifications of corporations:* Corporations may be classified as domestic or foreign, public or private, closely held, or Subchapter S.

(1) *Domestic versus foreign corporation:* A corporation is a *domestic* corporation in the state in which it is incorporated and a *foreign* corporation in every other state.

EXAMPLE: ABC Corporation, incorporated in Delaware, is considered a foreign corporation in New York but a domestic corporation in Delaware.

(2) *Public versus private corporation:* A *public* corporation is

a government-owned corporation. *Private* corporations are owned by individuals, not governments. The stock of some corporations is traded on a stock exchange. For purposes of corporate law, such corporations are still private, if not government owned, even though publicly traded.

EXAMPLE: General Motors is a private corporation even though its stock is traded on a stock exchange.

EXAMPLE: Amtrak is a public corporation.

(3) *Closely held corporation:* A closely held corporation is a corporation owned by a small number of shareholders.

(4) *Subchapter S corporation:* Small corporations with 35 or fewer shareholders may be formed as Subchapter S corporations. The S corporation is especially attractive to individuals who want to establish new businesses. The Tax Reform Act of 1986 included new incentives for individuals to consider S incorporation. The primary features of the S corporation are similar to any other type of corporation. First of all, the corporation must be formed; then all shareholders must agree that the corporation should become an S corporation. The S corporation has only one class of stock and must be a small business corporation.

EXAMPLE: Richard and Joanne decide to form a small business corporation that will specialize in tax consulting. They are the two shareholders, with each one owning 50 percent of the common stock. Once the corporation, Tax Specialties, Inc., was formed, Richard and Joanne found that all of the requirements to become an S corporation had been met. They completed appropriate forms to be filed with the Internal Revenue Service and later received IRS confirmation that the corporation had been approved as an S corporation.

2. *Formation of a Corporation:* Corporations are formed under state laws, not federal. The sale of stocks and bonds (both securities) may be controlled by the Securities Exchange Commission (federal) or state laws.

   a. *The role of the promoter:* A promoter is the person who organizes and forms a new corporation.

      (1) A promoter assembles the necessary assets and financing for the new corporation.

(2) A promoter seeks stock purchasers, known as subscribers to the corporate stock.

(3) A promoter is not an agent of the corporation to be formed since no principal is yet existing.

(4) A promoter owes fiduciary duties to fellow promoters and/or subscribers. This means that the promoter must act in good faith and without known personal gain. A promoter must disclose any situation of private gain even though the corporation may also receive a benefit.

EXAMPLE: A promoter must disclose his or her interest in a parcel of land being considered for the site of the new business.

(5) A promoter is allowed to make a profit if full disclosure is made, and there is subsequent acceptance by the new corporation.

EXAMPLE: Promoter C sells an owned building to the newly formed XYZ Corporation. C is allowed to keep his profit if a full disclosure was made and appropriate approval was received.

b. *Articles of incorporation:* A new corporation is formed by the filing of articles of incorporation with a state and receiving back a corporate charter. In effect, the articles of incorporation are the corporation's constitution and, as such, contain

(1) name of corporation being formed.

(2) address of corporation.

(3) duration of time the corporation is to exist.

(4) purpose (often stated in very broad terms such as "any legal purpose").

(5) the names of the incorporators of the new corporation.

(6) number and types of shares.

(7) the name of the statutory agent (a person appointed by the incorporators who is available to receive complaints and summonses if the corporation is involved in litigation).

EXAMPLE: Cajun Corporation's articles of incorporation

authorize 1,000 shares of voting common stock and 500 shares of nonvoting preferred stock.

    c. *First shareholders' meeting of new corporation:* The agenda of the first shareholders' meeting will include the issuance of stock to the subscribers and the election of the board of directors.

    d. *First meeting of board of directors:* Items of business for the initial board of directors meeting should include:

        (1) establishment of bylaws (the internal governing rules of the corporation).

        (2) election of officers.

        (3) general acceptance or rejection of preincorporation contracts of the promoters.

            (a) The corporation is not liable on such contracts unless the directors have approved adoption (implied or express) of such contracts.

            (b) The promoter continues personal liability even though a contract has been adopted unless it was a conditional contract (no liability to promoter if corporation is not formed or does not adopt) or a novation occurs (third party agrees to release the promoter from liability and looks only to the corporation for performance).

3. *The Role of the Shareholder:* A shareholder owns stock in a corporation but is not an agent of the corporation. Therefore, a shareholder cannot legally bind the corporation. No fiduciary duties are owed to the corporation or fellow shareholders (unless the shareholder has majority shareholder status).

EXAMPLE: A shareholder may own stock in every American car manufacturing corporation without breach of loyalty.

    a. *Primary powers of shareholders:*

        (1) Election and removal of directors (not officers).

        (2) Amending the articles of incorporation.

        (3) Amending bylaws (unless power delegated to the board).

        (4) Approval of mergers (Company A + Company B = Company A).

(5) Approval of consolidations (Company A + Company B = new Company C).

(6) Approval of extraordinary sales (not purchases) of assets.

EXAMPLE: Shareholders would not vote on the purchase of all new assembly-line equipment.

b. *The right to vote at shareholder meetings:* A shareholder may give voting rights to another by written authorization (a proxy).

c. *Other shareholder rights:*

(1) Shareholders may inspect the corporate books.

(2) Shareholders receive dividends when declared (shareholders do not declare dividends; directors do).

(3) Shareholders may be elected directors and/or officers.

4. *The Role of Corporate Directors:* Directors are elected by the shareholders of the corporation to serve in this capacity. Directors may be shareholders and/or officers.

a. *Fiduciary relationship to corporation:* Directors may not have major conflicts of interest and must act in good faith toward the corporation.

b. *Primary duties of the board of directors:*

(1) Election and removal of officers.

(2) Amending bylaws (unless shareholders retain right).

(3) Declaring dividends.

(4) Establishment of corporate policy.

c. *Director liability:* Directors are judged by the business judgment rule.

(1) Directors are not guarantors of corporate profit, so they are not liable just because the corporation suffered financial losses.

(2) The basic test is whether a board member exercised due care and good faith in making board decisions.

(3) Directors may be personally liable if they authorize improper actions.

EXAMPLE: Directors of ABC Corporation, a manufacturer, agree to allow the corporation to lend money to a major customer so the customer can build a personal swimming pool.

d. *Routine delegation:* The delegation of routine matters by the board of directors to an executive committee is permissible.

5. *The Role of Officers:* Officers are elected by the board of directors of the corporation. Officers may be shareholders and/or directors.

   a. *Fiduciary duties to corporations:* Officers owe the corporation good faith, full disclosure.

   b. *Agents of the corporation:* Officers of the corporation are agents of the corporation.

      (1) *Express powers:* Express powers are derived from the by-laws or board authorizations.

      (2) *Implied powers:* Implied powers are those powers necessary to implement express authorizations.

      (3) *Apparent powers:* Apparent powers are those derived from what officers of similar corporations would normally be expected to be able to do.

6. *Corporate Finances—Stock:*

   a. *Common stock:* Common stock represents ownership in a corporation. Each share of stock may earn a dividend only after all corporate obligations, including those to owners of preferred stock, are satisfied.

      (1) *Dividends:* Common shareholders have no priority as to dividends paid.

      (2) *Voting:* Generally there is one vote per share of common stock owned.

   b. *Preferred stock:* Preferred stock also represents ownership in a corporation that entitles the shareholder to certain advantages not available to owners of common stock. The owner of preferred stock is usually entitled to receive a dividend before owners of common stock.

c. *Par versus no-par stock:*

   (1) *Par stock:* Stock whose value for initial sales is established in the articles is known as *par stock.* The stock, when initially sold, could be greater than par value but not less.

   EXAMPLE: *ABC Corporation may sell $3-per-share common stock for $5, but not for $2.50. (Note that this rule applies only to the original issuance or sale of stock.)*

   (2) *No-par stock:* Stock without stated value in the articles is called *no-par stock.* It may be initially sold for whatever value the directors stipulate. This is often called *stated value stock.*

d. *Redeemable stock:* Redeemable stock is stock that can be reacquired at the option of the corporation (generally preferred stock).

e. *Convertible stock:* Stock that can be exchanged for shares of another class (such as preferred to common) at the option of the holder of the stock is known as convertible stock.

f. *Authorized shares:* Authorized shares refers to the number of shares authorized in the articles.

g. *Issued stock:* Stock actually sold by the corporation is called issued stock.

h. *Outstanding stock:* Outstanding stock is stock sold by the corporation and not reacquired.

i. *Treasury stock:* Stock sold by the corporation but subsequently reacquired is termed treasury stock.

   EXAMPLE: *Huskie Corporation has 5,000 shares of common stock authorized, has issued 3,500 shares, and reacquired 500 shares.*

Shares authorized	5,000
Shares issued	-3,500
Shares yet to be issued	1,500
Shares issued	3,500
Shares repurchased (treasury stock)	- 500
Shares outstanding	3,000

j. *Preemptive rights:* A shareholder may be allowed by the articles to retain his/her share of corporate ownership by having the right to purchase the same percentage of new stock being issued as that owned at present. This is called a *preemptive right*.

EXAMPLE: Mary owns 1,000 shares (of 10,000) of Northwood Corporation. If Northwood should issue 3,000 new shares of stock, then Mary would have a right to purchase 1,000/10,000 (or 10 percent) of the 3,000 shares (right to 300).

Preemptive rights generally exist in only small and/or closely held corporations.

EXAMPLE: No General Motors shareholders have preemptive rights in GM stock.

Business Entities 269

Chapter 11: Review Questions

PART A: Multiple-Choice Questions

DIRECTIONS: Select the best answer from the four alternatives. Write your answer in the blank to the left of the number.

_____ 1. A partnership is being sued by Jackson for injuries suffered in an auto accident. The evidence shows that Burns, an employee of the partnership, was negligent in causing the accident. In a court action

   a. Jackson would win against Burns only if Burns was not acting within the scope of employment.
   b. the partners would be jointly liable.
   c. the partnership would be liable if Burns was acting within the scope of employment.
   d. the partnership would win versus Jackson because Burns is not a partner.

_____ 2. Partner D of ABCD Company is retiring from the partnership. As to partnership debts that occurred prior to D's departure, D will not be liable if

   a. creditors were given actual notice of D's departure.
   b. ABCD Company is a nontrading partnership.
   c. new partner, E, agrees to cover D's share of debts.
   d. D receives a novation.

_____ 3. Partner X of the XYZ Partnership contributes vacant land for a store to the partnership as part of his capital contribution. The title to the property was left in X's individual name. X then sells the land to Burt without partnership knowledge or consent. The sale to Burt is binding on the partnership

   a. if Burt was a bona fide purchaser without knowledge of irregularity.
   b. because X had apparent authority to sell the land.
   c. because the land was never titled in the partnership name.
   d. because the other partners should have recorded the partnership title to the land.

4. R, S, and T form a new partnership. R contributes $50,000; S contributes $25,000; and T contributes expertise but no money. The partnership agreement is silent as to the sharing of profits. The partnership makes $30,000 profit in its first year, which it now wishes to pay partners.

    a. Partner T should receive nothing.
    b. Partner R should receive $10,000.
    c. Partner R should receive $20,000.
    d. Partner S should receive $15,000.

5. Partner A of the ABC Partnership assigns his interest in the partnership to Craig to cover a large personal debt.

    a. Craig is a new partner.
    b. Craig will be treated as a new partner.
    c. Craig has a right to share in the partnership management.
    d. Partner A still has a right to share in the partnership management.

6. The order of payment upon the termination of a general partnership is to

    a. pay inside creditors first.
    b. pay outside creditors first.
    c. pay back capital contributions first.
    d. divide profits first.

7. Alex is a promoter for a new corporation to be formed, the Denver Corporation. Which of the following statements is true?

    a. Alex is an agent for the Denver Corporation.
    b. The Denver Corporation will be liable for Alex's contracts made prior to incorporation.
    c. Alex owes fiduciary duties to the new corporation.
    d. Alex is considered a corporate officer.

8. A shareholder

    a. has limited liability.
    b. has implied authority to bind the corporation.
    c. has a right to vote for or against the payment of cash dividends.
    d. has a similar role as partners do in a partnership.

Business Entities

9. Oscar Superstar is an 80 percent shareholder of Bounce Corporation. Because of Superstar's professional ball-playing duties, he is neither a director nor an officer. On his way to the ballpark Superstar sees a building for sale and stops to sign a contract of purchase on behalf of Bounce Corporation for a new store.

   a. Bounce is liable on the contract.
   b. Bounce is not liable but would have been if Superstar had been a director.
   c. Bounce is not liable but would have been if Superstar had been a corporate officer.
   d. Bounce is not liable.

10. Best Corporation has 5,000 shares of stock authorized in its articles of incorporation. Best has issued 3,000 shares and has 2,500 shares now outstanding. Best Corporation possesses

    a. 500 treasury stock shares.
    b. 2,000 treasury stock shares.
    c. 2,500 treasury stock shares.
    d. 3,000 treasury stock shares.

11. The business judgment rule can best be described as

    a. a guarantee to shareholders against corporate losses.
    b. a standard of good faith.
    c. a rule excusing honest errors of judgment by a promoter.
    d. a suggestion of business conduct.

12. Shareholders of Vital Corporation are upset about the failure to receive a cash dividend and the corporate funds pledged by the management to the local United Way campaign. At a shareholders' meeting the shareholders could

    a. declare a cash dividend if sufficient moneys exist.
    b. fire the officers responsible for the United Way pledge.
    c. cancel the United Way pledge.
    d. remove directors if the meeting was specially called for that purpose.

PART B: Matching Sets

Matching Set 1

Match each fact statement (13-17) with the correct business entity(ies) (A-C). Write the letter of your answer in the blank to the left of each statement.

BUSINESS ENTITY/ENTITIES

A. Sole Proprietorship Only
B. Partnership Only
C. Both Sole Proprietorship and Partnership

FACT STATEMENTS

_____ 13. Unlimited potential personal liability exists.

_____ 14. Ownership implies the authority to make final decisions about the business's problems.

_____ 15. The laws of agency apply.

_____ 16. Ownership interest can be freely sold.

_____ 17. Tort liability is joint and several.

Business Entities

Matching Set 2

Match each fact statement (18-22) with the appropriate type of business entity (A-B). Write the letter of your answer in the blank to the left of each statement.

TYPES OF BUSINESS ENTITIES

A. Partnership
B. Corporation

FACT STATEMENTS

_____ **18.** All owners are presumed to have an equal voice in management.

_____ **19.** An owner can generally freely sell his or her ownership interest to a third person.

_____ **20.** An owner is said to have limited liability.

_____ **21.** The entity pays no federal income taxes.

_____ **22.** The owners are said to have fiduciary duties between themselves.

Matching Set 3

Match each fact statement (23-27) with the appropriate corporate persons (A-C). Write the letter of your answer in the blank to the left of each statement.

CORPORATION PERSONS

A. Shareholders
B. Board of Directors
C. Officers

FACT STATEMENTS

_____ 23. These persons decide whether to declare shareholder dividends and when.

_____ 24. These persons would normally have the authority to bind the corporation for the renewal of a lease.

_____ 25. They have the authority to change the articles of incorporation.

_____ 26. They have the authority to appoint and remove officers.

_____ 27. They generally do *not* owe fiduciary duties to the corporation.

Business Entities 275

PART C: Case Problems

DIRECTIONS: For each of the questions relating to the following case problem, select the best answer from the four alternatives. Write the letter of your answer in the blank to the left of the number.

Case 1

John Austin is contemplating opening an athletic store, Heflin Aerobics Sports, focusing primarily upon running, swimming, and biking. Austin already owns the property that will be used for the store. Austin will initially begin business without any other persons joining him as co-owners. From a previous business experience, Austin knows he wants to somehow retain control if and when he does accept co-owners. He presently expects future co-owners to also be managers of new store locations.

_____ 28. The easiest form of business for Austin to choose to begin business would be

        a. sole proprietorship.
        b. general partnership.
        c. limited partnership.
        d. corporation.

_____ 29. The form of business most compatible with Austin's goals and most appropriate for new co-owners would be

        a. sole proprietorship.
        b. partnership.
        c. limited partnership.
        d. corporation.

_____ 30. Assume Austin has formed a corporation. A prospective shareholder, Donna Mitchell, is willing to purchase stock only if she will secure preemptive stock rights. Mitchell's best source to address her concern would be

        a. the materials which Austin offered prospective investors while promoting the corporation.
        b. minutes of the early meetings of the corporate board of directors and shareholders.
        c. the corporate bylaws.
        d. the articles of incorporation.

Chapter 11: Solutions

PART A: Multiple-Choice Questions

Answer	Refer to Chapter Section
1. (c)	[B-6-c] The employee's negligence will cause the partnership to be liable if the employee was acting within the scope of employment.
2. (d)	[B-7-d] A partner who leaves a partnership is potentially liable for his/her share of partnership debts unless a novation occurs (the existing creditors agree to release D from potential personal liability and instead look to another party or parties, such as a new partner and/or the remaining partners).
3. (a)	[B-5-b(3)] Where real property is conveyed by a partner to the partnership, the partnership should transfer title into the name of the partnership. A third party, such as Burt, prevails against the partnership where the third party purchases such land (or building) in good faith believing that Partner X actually owns the property by himself.
4. (b)	[B-5-a(2)] Where a partnership agreement is silent as to the manner of sharing profits and losses, the Uniform Partnership Act calls for an equal sharing. T shares in profits and losses regardless of capital contribution.
5. (d)	[B-5-b(1)(d)] A partner's assigment of partnership interest is not considered a sale of the partner's interest. The assigning partner remains a regular partner. [Even if partner A purported to sell his interest, it would be ineffective because unanimous consent is required to admit a new partner.] Craig only has a right to partner A's share of profits and receives no management power and/or authority.
6. (b)	[B-8-a, b, c, d] The order of payment for a terminating partnership is as follows: a. Pay outside creditors (loans made by nonpartners). b. Pay inside creditors (loans made by partners). c. Pay back capital contributions. d. Divide partnership profits (or losses).

Business Entities

7. (c) [C-2-a] A promoter is someone involved in the creation of a new corporation. A promoter owes both prospective shareholders and the formed corporation fiduciary duties—full disclosure, fair dealing, and full accountability.

8. (a) [C-1-a(1) and C-5] Unlike a partner in a partnership, a shareholder of a corporation is treated as an investor and is liable only to the extent of capital contributions. A shareholder is not an agent of the corporation and has no authority to bind the corporation.

9. (d) [C-1-a(1) and C-5] A corporation is bound on those contracts properly entered into by its agents. A shareholder has no authority to bind the corporation as a shareholder. A director, acting as a director, is not an agent of the corporation.

10. (a) [C-6-i] Treasury shares are shares of stock which a corporation has issued (sold) but subsequently purchased back. Best Corporation has purchased back 500 shares.

11. (b) [C-4-c] The business judgment rule applies to the decisions made by board members. Basically, the rule relieves a director from liability for decisions where the director used reasonable care and honest error of judgment occurred.

12. (d) [C-3 and C-4] Shareholders are the owners of the corporation, but they are not the managers. Shareholders may remove directors of a corporation at a special meeting called for that purpose.

PART B: Matching Sets

Matching Set 1

13. (C) [A-1-c and B-5-a(3)] This is true for both.

14. (A) [A-3-d(1)] The sole proprietor is the principal. A partner acts as an agent when he or she acts on behalf of the partnership.

15. (C) [A-3-d and B-5-a(1)] It is possible for the sole proprietorship to have no agents, but principal-agency law still is applicable.

16. (A) [A-3-e] The fact that the ownership interest can be freely sold does not mean that there will be a buyer for certain.

17. (B) [B-6-c] Partnership tort liability can be joint and several.

278   Business Entities

Matching Set 2

18. (A)   [B-5-a(5)] Unless agreed upon otherwise, the UPA presumes that partners have equal management rights. (It should be noted that partners often do agree otherwise.)

19. (B)   [C-1-b(7)] Stock in a corporation is generally much easier to sell than a partnership interest since the sale of a partner interest will generally require the unanimous vote of all partners.

20. (B)   [C-1-b(2)] One of the greatest attributes of a corporation for shareholders is limited liability.

21. (A)   [B-3-a] Partnerships pay no federal income tax. Income tax liability for the partnership is paid by the individual partners dependent upon their share of profits and losses.

22. (A)   [B-6-a and Chapter 10] Partners owe fiduciary duties to each other and to the partnership business. A fiduciary duty is a responsibility to exercise rights and powers as a partner to benefit each other and the partnership. The laws of agency apply when a partner acts on behalf of the partnership.

Matching Set 3

23. (B)   [C-4-b(3)] The board of directors has the power to declare dividends.

24. (C)   [C-5-b(3)] Corporate officers, as agents, have that apparent authority normal to a business of the kind and magnitude involved.

25. (A)   [C-3-a(2)] Shareholders have the authority to change the articles of incorporation.

26. (B)   [C-4-b(1)] The board has the power to appoint and terminate officers.

27. (A)   [C-3] Shareholders do not normally owe fiduciary duties to the corporation.

PART C: Case Problems

28. (a)   [A-2] A sole proprietorship is the easiest form of business to begin.

29. (d)   [C] A corporation would be best for purposes of control and the ability of co-owners to be actively involved in the day-to-day business operations.

30. (d)   [C-6-j] Preemptive rights must be reserved in the articles of incorporation.

CHAPTER 12

Regulatory Law

OVERVIEW

This chapter focuses on government regulation of business by administrative agencies. The overall role of administrative agencies, antitrust laws, and several federal regulatory agencies is described and presented in detail. The candidate should review the following key points:

- The role and basic operations of an administrative agency.
- The basic scope of antitrust laws (enforced by both the Department of Justice and the Federal Trade Commission).
- The overall objectives of the following federal government commissions or agencies:

  Interstate Commerce Commission (ICC)

  Federal Energy Regulatory Commission (FERC)

  Federal Communications Commission (FCC)

  Environmental Protection Agency (EPA)

  Consumer Product Safety Commission (CPSC)

  Federal Trade Commission (FTC)

  Food and Drug Administration (FDA)

  Securities Exchange Commission (SEC)
- The purposes and functions of state public utility commissions
- The scope of the Freedom of Information Act (FOIA)

Information concerning other regulatory legislation can be found in the following chapters of this review manual:
- Magnuson-Moss Warranty Act (Chapter 4: Sales)
- FTC Holder in Due Course Rule (Chapter 5: Negotiable Instruments)
- Patents, copyrights, and trademarks (Chapter 6: Personal and Intellectual Property)
- Consumer credit protection acts (Chapter 8: Credit, Security, and Bankruptcy)
- Bankruptcy law (Chapter 8: Credit, Security, and Bankruptcy)
- Labor standards, labor relations, and employment discrimination laws (Chapter 13: Employment Law)

DEFINITION OF TERMS

ADMINISTRATIVE LAW JUDGE. An official who hears cases within an administrative agency.

BAIT AND SWITCH. The advertising ploy whereby the advertiser lures buyers into the store on the pretense of wishing to sell one item, whereas his/her objective is to have the consumer purchase another, often more costly, product.

CEASE AND DESIST ORDER. An administrative agency's demand that the defendant stop a certain action and not resume it (similar to a court's injunction).

CONSENT DECREE. An agreement whereby the defendant admits no guilt but agrees to pay damages, cease an action, and/or other remedial action.

DIVESTITURE. A court order that a corporation divest (sell) some of its particular operations and/or assets.

EXECUTIVE BRANCH. The President or governor and the administrative agencies thereunder (the bureaucracy).

FEDERAL TRADE COMMISSION (FTC). An administrative agency whose primary responsibility is to keep business competition fair, free, and open.

GENERAL COUNSEL. The person within an administrative agency who oversees agency enforcement prosecution.

INTERSTATE COMMERCE. Sales, purchases, or transit (commerce) among states.

INTRASTATE COMMERCE. Sales, purchases, or transit (commerce) within a state.

ISSUER. A seller of new securities.

PER SE VIOLATION RULE. A rule of antitrust conduct stating that some business arrangements are per se violations of antitrust laws without specific proof of their having hurt competition; the harm is presumed. (Per se means "inherently.")

PRICE DISCRIMINATION. A seller's sale of identical goods at different prices to different buyers without legal justification. (Robinson-Patman Act)

PRICE FIXING. The agreement by one party with one or more others as to the setting of a price of a good or type of good. (Sherman Act)

PROSPECTUS. A summarized version of the registration statement provided investors before purchase of securities.

Regulatory Law

REGISTRATION STATEMENT. A statement filed by the issuer with the Securities and Exchange Commission to gain approval of the sale of new securities.

RULE OF REASON. A rule of antitrust conduct stating that only unreasonable restraints of trade shall be considered illegal.

SECURITY. The evidence of ownership in a business enterprise such as a stock certificate.

16b INSIDER. Officer, director, or shareholder of 10 percent ownership shares.

10b-5 INSIDER. Anyone using proprietary (inside, nonpublic) information to make an investment decision.

TREBLE DAMAGES. Triple the amount of actual damages given in some lawsuits to strongly discourage certain kinds of wrongful actions. A statute must authorize treble damages; most antitrust statutes do just that.

A. Administrative Agencies

An administrative agency is a subdivision of the government with expertise and jurisdiction to regulate a specialized area of government operation.

Figure 12-1
Relationship of Administrative Agencies
to Legislative and Judicial Branches

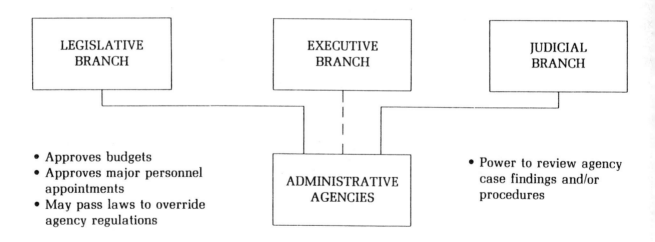

1. *Relationship to Other Branches of Government:* Administrative agencies are often considered the fourth branch of government because of their significant impact on everyday life. In fact, administrative agencies fall under the jurisdiction of the Executive Branch (the President). Figure 12-1 illustrates the branches of government and their interrelationship with administrative agencies.

2. *Administrative Agency Functions:* Administrative agencies have been

established for many specialized areas of government and/or governmental regulation. All existing agencies encompass basic similarities in the types of functions performed. Administrative agencies generally encompass similar executive, legislative, and judicial functions performed by the three branches of government.

EXAMPLE: The administrative agency may issue regulations interpreting statutes, enforce existing statutes and regulations under the agency's jurisdiction, and/or determine liability for failure to comply with statutes/regulations.

3. *Administrative Agency Configuration:*

   a. *Establishment of commission or board:* As a general rule, administrative agencies are headed by a commission or board.

      (1) The commission or board is composed of an odd number of members, usually from five to seven.

      (2) Members are appointed by the President and approved by Congress. The majority of board members are usually of the same party in control of the Presidency.

      (3) Members serve set terms of office, often four years; and members can be removed by the President only for wrongdoing.

   b. *General counsel:* Agencies usually have a general counsel, appointed by the President, charged with deciding which cases should be brought by the agency.

   c. *Regional agency offices:* Administrative agencies often have regional offices at different locations around the country. A regional office administers agency matters for a given geographical area.

      EXAMPLE: Alice claims she has been discriminated against in promotion by her employer because of her sex. Her complaint would be processed and prosecuted by a regional office of the Equal Employment Opportunity Commission (EEOC) in Chicago if she is working in the Chicago area.

   d. *Administrative law judge:* Administrative law judges (ALJs) within each agency hear administrative cases brought by the agency.

      (1) An administrative law judge hears witnesses and receives evidence in a similar manner as a court. The ALJ, however, is not a judge in the judicial branch.

Regulatory Law

(2) An ALJ's decision is reviewable by the full board or commission of the agency.

e. *Court review and/or enforcement:* Decisions of ALJs can be appealed to the full board or commission of an administrative agency, as discussed. An appeal is thereafter possible from the board or commission to a court of appeals. The court will not hear any witnesses or admit new evidence.

B. Antitrust Laws

1. *Applicable Statutes:* Three major acts make up the federal antitrust laws:

    a. *Sherman Act:* Antitrust legislation enacted in 1890 (see Section B-5 of this chapter).

    b. *Clayton Act:* Antitrust legislation enacted in 1914 (see Section B-6 of this chapter).

    c. *Robinson-Patman Act:* Antitrust legislation enacted in 1936, actually an amendment to the Clayton Act (see Section B-7 of this chapter).

2. *Major Objectives of Antitrust Laws:* The major objectives of antitrust legislation include

    a. *A competitive society:* The preservation, protection, and promotion of a competitive society.

    b. *Economic opportunity:* Many smaller, independent businesses are favored over fewer, larger businesses in an industry.

    c. *Protection of the public:* The public is to be protected against monopolistic control of the economies (protected against monopolies).

3. *Types of Offenses:* Antitrust violations are one of two types of offenses:

    a. *Rule of reason violations:* In these types of alleged violations the defendant(s) can attempt to show that the alleged improper conduct is not an unreasonable restraint of trade.

    EXAMPLE: Favoring one buyer over another because of savings resulting from a quantity order would not be price discrimination.

    b. *Per se violations:* In these types of violations, once improper conduct is shown there can be no defense raised and recognized by the defendant.

EXAMPLE: Price fixing between two major competitors would be a per se violation.

4. *Possible Sanctions (Punishments) and/or Remedies:* Possible sanctions and/or remedies for antitrust violations are as follows:

   a. *Civil:* Civil remedies can be sought by the federal government (FTC or Department of Justice), competitors, victims, or state governments. Remedies include

      (1) *Injunction:* A court ordering a person or company not to do something.

      (2) *Treble damages:* Actual damages incurred times three.

      EXAMPLE: If actual damages were $5 million, the winning plaintiff would receive $15 million.

      (3) *Divestiture:* A court order that a corporation divest (sell) some of its particular operations and/or assets.

      EXAMPLE: Ford Motor Company was required to divest itself of Autolite, a manufacturer of automobile lights.

   b. *Criminal:* Criminal prosecution can only be brought by the federal government (Department of Justice) and only for alleged violations of the Sherman or Robinson-Patman Acts. Possible sanctions include

      (1) Treble damages.

      (2) Fine(s).

      (3) Prison sentence(s).

5. *Violations Under the Sherman Act:* Violations under the Sherman Act can involve the sale of either goods or services. Violations include

   a. *Price fixing (per se violation):* Price fixing occurs when two or more competitors agree on the price at which to sell goods or services.

      EXAMPLE: It would be price fixing for two competing airlines to agree to a price for the Dallas-to-Chicago air route. (It is not a violation for one to match the other without an agreement.)

Regulatory Law 285

      b. *Horizontal territorial allocation (per se offense):* This would take place when two or more competitors agree to divide sales territories.

      EXAMPLE: It would be a per se violation for one soft drink company to agree to only sell east and another to only sell west of the Mississippi River.

      c. *Vertical territorial allocation (rule of reason offense):* An agreement among companies to provide goods or services needed for the operation of a particular business can be a violation if the business owner attempts to create a monopoly or monopolize any market. Franchises are not considered a violation but are seen as reasonable even though this form of business organization involves all functions, goods, or services needed for the operation of the business. A franchise is purchased from a parent organization which has already established policies and procedures. In other words, controls are already in place for the franchisee to follow.

      EXAMPLE: It is not a violation for McDonald's to create different sales territories for McDonald's Restaurants in St. Louis. It would be a per se violation if McDonald's divided St. Louis with Burger King (an example of a horizontal territorial allocation).

      d. *Monopoly (rule of reason offense):* An illegal monopoly is one that has the *power* and the *intent* to control prices and/or exclude competition.

      EXAMPLE: Regional telephone companies were divested from AT&T because of the telephone company's monopoly power in the telephone market.

6. *Clayton Act Violations* (not applicable to sales of services): The Clayton Act has some overlap with the Sherman Act. Common violations include

      a. *Tying contracts (rule of reason offense):* A tying contract occurs where seller uses control of one market item to require buyers of that item to buy another item which the seller does not control.

      EXAMPLE: Years ago IBM was found to have improperly tied the lease of IBM punch card machines to the usage of IBM punchcards. But for this tying arrangement the lessee would have been able to easily acquire proper punch cards from a number of sources.

      b. *Reciprocal dealing contracts (per se offense):* It is a violation for a stronger contracting party to require a weaker party to sell to it or buy from it as a condition of the stronger party buying or selling.

EXAMPLE: It would be a violation for General Motors to require a supplier of steering wheels to buy only GM vehicles as a condition of doing business with GM. (As a practical matter, the supplier would likely buy GM vehicles if GM were a significant customer.)

    c. *Improper mergers (rule of reason offense):* A merger of two or more companies into one company is illegal where the reasonable probability or effect would be to substantially lessen competition or tend to create a monopoly.

EXAMPLE: Mobil Oil was not permitted to merge with Marathon, another oil company (which was subsequently acquired by U.S. Steel).

7. *Robinson-Patman Act (price discrimination/rule of reason defense):* The Robinson-Patman Act applies only to price discrimination—charging a buyer a different price for the same merchandise of identical grade or quality than the price charged another buyer for the same goods.

EXAMPLE: ABC Company sells the same ladder for $20 to Joe's Hardware, a little hardware store, and $18 to K-Mart, a large retail corporation. This would be an offense unless covered by a recognized defense (most probably a permissible discount because of proven savings by volume of sales).

    a. *Overview of the act:* The primary features of this legislation include the following elements:

        (1) Permits criminal prosecution.

        (2) Is not applicable to the sale of services.

        (3) Does not apply to sales by retailers to consumers.

    b. *Violation (rule of reason offense):* It is a violation to knowingly give or receive a price discrimination.

    c. *Defenses:* Appropriate defenses include the following:

        (1) *Meeting the price of competitor.*

            EXAMPLE: American Airlines matches a fare rate charged by Delta between Dallas and Chicago.

        (2) *Functional or quantity discount.*

Regulatory Law

EXAMPLE: Ladders to be sold in K-Mart stores are delivered to central K-Mart location. From that location K-Mart trucks distribute the ladders to retail stores.

(3) *Change in market conditions.*

EXAMPLE: Santa Claus outfits are more valuable before Christmas than afterwards.

(4) *Change in marketability of item involved.*

EXAMPLE: Fruit about to rot is worth less than fresh ripe fruit.

C. **Government Regulatory Agencies**

Within the executive branch of government exist a number of government regulatory agencies established for specific purposes through legislative acts. Some of these regulatory agencies are supervised directly by the President of the United States; others report directly to cabinet departments of the executive branch. Those regulatory agencies highlighted in this section represent some of the more influential agencies in power at this time.

1. *Interstate Commerce Commission (ICC):* The Interstate Commerce Commission (ICC) was established in 1887 and is one of the oldest of the federal administrative bodies. The ICC is presently subject to much deregulation by Congress. The requirement for ICC jurisdiction is that the carrier be engaged in interstate commerce. This is met by crossing state lines. ICC powers include investigation of interstate commerce and the establishment of rules and regulations governing interstate commerce.

   a. *Interstate commerce:* ICC investigations relate to interstate carriers and freight forwarders.

   EXAMPLE: The ICC will investigate allegations of prejudicial rate-fixing between transit users.

   b. *Rules and regulations:* Establishment of rules and regulations concerning interstate shipments, keeping of accounts, and responsibilities to users are primary powers of the ICC.

   EXAMPLE: Railroads engaged in interstate commerce are required to maintain accounting books in a prescribed, uniform manner.

   EXAMPLE OF NEW ICC REFORM: Trucking companies have

recently been exempted from such accounting rules.

    c. *Other responsibilities:* The ICC is responsible for the establishment and review of

        (1) *Certificates of public convenience:* The ICC award of a right to do business over a given route.

        (2) *Rates, fares, and charges* to be legally allowed.

        (3) *The number of carriers* to be permitted per given route.

        (4) *Approval before a merger* may occur between two or more interstate railroads or between two or more interstate motor carriers.

        (5) *Approval of any sale or purchase* of an ICC-granted route from one business to another.

2. *Federal Energy Regulatory Commission (FERC):* The Federal Energy Regulatory Commission is an independent regulatory agency, established within the Department of Energy.

    a. *Responsibilities:* The FERC is empowered with many of the responsibilities of the former Federal Power Commission. Primarily, its charge includes the following priorities:

        (1) *Monitoring electrical rates:* The FERC establishes and monitors rates charged for electricity.

        (2) *Monitoring rates for pipeline transportation:* The FERC establishes and monitors rates charged for the transportation of oil and gas by pipeline.

    b. *General organization:* The FERC was established within the Department of Energy as part of the Department of Energy Organization Act enacted by Congress on August 2, 1977. The head of the FERC is responsible only to the President of the United States. The Economic Regulatory Administration (ERA), a division within the Department of Energy, is responsible for administering many of the directives handed down by the FERC. The ERA also has the power to order that electrical utility companies convert their operations to use coal instead of scarcer oil and natural gas resources.

    EXAMPLE: In 1978, one of the ERA's first activities was to hold hearings to set rates for oil transported through the Trans-Alaska Pipeline.

Regulatory Law

3. *Federal Communications Commission (FCC):* In essence, the Federal Communications Commission regulates all interstate communication except the awarding of cable television franchises which local government units generally award. The FCC has the preemption power to decide franchise cable license awards but has chosen not to exercise this power.

   a. *Areas of communication under FCC jurisdiction:* Specific communication areas directly under the jurisdiction of the FCC include

   (1) Telephone (interstate operations)

   (2) Radio (licensing and operations)

   (3) Television (licensing and operations)

   (4) Cable television (operations only)

   (5) Communication satellites

   (6) Telex

   (7) Mobile telephone service

   b. *Functions of the FCC:* The FCC's primary functions at the present time are quite broad and include the following specific operations:

   (1) Establishing rules and regulations governing those matters over which the FCC has jurisdiction.

   EXAMPLE: The prime-time-access rule, also known as the family viewing hour, reserves one evening hour per day to local television stations to program nonnetwork shows.

   (2) Granting and renewing licenses to operate (awarding of certificates of public necessity).

   EXAMPLE: The FCC grants licenses to television and radio stations.

   (3) Investigating potential violations of FCC regulations and rules.

   EXAMPLE: The FCC investigates charges of outrageous conduct by radio station disc jockeys. Fines or even revocation of licenses may result.

c. *Limitations of FCC powers:*

   (1) *Regulation of radio/television programming:* The FCC regulates radio and television to determine what constitutes the public interest. The FCC may prevent the airing of certain programs or commercials on television (example: cigarette advertisements), require equal time for political candidates, and impose fairness standards. The FCC may not specifically detail what overall scheduling and programming radio and television stations will follow.

   (2) *Effect on network policies:* The FCC seldom becomes concerned with individual stations until it is time for license renewal (every five years for television stations and every seven years for radio stations). Accordingly, the FCC's policies appear to affect network policies more directly than individual stations.

d. *Trends of the FCC:*

   (1) The FCC is in the process of lessening or removing regulations in many areas.

   EXAMPLE: The FCC has greatly relaxed the licensing requirements for pay TV (where a television station transmits a scrambled signal that can only be unscrambled with a decoder machine.

   (2) Radio and television station license renewals are likely to remain under close FCC scrutiny.

   (3) As new communications technology surfaces, it is probable that the FCC jurisdiction will be expanded to apply.

   EXAMPLE: The FCC jurisdiction was broadened to include communication satellites and mobile telephone services as these technologies evolved.

   (4) The FCC favors a maximum diffusion of control of radio and television stations. Local control and ownership will generally prevail over nonlocal control in the granting of station licenses.

e. *FCC jurisdiction:*

   (1) The FCC has primary jurisdiction to resolve disputes concerning interstate communications matters.

Regulatory Law

> *EXAMPLE: An allegation of improper conduct by a radio station would be tried before an administrative law judge for the FCC and not a court.*

    (2) Federal courts may be utilized only on appeal of FCC rulings.

4. *Environmental Protection Agency (EPA):* The Environmental Protection Agency was established in 1970 to consolidate the federal government's efforts in protecting the environment.

   a. *Functions of the EPA:*

      (1) *Regulation of external pollutants:* The EPA regulates industry as to external pollutants.

         (a) Pollutant discharges of factories, such as smokestack pollution at a steel plant.

         (b) Pollutant discharges of consumer goods, such as auto emission standards.

      (2) *Types of external pollutants:* The EPA's regulation of external pollutants by industry includes the following types of pollution:

         (a) Air

         (b) Water

         (c) Pesticides

         (d) Solid waste (land pollution)

         (e) Noise

         (f) Radiation

   b. *Civil or criminal sanctions:* The EPA monitors pollution discharges. If discharges exceed the discharge standards, then the violator is subject to civil or criminal sanctions.

      (1) *Civil sanctions:* Fines, injunctions, and/or seizure.

      (2) *Criminal sanctions:* Fines and/or imprisonment.

   c. *Environmental impact studies:* Federal agencies are required to perform environmental impact studies before federal dollars are spent on programs which will affect the environment.

5. *Consumer Product Safety Commission (CPSC):* Consumer product safety protection legislation is monitored by the Consumer Product Safety Commission (CPSC).

   a. *Consumer Product Safety Act:* The overall purpose of the act is to protect the public from dangerous products and to provide for the evaluation of product safety hazards.

   b. *Major functions of the CPSC:*

      (1) Establishes *consumer* product safety standards.

      (2) Analyzes product injury data (investigation).

      (3) Enforces consumer product safety standards:

          (a) Quality of the product.

          (b) Design of the product.

          (c) Labeling of the product (warnings).

          (d) Performance of the product.

          (e) Manufacturing of the product.

      (4) Establishes industry standards:

          (a) Notice of proposed standards must be given to the public.

          (b) Public hearings are held by the CPSC.

      The CPSC must evaluate the cost of a proposed product safety standard in relation to the expected consumer benefit.

      EXAMPLE: The CPSC wishes to require a reduction of potentially dangerous microwave oven leakages. The CPSC would have to calculate the probable costs to the microwave manufacturing industry and contrast this to the protected consumer benefit. In short, the CPSC would have to conduct a cost-benefit analysis.

   c. *Product injury analysis function--investigation:* The Injury Information Clearinghouse of the CPSC serves three primary purposes:

      (1) *Data collection:* Data on injuries, illness, or death caused by various consumer products is collected.

      (2) *Cooperation from manufacturer:* Manufacturer cooperation

Regulatory Law

is sought in voluntarily correcting, removing, and/or stopping the manufacture of a defective consumer product.

(3) *Public warnings:* Consumer warnings are issued to the public about dangerous products.

d. *Enforcement of Consumer Product Safety Act:*

(1) *Hearings:* Administrative hearings are similar to those described concerning the FTC.

(2) *Remedies:* Possible remedies include requiring the manufacturer to

(a) provide notice and/or warning of a defective consumer product to consumers.

(b) repair or replace a defective product or provide a refund to consumers.

(c) recall a product for repair or replacement.

6. *The Federal Trade Commission (FTC):* The Federal Trade Commission is a federal administrative agency whose primary responsibility is to keep business competition fair, free, and open. In essence, the FTC is a "watchdog" over business conduct and activity.

a. *Areas of commerce:* The areas of commerce regulated by the FTC include

(1) advertising.

(2) antitrust laws (Clayton Act and Robinson-Patman Act).

(3) consumer credit.

(4) product safety.

(5) unfair methods of competition.

b. *General organization:* The FTC is similar in overall organization to government regulatory agencies. As is the case for other administrative agencies, the FTC commissioners are nominated by the President and approved by the Senate. There are five commissioners who serve seven-year terms.

c. *Functions of the FTC:*

(1) *Regulation:* The FTC makes rules (regulations) which implement and/or interpret laws of Congress. Regulations have the force of law.

(2) *Advice to businesses:* The FTC gives advice and provides guidelines to businesses and/or industries.

(3) *Investigation of business practices:* The FTC investigates activities and practices that may be in violation of FTC regulations or statutes.

(4) *Hearings:* The FTC conducts adjudicative hearings to determine whether violations actually exist. Hearings may result from FTC-initiated investigations or from actions commenced by third parties such as consumers or competitors.

d. *The FTC's role in regulation of advertising:*

(1) *Substantiation of product claims:* All product claims must be capable of being substantiated as true and not unfair or deceptive.

EXAMPLES:

A product endorsement by a famous person is illegal if the product is not actually used by that person.

A claim of consumer preference must be through a fair and actual objective determination.

Competitor price comparisons must not be deceptive or misleading. (Comparing a "stripped" car price vs. a competitor's make "fully loaded" would be misleading.)

Advertising special and/or sale prices which, in fact, are not special or sale prices is deceptive.

Advertising a product just to lure customers in to get them to buy a different or more expensive product (bait and switch) is deceptive. (A store advertises a low price on a basic white washing machine, but only has in stock or sells more expensive machines.)

Usage of simulation vs. actual showing of the product, without adequate disclosure, is unfair and deceptive.

(2) *Issuance of industry-wide rules:* The FTC may issue industry-wide rules regulating commercial advertising. (This

Regulatory Law 295

> power has been a very controversial matter before Congress.)
>
> (3) *Issuance of cease and desist orders:* The FTC can issue cease and desist orders preventing and/or forbidding deceptive and/or unfair advertising.
>
> *EXAMPLE: The FTC could order an advertisement discontinued where a professional ball player claims he always eats a certain cereal whereas, in fact, he does not.*
>
> e. *Regulation of antitrust activity:* (See Section B of this chapter for an explanation of antitrust laws.)

7. *Food and Drug Administration (FDA):* The objective of the Federal Food, Drug, and Cosmetic Act is to exclude impure, defective, or misbranded food, drugs, and/or cosmetic products from interstate commerce. The act is enforced by the Food and Drug Administration (FDA). [Generally, states also enact and enforce health standard laws.]

   a. *Enforcement powers of the FDA:*

   (1) The seizure of defective products.

   (2) Securing injunctions against the creation, handling, and/or storage of defective products.

   (3) Bringing civil actions for money damages and/or fines.

   (4) Bringing criminal actions against violators.

   b. *Product evaluation by the FDA:*

   (1) Tests and certifies new drugs.

   (2) Tests products overall to discover impure, defective, or mishandled food, drug, and/or cosmetic products.

   (3) Investigates manufacturing, processing, and handling procedures relating to health standards.

   EXAMPLE: The FDA may inspect food warehouses to insure that foods handled therein are not subject to rodents, cockroaches, or other pests.

8. *Securities and Exchange Commission (SEC):* In order to protect the investing public, the Securities and Exchange Commission (SEC) was established to ensure disclosure of relevant, accurate, and truthful

information by sellers of new securities. In addition, the SEC has the authority to establish rules needed to ensure the integrity of the securities market and protect the investing public from fraud and/or manipulation in the sale or purchase of securities. The three major legislative acts involving the SEC are the Securities Act of 1933 (The Truth in Securities Law), the Securities Exchange Act of 1934, and the Foreign Corrupt Practice Act of 1977.

    a.   *The Securities Act of 1933:* This act, also known as the Truth in Securities Law, regulates the issuance (sale) of new securities to investors.

             (1)   *Securities:* Essentially, a security is an investment. In order for the investment to be called a security, the investor

                  (a)   must not be actively engaged in the management of the business.

                  (b)   must be expecting investment returns (profits) primarily from the efforts of others.

                  EXAMPLE: The buyer of an IBM bond does not expect nor receive the right to be actively involved in the management of IBM.

              Unless an exemption applies, a seller of new securities must receive SEC approval before offering new securities to the public.

              EXAMPLES OF SECURITIES:

              Stock of a corporation.

              Bonds (where some of the seller's assets are put up as security to ensure payment of the debt.)

              Debentures (where no specific seller's assets are put up to secure repayment of the debt).

              Limited partnership interest.

              Real estate investment trust interest (REIT).

              In some cases, a franchise business (where the franchisee's actions are so completely controlled by the franchisor).

             (2)   *Procedure for SEC approval of new security sales:* The procedure for obtaining SEC approval of the sale of new

securities includes the following:

(a) The seller must file a *registration statement* with the SEC. The registration statement provides basic information as to the seller's operations, the proposed use of the moneys to be received, and the manner of distributing the new securities. It must include financial statements, certified by a CPA as to accuracy and truthfulness.

(b) The SEC reviews the registration statement. Only 20 days are allowed to review it unless additional information is needed.

(c) The SEC only evaluates the registration statement to determine if sufficient information exists so as to enable the prospective investor to decide to buy or not to buy.

EXAMPLE: New Fangle Corporation wishes to sell stock to raise money to produce silver widgets. If the SEC approves the registration statement, it does not mean that the SEC believes it to be a good idea or a good investment. SEC approval simply means enough information is available for the investor to make a purchase decision.

During the SEC review process, the seller may not make any offers nor accept any sales.

(d) If the SEC approves the sale offering, the seller sells to the public through usage of a prospectus. A prospectus provides basic information to prospective purchasers. In essence, a prospectus is a summarized registration statement and constitutes the official offering of a security for sale to the public. Announcement of offerings generally appear in "tombstone ads."

EXAMPLE: Look at the Wall Street Journal, *near the market reports, for examples of "tombstone ads."*

(e) The potential sellers of new securities who are required to file with the SEC include

- *An issuer:* Normally, the entity (business) selling the security.

- *An underwriter:* The distributor of an issuer's securities.

- *A broker:* An individual who acts in the role of an underwriter.

(3) *Exempted securities:* The seller of exempted securities need not file with the SEC regardless of the amount of money involved. Some types of exempted securities include

   (a) securities being sold by any governmental body or agency.

   (b) commercial paper (checks, notes) which is payable within nine months.

   (c) securities of charitable nonprofit organizations, for example, private schools, churches, Girl Scouts.

   (d) small public offerings (SEC Regulation A):

   - The offering must not be greater than $1.5 million issuance.

   - An offering circular must be provided prospective purchasers (similar in nature to a prospectus but in more condensed fashion).

   - There may be any number of offerees or purchasers.

   (e) Regulation D, Rule 242:

   - There are $5 million of issuances per 12-month period.

   - The offering is limited to 35 purchasers.

   - Less detailed information than the prospectus or offering circular must be provided prospective buyers.

   (f) Exchanges between the issuer and its existing security holders:

   - It is presumed that existing security holders are already knowledgeable.

   - The rule covers stock splits, reorganizations.

   (g) Intrastate offerings (seldom utilized):

   - Securities offered and sold exclusively to residents of issuer's state of incorporation.

- Good faith on behalf of issuer is no defense where there is an out-of-state offeree or purchaser.

(4) *Potential liability under the 1933 Act:* Antifraud provisions apply to any seller(s) of securities using telephone or mail (interstate communications) to defraud prospective or actual purchasers.

   (a) Civil or criminal violations are possible.

   (b) Who may sue?

   - Any party who can show actual knowledge of a false statement or a misleading omission in the registration statement and/or prospectus.

   - It is sufficient that the plaintiff simply purchased the security. There is no need to prove direct reliance.

   (c) Who may be sued?

   - The issuer.

   - Any person who signed the registration statement.

   - All directors named in the registration statement.

   - Any expert providing attributed statements in the registration statement. Such experts are likely to be CPAs, attorneys, engineers, or other professionals.

   (d) Burden of proof is on the defendant(s) after plaintiff shows actual knowledge of false statement or misleading omission and damages.

   (e) Due diligence is the major available defense:

   - A reasonable investigation was undertaken before signing the registration statement.

   - In good faith, the registration statement was believed to be true.

b. *The Securities Exchange Act of 1934:* This act created the Securities and Exchange Commission (SEC). Primary purposes of the act include the following:

   (1) *Proxies:* The act applies to proxies (granting of authority to another to vote one's shares) and tender offers (offers to purchase the shares of a corporation).

(2) *Required reporting:* Regular reports are required from companies which have total assets in excess of $5 million and 500 or more shareholders.

(3) *Rule 16b:* Rule 16b prohibits short-swing profits of *insiders* (officers, directors, and principal shareholders representing 10 percent or more of the ownership; trader on security exchange).

   (a) Insiders may not sell, then buy; or buy, then sell, within a six-month period.

   EXAMPLE: John, a 16b insider, purchased 50 shares of Ace stock on January 9. John may not sell any Ace stock for six months thereafter, or he will lose his profits.

   (b) Insider gains belong to the corporation.

   (c) Losses averted belong to the corporation if the insider should thereafter repurchase corporate stock.

(4) *Rule 10b-5:* Rule 10b-5 prohibits insider usage of knowledge.

   (a) An insider is defined as anyone with proprietary (inside) knowledge, whether involved with the corporation or not. Insider information is information not generally available to the public in the purchase or sale of securities.

   EXAMPLES:

   Corporation clerical workers typing information

   "Tippees"—people given tips

   Anyone who knows and uses inside information

   (b) An insider must allow inside news to be publicly released and disseminated before acting personally in buying or selling.

   (c) A violation of 10b-5 results in loss of the profits to any party injured by the sale to the insider.

   (d) The plaintiff must prove that the defendant

   - had actual knowledge of the falsity.

Regulatory Law 301

- used reckless disregard of the truth in making a false statement.

- intentionally made a material omission or false statement.

(e) The question posed by 10b-5 is whether a prudent investor would be expected to respond to such information if already inclined to buy or sell the security.

(f) Plaintiff need not prove actual reliance.

EXAMPLE: Tom buys 100 shares of ABC stock from Ken without telling Ken that ABC Corporation will announce a major oil field discovery in three days. If the stock should thereafter go up, the profits would rightfully belong to Ken.

c. *The Foreign Corrupt Practice Act of 1977:* An amendment to the 1934 Act, this law prohibits all United States corporations (their officers, agents, or employees) from bribing foreign governmental or political officials.

(1) The act imposes internal control requirements for corporate financial statements so as to allow the SEC to better detect possible bribing violations.

(2) Criminal fine and/or imprisonment is possible for violators of this law.

D. The Freedom of Information Act (FOIA)

1. *Objectives of the FOIA:*

    a. *Access to public information:* The FOIA permits the public as complete an access as possible to public information held by the federal government.

    b. *Prevention of withholding information:* The FOIA prevents government agencies from unjustifiably withholding information that is of public interest without proper justification.

2. *Procedures for Requesting Government Information:*

    a. *Granting of request:* A written request must be granted, if no exemption applies, regardless of motive, interest, or intent of the requestor.

(1) If a portion of the requested information is exempted, the agency must still send the nonexempted portion.

(2) Courts ultimately determine whether an exemption may be relied upon by the government.

    b. *Response to request:* Information must be supplied the requestor within 10 days or an explanation as to why the information is not supplied.

    c. *Appeal:* The requestor may appeal agency denial of information.

    d. *Costs:* The government may charge the requestor for the costs of search and the cost of copies.

3. *Exemptions:* Exemptions are defenses for the government to justify not making disclosures. The following are examples of allowable exemptions:

    a. *National security:* National security reasons require that no disclosure be made.

    b. *Internal personnel rules:* Requested information applies to purely internal personnel rules of the agency.

    c. *Statute:* An existing statute prevents disclosure.

       EXAMPLE: Section 6103 of the Internal Revenue Act prohibits the Internal Revenue Service from disclosing tax return information of taxpayers to the public.

    d. *Medical or personnel file:* Information sought constitutes the medical or personnel file of an individual.

    e. *Investigative file:* The requested file is a law-enforcement investigative file.

4. *Reverse FOIA Request:* This is the request of a business to the government *not* to release information to a competing business. The purpose of the request is to obtain more information about a competitor's business practices.

    a. *Agency discretion:* The decision to release information is a matter of agency discretion.

    b. *Action preventing disclosure:* The supplier of the information may bring an action against the government agency to prevent such disclosure.

Regulatory Law

EXAMPLE: Burroughs Corporation successfully prevented the government from disclosing Burroughs's input to the government to a Burroughs competitor. Burroughs proved disclosure would expose it to substantial injury to its commercial, financial, and competitive positions.

E. **State Public Utility Commissions**

State public utility commissions have jurisdiction over intrastate rates, routes, and services for gas, electricity, water, common carriers, and telephone communications. The state commissions have no authority as to interstate utility rates, routes, and/or concerns. A state must be careful not to burden interstate commerce unduly with its state laws.

EXAMPLE: Louisiana was not permitted to tax the passage of offshore oil extracted beyond its state coastline authority.

1. *Purposes of State Utility Regulation:*

    a. *Licensing of utility services:* State public utility commissions provide certificates of necessity.

    b. *Utility services:* Commissions prescribe mode and manner of utility service to the public.

    c. *Rates, services, and operations:* Commissions also establish rates, variety of services, and means of operations for utilities as well as later review.

    EXAMPLE: An electrical utility company must secure state approval for any rate increase.

    d. *Issuance of certificates of necessity:* A certificate of necessity is a right to do business and to compete. It may be an exclusive or a nonexclusive right.

        (1) Exclusive franchise right.

        EXAMPLE: Awarding intrastate electrical franchise for a given part of the state to an electrical company.

        (2) Nonexclusive franchise right.

        EXAMPLE: Establishing two independent carrier routes between two in-state cities.

2. *State Delegation of Utility Regulation:*

      a. States may delegate regulatory powers to local government units (cities, counties).

      b. Some regulatory areas are fully delegated to local government units such as the awarding of cable television franchises.

3. *Tariffs:* Tariffs are descriptions of available services, equipment, rates, rules, and regulations between the user and the utility company.

      a. *Tariff approval:* Tariffs must be approved by the appropriate utility commission and publicly filed.

      b. *The effect of tariffs:* Tariffs have the effect of law.

      c. *A tariff rate-change procedure:*

          (1) Request for new tariff rate filed with the appropriate utility commission.

          (2) Public notice of hearing is made.

          (3) Memorandum and evidence of need are submitted by the utility company.

          (4) Commission conducts a public hearing to establish the need for a rate hike. The following factors are generally considered:

              (a) Operating expenses.

              (b) Past earnings or losses.

              (c) Apparent need.

              (d) Potential effect on the user.

          (5) After the finding of fact is concluded by the commission, the tariff request may be denied, partially approved, or fully approved.

Regulatory Law 305

Chapter 12: Review Questions

PART A: Multiple-Choice Questions

DIRECTIONS: Select the best answer from the four alternatives. Write your answer in the blank to the left of the number.

_____ 1. Administrative agencies are

    a. part of the legislative branch.
    b. part of the judicial branch.
    c. part of the executive branch.
    d. in fact a fourth branch of government.

_____ 2. Witnesses will be heard and evidence admitted in an administrative agency matter at which stage?

    a. Before the administrative law judge.
    b. Before the agency board itself.
    c. Before the federal court of appeals.
    d. Witnesses are never heard in an administrative agency matter.

_____ 3. A criminal violation for monopoly activity is possible under the

    a. Sherman Act.
    b. Clayton Act.
    c. Robinson-Patman Act.
    d. FTC Act.

_____ 4. Arrow Corporation and Phoenix, Inc. have been charged with price fixing. Which of the following statements is correct?

    a. Price fixing is a Robinson-Patman Act violation.
    b. Arrow and Phoenix should prevail if the alleged price fixing actually resulted in lower consumer prices.
    c. Price fixing is a per se rule violation.
    d. Price fixing cannot result in a criminal trial.

5. A situation where a seller will only sell you product A if you agree to also buy product B, a product readily available elsewhere, is called

   a. a tying contract.
   b. a vertical territorial allocation.
   c. a horizontal territorial allocation.
   d. price discrimination.

6. Martin, Inc. has been charged with price discrimination to buyers Smith and Pace. Which defense below would *not* be recognized?

   a. Martin is a retailer.
   b. Martin's price to Pace was because the particular product was damaged by water from a flood.
   c. Pace's price reduction was because of a functional discount.
   d. Smith was selling Martin's product at a discount causing Pace to lose sales.

7. Which antitrust act applies to both the sale of goods and the sale of services?

   a. Clayton Act
   b. Robinson-Patman Act
   c. Securities Act of 1933
   d. Sherman Act

8. The FTC has authority to act in each of these areas except

   a. product safety.
   b. consumer credit.
   c. food impurities.
   d. antitrust actions.

9. The following remedies for unsafe products may be sought by the Consumer Product Safety Commission except for

   a. warnings on products and/or packages.
   b. treble damages.
   c. requiring manufacturers to replace products.
   d. requiring manufacturers to provide a refund.

10. Which of the following agencies deals with the regulation of the sale and exchange of stock?

    a. Federal Trade Commission
    b. Interstate Commerce Commission
    c. Securities and Exchange Commission
    d. Federal Communications Commission

Regulatory Law

11. The Securities Act of 1933 accomplished which of the following?

    a. Creation of the Securities and Exchange Commission.
    b. Regulation of issuance of new securities.
    c. Established rules as to insiders.
    d. Established the Foreign Corrupt Practice Act.

12. The following are all securities under the Securities Act of 1933 except

    a. corporate stock.
    b. bonds.
    c. limited partnership interest.
    d. checks.

13. A prospectus approved by the SEC assures a prospective investor that

    a. the sale will be free of any fraud.
    b. the offered security is at least not a bad investment risk.
    c. the SEC has reviewed the prospectus for adequacy of investor information.
    d. the SEC will stand behind any losses suffered.

14. The FCC has jurisdiction to do all of the following things except

    a. require the showing of specific programs.
    b. require one hour of prime-time television access for local television stations.
    c. require an opportunity for opponents of a major issue to rebut on a television show.
    d. require equal time for all qualified candidates for a public office.

15. The granting of a specific route by the ICC is called a

    a. certificate of public necessity.
    b. certificate of public convenience.
    c. forwarder's certificate.
    d. controlled airspace.

16. A state public utility commission would potentially have jurisdiction over

    a. licensing of television stations in the state.
    b. the interstate telephone rates for its residents.
    c. the rates for electricity sold to its residents.
    d. federal clean water laws.

PART B: Matching Sets

Matching Set 1

Match each antitrust violation (17-20) with the correct applicable antitrust rule of review (A-B). Write the letter of your answer in the blank to the left of each number.

ANTITRUST RULES

A. Rule of Reason
B. Per Se Rule

ANTITRUST VIOLATIONS

_____ 17. Price discrimination

_____ 18. Price fixing

_____ 19. Horizontal territorial allocation

_____ 20. Monopoly

Regulatory Law

Matching Set 2

Match each fact statement (21-24) with the applicable administrative agency with jurisdiction over the matter (A-B). Write the letter of your answer in the blank to the left of the statement.

ADMINISTRATIVE AGENCIES

A. Federal Trade Commission
B. Consumer Product Safety Commission

FACT STATEMENTS

_____ 21. A celebrity claims in an advertisement to regularly use a particular home riding lawn mower but he does not.

_____ 22. A number of individuals have been injured playing with yard darts.

_____ 23. The label on a bathroom cleaner fails to indicate its toxicity.

_____ 24. A car engine additive product is advertised as being the equivalent of lead gasoline; it is not.

PART C: Case Problems

DIRECTIONS: For the questions relating to the following case problem, select the best answer from the four alternatives. Write the letter of your answer in the blank to the left of the number.

Case 1

Star Corporation is an independent oil refining company. Star needed money for expansion of refining capacity so it filed a registration statement and a prospectus with the SEC to sell $10 million worth of stock. Star failed to disclose an ongoing major investigation by the EPA concerning air pollutant emissions at their major refinery. Oswald Oil, another independent oil refining company, is seeking to acquire Star Corporation.

_____ 25. Concerning the registration statement and prospectus

    a. the registration statement provides information as to the seller's operations.
    b. the SEC reviews the registration statement to approve it as to its soundness of investment.
    c. the SEC may accept offers but not sales during the SEC review process.
    d. the registration statement is what is actually given investors.

_____ 26. The EPA could seek all of the remedies listed below against Star Corporation except

    a. criminal fines.
    b. an injunction to stop the emissions.
    c. imprisonment of responsible corporate officers.
    d. treble damages.

_____ 27. Oswald Oil's planned acquisition of Star Corporation might be challenged on grounds

    a. that the effect could be to substantially lessen competition.
    b. that Oswald would have a monopoly.
    c. of price discrimination.
    d. of price fixing.

Chapter 12: Solutions

PART A: Multiple-Choice Questions

	Answer	Refer to Chapter Section
1.	(c)	[A-1] Administrative agencies are often considered the fourth branch of government but actually are part of the executive branch.
2.	(a)	[A-3-d] Administrative law judges act as the equivalent to trial judges in hearing administrative cases.
3.	(a)	[B-4-b and 5-d] Monopoly is a violation under the Sherman Act. Criminal prosecution is possible under the Sherman Act.
4.	(c)	[B-5-a] Price fixing is a per se violation under the Sherman Act. It does not matter whether the agreed upon price is a fair price.
5.	(a)	[B-6-a] The described actions would result in a tying contract.
6.	(d)	[B-7-c] The fact that Smith is selling the product at a discount is not an acceptable reason for Martin to sell the same product at a lesser price to Pace.
7.	(d)	[B-5] The Sherman Act is the only antitrust act which applies to both the sale of goods and the sale of services. (The Clayton and Robinson-Patman Acts apply only to the sale of goods.)
8.	(c)	[C-6-a] The FTC has broad authority but not over food impurities.
9.	(b)	[C-5-d] Treble damages are not available for violations of the Consumer Product Safety Act.
10.	(c)	[C-8] The SEC is the federal administrative agency responsible for overseeing the issuance of new securities.
11.	(b)	[C-8-a] The regulation of the issuance of new securities came into the law with the Securities Act of 1933.

12. (d) [C-8-a(1)] Checks are not an example of securities; they are not considered an investment.

13. (c) [C-8-a(2)(d)] The SEC reviews the registration statement and prospectus to determine the adequacy of investor information so that an investor can reasonably decide whether to invest.

14. (a) [C-3-c(1)] The FCC cannot require the showing of specific programs.

15. (b) [C-1-c(1)] The ICC regularly issues certificates of public convenience, the right to do business over a given route.

16. (c) [E] State utility commissions are primarily involved with setting rates and awarding service areas for in-state service of customers.

Regulatory Law 313

PART B: Matching Sets

Matching Set 1

17. (A) [B-7-c] There are some reasons which can be raised in defense of the price discrimination allegation. Examples include a changing market, the seller is a retailer, the favored buyer has received a functional discount.

18. (B) [B-5-a] Price fixing is a per se rule. If price fixing is proved, the violation is proved and no defense or excuse is permitted.

19. (B) [B-5-b] Horizontal territorial allocation offense is a per se violation.

20. (A) [B-5-d] Monopoly is a rule of reason offense. There are reasons which can be raised which mitigate against a finding of illegal market concentration. For example, an electric utility which serves an area with the consent of the municipal or state public utility commission.

Matching Set 2

21. (A) [C-6-d(1)] Unfair advertising claims are a matter addressed by the FTC.

22. (B) [C-5-a] The CPSC has already regulated against the sale of yard darts because of consumer injuries.

23. (B) [C-5-b(3)] Labeling of a consumer product, including the posting of appropriate warnings, is a matter of CPSC regulation.

24. (A) [C-6-d(1)] Labeling relating to product performance is regulated by the FTC.

PART C: Case Problems

        25. (a)   [C-8-a(2)(a)] A registration statement provides background information about the issuer including information about the issuer's operations.

        26. (d)   [C-4-b] Treble damages are not available for a breach of environmental laws.

        27. (a)   [B-6-c] A merger between two companies may be challenged on grounds that the effect of the merger could be to substantially lessen competition.

CHAPTER 13

Employment Laws

OVERVIEW

Labor laws are divided into three separate parts: (1) laws regulating employment, (2) laws governing employment discrimination, and (3) laws pertaining to labor-management relations (private sector). Some of these laws are federal; others are state.

Laws regulating employment include such legislation as social security, minimum wage, overtime, unemployment compensation, workers' compensation, and occupational safety and health legislation. The candidate should be able to easily distinguish these different laws and set forth the applicable requirements of each one.

Laws governing employment discrimination deal with all aspects of employment discrimination--race, color, sex, religion, and national origin (included in Title VII) as well as discrimination in regard to age or handicaps. The candidate should be familiar with the various types of discrimination, bona fide occupational qualifications, and the role of the Equal Employment Opportunity Commission in monitoring employment practices.

Labor-management relations law deals with legislation covering the private-sector work force. The candidate should basically understand what the National Labor Relations Act is, the role of the National Labor Relations Board, the role of an arbitrator, how a union may be recognized, and what is meant by unfair labor practices.

This subject matter area is quite broad and detailed. Included here is a basic overview of labor laws as they are most likely to be covered on the CPS Examination.

DEFINITION OF TERMS

AGE DISCRIMINATION IN EMPLOYMENT ACT (ADEA). The law prohibiting employment discrimination on the basis of age for persons over the age of 70 and employers with 19 or more employees.

BONA FIDE OCCUPATIONAL QUALIFICATION (BFOQ). In limited situations, an employer is permitted to discriminate on the basis of sex, religion, or national origin if any of these characteristics are required as occupational qualifications.

EMPLOYEE RETIREMENT INCOME SECURITY ACT (ERISA). A federal pension law; an employer is not required to have a pension plan for employees, but ERISA applies if the employer does have a pension plan for employees.

EQUAL EMPLOYMENT OPPORTUNITY COMMISSION (EEOC). The administrative agency that oversees the enforcement of Title VII and other employment discrimination laws.

EQUAL PAY FOR EQUAL WORK ACT. An amendment to the Fair Labor Standards Act that requires equal pay for women who are performing work substantially equal to that of men; also known as the Equal Pay Act.

FEDERAL INSURANCE CONTRIBUTION ACT (FICA). The federal legislation that created the social security system.

LANDRUM-GRIFFIN ACT. Federal legislation that established rights of individuals with union and union internal affairs.

NATIONAL LABOR RELATIONS ACT (NLRA). The federal act that deals with private employer-union relations.

NATIONAL LABOR RELATIONS BOARD (NLRB). The administrative agency established by the National Labor Relations Act that oversees and monitors union-management relations in the private sector.

OCCUPATIONAL SAFETY AND HEALTH ACT (OSHA). Federal law that provides for the establishment of health and safety standards for the workplace.

RIGHT TO WORK. One of the provisions of the National Labor Relations Act that permits states to decide whether union shops may exist and whether an employee can be forced to join a union as a condition of continued employment.

TAFT-HARTLEY ACT. Federal legislation that established free-speech rights for employees and identified union unfair labor practices.

TITLE VII—CIVIL RIGHTS ACT OF 1964. The law that prohibits employment discrimination on the basis of race, color, religion, sex, or national origin.

UNEMPLOYMENT INSURANCE. Payments made to employees because of involuntary severance from work; to qualify, the employee must have worked a minimum number of weeks and be ready, able, and willing to take equivalent new employment.

UNFAIR LABOR PRACTICES. Management and union practices that are deemed to be unfair and illegal as set forth in the National Labor Relations Act.

WAGNER ACT. The first comprehensive labor act to regulate private employment; this act provides protection for employees to engage in concerted union activity.

Employment Laws 317

WORKERS' COMPENSATION. Laws passed in most states to pay money to employees who are injured on the job, even though the employee failed to follow directions and/or was negligent as long as there was no intentional infliction of injury.

A. Federal Laws Regulating Employment

Federal laws regulating employment include laws regulating minimum wage and overtime pay (Fair Labor Standards Act), unemployment compensation, social security, and occupational safety and health (Occupational Safety and Health Act).

1. *Fair Labor Standards Act:* This act, also known as the Wage and Hour Law, established the requirements for an employer to pay employees a minimum wage and "time and a half" for overtime worked over 40 hours per week. To limit child abuse, the act provides rules limiting the use of children in employment. In addition, the act was amended in 1963 to require equal pay for men and women who are performing equal work (the Equal Pay Act, see Section C-2 of this chapter).

   a. *Employees covered by the act:* Employees involved in interstate commerce or producing goods for interstate commerce are covered by the act. As a practical matter, very few private employers are able to escape application of the act on this basis. Those who might will generally be covered by a similar type of state law. The act applies to both union and nonunion employees.

   b. *Minimum wage:* Each year Congress reviews and sets the minimum wage employers are required to pay to employees. In figuring the minimum wage, an employer may include the reasonable value of room and board (if furnished), tips, commissions, and bonuses. In addition, an employee may be paid according to piece rate (payment for units handled or worked) so long as the probable earnings equate to the minimum wage.

   c. *Overtime pay:* An employee who works over 40 hours in a week's time is due time and a half by the employer. This means that if an employee makes $5 an hour, he/she will be due $7.50 per hour for each hour worked beyond 40 in a week. It is important to note that this law does not require time-and-a-half pay for hours worked in excess of eight hours per day.

   EXAMPLE: Sara works 12 hours on Monday, Tuesday, and Wednesday and four hours on Thursday. Sara would not be entitled to any overtime pay under the act. (Sara's company may pay overtime over eight hours worked, but this is not required by the act.)

d. *Exemptions to minimum wage and overtime payment requirements:* Employees in the following categories are not covered by the minimum wage and overtime pay provisions of the act:

(1) Fishing industry.

(2) Seasonal employees.

(3) Executive, professional, managerial, and supervisory personnel.

(4) Outside salespersons.

(5) Partial exemptions for learners, apprentices, students, and handicapped persons.

e. *Child-labor laws:* In order to reduce the likelihood of abuse of children at work, the act generally prohibits the employment of children under the age of 16. Two exceptions apply:

(1) *Age exceptions:* Children who are age 14 or 15 may do light work such as clerical or sales work so long as limited hours exist that do not conflict with school hours.

(2) *Work exceptions:* Newspaper delivery, child actors, children who work for their parents, and agricultural work are work exceptions according to the act.

f. *Equal Pay for Equal Work Act:* This act is an amendment to the Fair Labor Standards Act and requires equal pay for women who are performing work substantially equal to that performed by men. A detailed explanation of the Equal Pay Act is included in Section C-2 of this chapter.

g. *Enforcement/remedies:*

(1) *Civil actions:* Among the available civil remedies are back pay, fines, and injunction. In addition, the government may seize goods moving in interstate commerce that were made in violation of child labor laws.

(2) *Criminal actions:* Fines and/or imprisonment may occur in exceptional cases.

2. *Unemployment Insurance (Part of the Social Security Act):* Unemployment insurance, as its name implies, is for workers who, without fault, become unemployed. The federal unemployment insurance coverage was implemented to spur the creation of such benefit programs by states

at the state level. All states today have unemployment insurance programs. Employers are permitted to take as a credit a percentage of the state unemployment tax permitted.

    a. *Calculation of amount owed:* An employer's tax is dependent upon unemployment claims made against it. A good claims record will result in lower employer-required payments. In addition, the employer is permitted to offset a percentage of the state payment, as discussed in the preceding paragraph.

    EXAMPLE: Fast-food businesses often have a very high turnover rate, which results in a higher unemployment rate than more stable employment businesses.

    b. *Special exemptions:* Family employees working in the family business and agricultural employees for small farm operations are not covered by the law.

    c. *Requirements to receive unemployment benefits:* An employee who loses his/her job is entitled to compensation only if he/she has worked a minimum number of weeks and is ready, able, and willing to take equivalent new employment. It is not necessary that the terminated employee be in financial need of the benefits.

    EXAMPLE: Scott, a bartender, is laid off by a bar because of slow business. Scott is eligible for unemployment benefits even if he is independently wealthy so long as he has earlier worked a minimum number of weeks.

    d. *Disqualification:* In most states, an employee who was discharged for good cause, quit voluntarily (unless to take a better job), or refuses to accept equivalent work will be ineligible for benefits. In other states, the applicant may be penalized before receiving benefits if termination has been based on one of these reasons.

    EXAMPLE: If Scott, in the above example, refuses to take a bartender position in a similar type of bar in a similar area, then he will lose his unemployment benefits.

3. *Social Security (FICA):* The social security system has undergone great scrutiny and has had many changes made by Congress because of the concern over its financial stability. The following are the basic aspects of the system:

    a. *Benefits covered:* The benefits covered by the social security system include

        (1) Medicare.

(2) Retirement.

(3) Disability.

(4) Death benefits to surviving family members.

    b. *Employees covered:* This area of the law has undergone great change. Formerly, government employees were exempt from social security taxes (except the military), but this has now been changed as to new employees in state or federal government.

        (1) If covered, an employee does not have a choice to opt out of the social security system.

        (2) Self-employed persons are not exempt from coverage.

    c. *Computation of withholding rates:* Congress has the authority to set the rates and earning limits for the collection of the social security payments due. The following contributions are required:

        (1) *Employee:* An employee has his/her FICA contribution deducted at the time of payment by the employer. If the employer should fail to deduct the employee's contribution, then the government will assess the employer for the amount.

        (2) *Employer:* The employer is required to pay an additional amount for each employee.

        (3) *Self-employed individual:* The rate for self-employed individuals is approximately double that of the individual employee rate.

4. *Employee Retirement Income Security Act (ERISA):* ERISA was passed in 1974 in an attempt to better regulate private pension plans. ERISA does not require an employer to establish a pension plan or set any minimum level of benefits if a pension plan is established.

    a. *Purposes of the act:* The primary purposes of ERISA include the following:

        (1) To ensure that an employer's pension plan, if one exists, does not favor management and is sufficiently broad-based in employee coverage.

        (2) To ensure that an employee will have his/her interest *vest* without the passage of an unreasonable amount of time. (*Vest* means that the employee has the legal right to receive those payments that have been contributed into the pension on his/her behalf by the employer.)

Employment Laws

(3) To establish financial control rules relating to pension trust funds.

(4) To provide pension termination insurance via the Pension Benefit Guaranty Corporation (PBGC).

    b. *Pension Benefit Guaranty Corporation (PBGC):* This federal corporation provides protection to pensions in a similar fashion to the Federal Deposit Insurance Corporation's protection of bank savings accounts. If a covered pension plan should have insufficient assets to make the required payments to beneficiaries, then the PBGC would cover the deficient amounts.

5. *Occupational Safety and Health Act:* This act is administered by the Occupational Safety and Health Administration (OSHA) under the Secretary of Labor. Established in 1970, OSHA received much media attention for its workplace rules, which were often contradictory, unclear, and unnecessary. Today OSHA has attempted to reduce its exhaustive set of miscellaneous rules and instead concentrates more on major problem areas.

    a. *Purposes of the act:* There are two major purposes of this legislation:

(1) To ensure safe workplaces for employees.

(2) To establish safety and health standards for the workplace.

    b. *Workplace inspections:*

(1) By law, OSHA investigators must not inform an employer of a pending investigation. The purpose of this rule is to reduce the likelihood that the employer will cover up problems that would otherwise have been detected and ordered remedied.

(2) OSHA investigations may be prompted by employee complaints or by the initiation of OSHA alone. An employee cannot be subjected to retaliation by the employer.

(3) An employer has the right to insist that an OSHA investigator secure a search warrant before being granted access to the plant. As a practical matter, a search warrant is very easily obtained by the investigator.

(4) If OSHA violations are found during the inspection, then the employer is given a *citation* (notice of violation). A citation recites the alleged violations and what OSHA is demanding the employer to do to rectify the situation. An employer may appeal.

c. *Potential penalties:*

(1) *Civil actions:* Fines (where greater than ten violations are found) and temporary injunctions are possible. A *temporary injunction* is issued where such danger exists that could cause great bodily harm or the possibility of death.

(2) *Criminal actions.*

d. *New directions for OSHA:* Because of the tremendous amount of criticism of OSHA operations and rules, OSHA has undergone a major reorganization.

(1) *Fewer inspections:* OSHA now permits small businesses or businesses with few problems in the past to conduct their own investigations. Results of these investigations are sent to OSHA, which always reserves the right to yet make an actual investigation. Inspections in the more dangerous industries have continued.

(2) *Greater focus upon health standards:* OSHA initially stressed safety standards almost exclusively.

B. **State Legislation—Workers' Compensation**

1. *Purpose of Legislation:* The purpose of workers' compensation is to provide coverage to employees who are incapacitated because of accidental injury, disease, or death incurred while on the job.

2. *Employer Requirements:* The state fund method requires that payments be based on claims experience and the number of employees. All states have state fund plans, but employers may be able to self-insure.

3. *Employee Eligibility for Benefits:* An employee becomes eligible for benefits if accidental injury, disease, or death was incurred while on the job.

a. *Liberal interpretation:* Courts liberally construe "while on the job" so as to give employee compensation.

EXAMPLE: *An employee kicked the plant cafeteria vending machine after it took his money without returning the desired soda. The employee recovered workers' compensation for a broken foot which resulted from the kick.*

b. *Recovery of workers' compensation:* The employee recovers even though the injury occurred because he/she negligently failed to follow directions.

Employment Laws

C. Employment Discrimination

Laws governing employment discrimination deal with all aspects of employment discrimination—race, color, sex, religion, and national origin (included in Title VII of the Civil Rights Act of 1964), as well as age or handicaps. Employment discrimination legislation and executive orders have been created to augment the Constitution. As such, they provide the means and/or procedures for effective redress of employment discrimination problems.

Employment discrimination laws generally prohibit discrimination in hiring, compensation, employment terms and conditions, promotion, retention, and discharge. In essence, no discrimination is to be tolerated in any aspect of employment.

1. *Title VII:* Title VII of the Civil Rights Act of 1965 brought fundamental changes to employment. The act created the Equal Employment Opportunity Commission (EEOC) to promulgate and enforce employment discrimination regulations for employers with 15 or more employees.

    a. *Coverage of act:* Title VII prohibits discrimination in any form of employment based upon

       (1) Race.

       (2) Color.

       (3) Religion.

       (4) Sex.

       (5) National origin.

    b. *Scope of coverage:* An employer may not discriminate in hiring, retaining, promoting, or laying off persons.

       (1) In assessing the employer's conduct, a court can consider the disparate (unequal) impact on the workforce of the employer's employment practices.

       (2) A court will look with great scrutiny on any employment requirements that have the effect of eliminating a protected minority group, such as an applicant's arrest record, education (unless relevant to the position), marital status, religion.

       (3) Applicants are not to be summarily refused simply because of preconceived notions. Applicants should be considered individually and tested against relevant work expectations.

EXAMPLE: Utility companies formerly often denied employment opportunities to women on work crews because the work was dangerous and/or involved hard work or lifting.

(4) Employers must attempt to make reasonable accommodations for persons claiming religious discrimination.

EXAMPLE: It is generally considered reasonable to expect an employer to accommodate a full-time employee's day of worship.

c. *Bona fide occupational qualifications (BFOQs):* In very limited situations involving reasonable business necessity, an employer may legally discriminate based on sex, national origin, or religion.

(1) This limited defense is called the bona fide occupational qualification defense.

EXAMPLE: A Catholic church could limit employees to Catholics.

EXAMPLE: A theater could require that Cleopatra be a woman.

EXAMPLE: The owner of a French restaurant could insist upon French natives to be employed as waiters and waitresses; however, he/she could not then reject a black French native.

(2) The BFOQ defense is *not* available for discrimination involving race or color.

d. *Enforcement/procedure for relief from discrimination:* The overall enforcement of Title VII is through the Equal Employment Opportunity Commission (EEOC).

(1) *Filing of complaints:*

(a) Complainants must first file their complaints with a state equivalent of the EEOC, if it exists.

(b) If a complaint is filed with a state or local agency, the EEOC cannot act until that agency has had 60 days to resolve the matter.

(2) *Role of the EEOC:* The EEOC may be involved in any of the following activities designed to assist with a solution:

Employment Laws

        (a) Investigation of the complaint.

        (b) An attempt to reach an administrative solution with the employer.

        (c) Filing of suit against the employer on behalf of the claimant(s).

        (d) Dismissal of the complaint.

    (3) *Private action:* If the complainant fails to achieve the desired relief after the preceding steps are taken, a private lawsuit may be brought against the employer by the employee(s).

  e. *Burden of proof:*

    (1) *Prima facie case of discrimination:* Plaintiff, whether complaining employee(s) or EEOC on behalf of complaining employee(s), must establish a prima facie case of discrimination.

    EXAMPLE: Charles, a black laborer, applied for a job with ACE Corporation. Although qualified, Charles was not hired and the job remained open.

    EXAMPLE: Karen was qualified to receive a promotion with ACE Corporation. Ken was promoted instead, even though he had lesser experience and qualifications.

    (2) *Employer accountability:* The employer has the burden to account for the apparent discrimination.

  f. *Potential remedies:*

    (1) Injunction prohibiting illegal action.

    (2) Damages (back pay).

    (3) Reinstatement if improperly fired or forced out.

    (4) Promotion to position improperly denied.

    (5) Other remedies suitable to redress the employer's wrongdoing.

2. *Equal Pay for Equal Work Act:* This act, a part of the Fair Labor Standards Act, requires equal pay regardless of sex for equal work. The term *equal work* means that two or more employees are doing substantially equal work under similar working conditions.

EXAMPLE: A man is paid 25 cents more per hour than the women on an assembly line because he is required to empty a 50-gallon drum twice a day. A court would probably find that this is not enough difference to justify the greater pay. (Perhaps the drum could be emptied more often, smaller drums could be utilized, or a mechanical device such as a two-wheeled cart could be used.)

    a.   *Permitted pay differences:* A difference in pay between sexes is permissible if due to piecework rates of production (quantity of production), seniority on the job, or merit. There might still be a violation of Title VII, however, because of the discriminatory effects of the seniority system.

    b.   *Remedy for violation:* If an equal pay violation is found, then the wages of the discriminated-against employees will be raised to the wages of the favored sex. (The reverse <u>never</u> occurs: the higher wage earners are never reduced to the wage rates of the discriminated-against workers.)

3.   *Age Discrimination in Employment Act (ADEA):* Even though the Age Discrimination in Employment Act (ADEA) was not a part of Title VII, the Equal Employment Opportunity Commission is the enforcing agency. The ADEA applies to employees over the age of 70 and employers with 19 or more employees. (Note: The original law applied to employees between the ages of 40 and 70 years of age.)

    a.   *Effect:* There is no mandatory retirement or discrimination in regard to hiring, promotion, and retention because of age if at least 40 years old.

    b.   *Exceptions:*

        (1)   Exceptions include certain occupations such as airline pilots, police, and firemen where innocent third parties rely on critical physical skills.

        (2)   A bona fide executive and/or high policy maker of a private company can be forced into early retirement if he/she will be receiving a pension of $27,000 or more per year.

    c.   *Potential damages:*

        (1)   Reinstatement in position.

        (2)   Back pay.

(3) Attorney fees.

4. *Rehabilitation Act of 1973:* This legislation requires employers who participate in government contracts to make reasonable accommodation to employ and promote qualified handicapped individuals. The Equal Employment Opportunity Commission (EEOC) has the power of enforcement for this legislation, even though this act is not a part of Title VII. The act seeks to have employers meet the individual needs of handicapped persons.

   a. *Coverage:*

   (1) Federal government employees are covered under this act.

   (2) Employers with federal government contracts of $2,500 or more per year are also included within this act.

   (3) Extended coverage occurs as a general contractor with a government contract is required to make its subcontractors agree to follow the act.

   b. *Requirements for covered employer:* Employers who participate in government contracts of $2,500 or more per year are required to take affirmative action in employing qualified handicapped individuals.

   (1) *Affirmative action:* Employers must take affirmative action to hire, promote, and retain handicapped employees.

   (2) *Employment:* The legislation applies to all levels of employment.

   (3) *Accessibility to work:* Working conditions and accessibility for handicapped individuals must be remedied as necessary to accommodate the handicapped person. Such remedies must not pose an undue hardship for the employer.

   c. *Qualifications for employment:* For employee coverage, the handicapped individual must be able to show that he/she is otherwise qualified for the job.

   (1) The individual must be able to perform the job or perform with reasonable accommodations.

   (2) Alcoholics and drug abusers are specifically not covered under the act. Persons with symptomatic HIV infection (AIDS) now are covered by regulation.

d. *Damages:* The government may require the following damages as settlement:

(1) *Severance:* The government may sever the contract with the employer.

(2) *Hiring or reinstatement:* The government may require hiring or reinstatement of minority workers.

(3) *Payment of back wages:* The government may require back wages to be paid.

5. *The Americans with Disabilities Act (ADA):* The Civil Rights Act of 1964 will be extended in 1992 to cover the physically and mentally disabled, including AIDS patients, cancer patients, and treated, recovering substance abusers. Individuals with emotional disorders, however, are excluded. Businesses must make reasonable accommodations to workers and job applicants with disabilities unless the required changes present an undue hardship for the business. The act is considered the most comprehensive civil rights legislation in 30 years.

   a. *General areas of the act:* The provisions of the act range from public services and building codes to employment practices concerning physically and mentally disabled persons.

   (1) *Public services:* One of the major provisions of the act mandates that disabled persons not be excluded from participating in any municipal activities. Disabled persons cannot be denied services provided routinely for other citizens. Building codes will need to be modified to include accommodation for disabled persons.

   EXAMPLE: Public transportation must be available and accessible for those citizens with a disability.

   (2) *Employment:* Employers cannot discriminate against an applicant on the basis of the disability if the person can perform the basic responsibilities of the job. Employers must make reasonable accommodation to assist the disabled employee.

   EXAMPLE: Job duties may need to be restructured so that the employee can perform these duties. Such restructuring must not cause the employer an undue hardship, however.

   EXAMPLE: Office equipment may need to be modified for the disabled person.

Employment Laws

b. *Passage of the act:* The legislation was passed in July, 1990, with provisions taking effect July 26, 1991, except for the employment sections. Those sections take effect July 26, 1992, for employers with 25 or more workers.

The President's Committee for Employment of People with Disabilities states that two-thirds of the nation's disabled adults are unemployed, and the majority receive public assistance. Therefore, the ADA is seen as a national response to the specific needs of an important group of citizens.

D. Labor-Management Relations (Private Employers)

Labor-management relations law deals with legislation covering the private-sector work force. The National Labor Relations Act (NLRA) covers labor-management relations of private employers. This act consists of the Wagner Act (1935), the Taft-Hartley Act (1947), and the Landrum-Griffin Act (1959).

1. *The National Labor Relations Act (NLRA):*

    a. *Administration of the act:* The NLRA is enforced by the National Labor Relations Board (NLRB).

    (1) The board is composed of five members.

    (2) A general counsel oversees operation of the NLRB and all investigations.

    (3) Regional offices exist to handle NLRA matters.

    b. *Coverage of the act:* Any employer engaged in private business affecting commerce is potentially covered. A business "affects commerce" if it is involved in interstate selling and/or purchasing.

    c. *Purposes of the NLRA:*

    (1) Protect employees in forming, joining, and being members of a union, or the alternative, their refraining from being so involved.

    (2) Ensure fair union election.

    (3) Enforce collective bargaining obligations.

    (4) Oversee unfair labor practices of management or the union.

2. *The Wagner Act (1935):* The Wagner Act established union election procedures and the requirement that employers must bargain in good faith with the winning union. The National Labor Relations Board (NLRB) was established. The act identified unfair labor practices of employers and the right of employees to assist, form, and join a union.

3. *Taft-Hartley Act (1947):* The Taft-Hartley Act identified union unfair labor practices. The act also created the Federal Mediation and Conciliation Service.

   a. *Free speech:* The act established the right of the employer to engage in free speech so long as "no threat of reprisal or force or promise of benefit" is made.

      EXAMPLE: It is all right for an employer to tell employees that he/she hopes the employees will vote against a union. It is wrong to threaten retaliation.

   b. *Union shop:* The employee also has the right to refrain from union involvement except to the extent of required membership by union shop. A *union shop* is where the collective bargaining agreement requires employees to join the recognized union as a condition of employment.

      EXAMPLE: Most union shop agreements require a new employee to join the union within 30 days of work.

   c. *Right-to-work law:* The act established the right of states to outlaw union shops in their states (known as the right-to-work law).

      EXAMPLE: In a right-to-work state, an employee could choose not to join the UAW, for example, even though it represents the plant employees at a General Motors plant.

      Workers choosing not to belong to the union are still covered by the union collective bargaining agreement and must be represented by the union if proper grievance is filed.

4. *Landrum-Griffin Act (1959):* The Landrum-Griffin Act essentially deals with the internal operation and management of unions and establishes specific union member rights, such as

   a. *Election of union officers:* Union members have the right to vote.

   b. *Conduct of meetings:* Union members have the right to attend and vote.

   c. *Management of union funds.*

Employment Laws

5. *Means and Effect of Union Recognition:*

   a. *Voluntary recognition of union:* Voluntary recognition of a union by the employer may occur where the union represents a majority of employees in the particular bargaining unit.

      (1) The bargaining unit is the particular grouping of employees.

      (2) The bargaining-unit employees must have sufficient common interests.

   b. *Involuntary recognition of union:* Involuntary recognition of a union occurs in situations where

      (1) a union wins a union election.

      (2) an employer engaged in such grievous unfair labor practices that a fair election was and/or is impossible.

      EXAMPLE: *Mass firing of a group of employees because of union favoritism prior to an election.*

   c. *Union recognition:* The effect of union recognition is that the union represents all employees within the bargaining unit.

6. *The Election Process:*

   a. *Order for election:* A union receiving authorization cards from 30 percent or more employees within a proposed bargaining unit will cause the NLRB to order an election.

   b. *Union election:* The NLRB investigates the proposed bargaining unit and, if appropriate, orders and conducts a union election at the employer's plant.

      EXAMPLE: *The NLRB generally holds that a single store within a chain is still an appropriate bargaining unit.*

   c. *Majority vote:* The union must secure the vote of a majority of the employees of the proposed bargaining unit *who vote.*

      EXAMPLE: *Union A wins if it secures 150 votes to 145 no-union votes even though 20 employees abstain from voting.*

   d. *Union campaign:* During the union campaign period, an employer may not

      (1) spy on employees.

(2) take polls of employees.

(3) offer new benefits or change existing working conditions.

(4) fire any employee because of union sympathy.

(5) restrict or forbid solicitation or distribution of information during working hours, if similar activity previously allowed for nonunion purposes such as the United Way.

   e. *Refusal of employer to recognize union:* An employer may refuse to recognize a union voluntarily and require the union to seek an election even though the union can show a majority interest via authorization cards.

   f. *New election ordered:* If either management or the union engages in activities that cause the other party to lose unfairly, then a new election may be ordered.

   EXAMPLE: An employer illegally polls employees regarding their views of the union.

7. *Unfair Labor Practices by Employer:*

   a. *Interference with employee's rights:* The employer may not interfere with the employee's rights to form, join, or belong to a union.

   b. *Domination of union:* The employer may not dominate the union.

   EXAMPLE: An employer may not establish a union for its employees.

   c. *Discrimination:* The employer may not discriminate in the hiring or firing of an employee because of union activity and/or affiliation.

   d. *Refusal to bargain in good faith:* The employer may be unwilling to bargain in good faith.

8. *Unfair Labor Practices by Union:*

   a. *Refusal to bargain in good faith:* Union representatives refuse to bargain in good faith.

   b. *Striking:* Where a no-strike clause exists, the union will exhibit an unfair labor practice by striking.

   c. *Picketing:* Certain types of picketing may be seen as unfair practice.

Employment Laws 333

9. *The Role of the Arbitrator:*

   a. *Settlement of disputes:* It is quite common for collective bargaining agreements to include a clause requiring disputes to be settled by an arbitrator.

   b. *Arbitration clause:* Where an arbitration clause exists and applies, a union may not strike where the matter is resolved by the arbitrator.

   c. *Unfair practices:* It is possible for an arbitrator to decide a matter that is also an unfair labor practice.

   d. *Ruling:* An arbitrator's ruling has the same force of law as does a court decision or NLRB decision.

10. *Potential NLRB Remedies:* The NLRB may utilize any of the following remedies:

    a. *Injunction:* The NLRB may issue an injunction.

    b. *New election:* The NLRB may order a new election.

    c. *Union recognition:* The NLRB may require an employer to recognize a union.

    d. *Good-faith bargaining:* The NLRB may order bargaining in good faith.

    If the offending party refuses to comply, the enforcement will be ordered via the federal courts of appeal.

E. **Emerging Employment Issues**

During the late 1980s and early 1990s a number of new employment issues began to emerge. These issues are being addressed by both statute and court cases.

1. *Decline of the Employment At-Will Doctrine:* At common law an employer had the power to fire any worker not subject to an employment contract for any reason (or no reason). Employees without a contract subject to such removal were known as employees at-will.

   EXAMPLE: John is hired as an assembler at ABC Manufacturing Company. John is not covered by a collective bargaining agreement and not hired for a set period of time. John could be freely terminated at any time under the common law.

EXAMPLE: Referring to the above example, John is covered by a collective bargaining agreement. Now John can probably not be discharged unless just cause reasons exist.

    a. *Limitation of employer powers:*

        (1) Employment discrimination laws have greatly reduced the ability of employers to discharge employees for impermissible discriminatory reasons.

        EXAMPLE: It would be a violation of Title VII for an employer to fire a person because of race or sex.

        (2) Court cases and, in some states, state statutes have begun to limit employer termination rights as to other discharges that are contrary to public policy or employee handbooks.

        EXAMPLE: An employee is given a subpoena for jury duty. The employer tells the employee that he/she will be fired if the employee reports for jury duty. The employee reports to court for jury duty. The employee is subsequently fired. The court may reinstate and/or award damages.

        EXAMPLE: The employee handbook states that an employee is probationary for the first six months of service and then becomes permanent. Permanent *may be interpreted as meaning that the employee cannot be removed without cause.*

    b. *Emphasis on proper employment practices:* The employment at-will doctrine is slowly eroding, primarily by state court decision precedents. The emerging abolition of the doctrine, however, has caused employers to put greater emphasis upon proper employment practices policies.

2. *Employee Privacy Issues:* A number of new employee privacy issues have arisen during the 1980s. These include the following:

    a. *Lie detector tests:* The Employee Polygraph Protection Act of 1988 forbids the usage of polygraph (lie detector) tests in most situations of employment, including hiring.

    b. *Drug testing:*

        (1) Employer drug testing of employees has dramatically increased as a result of a number of reasons including the Drug-Free Workplace Act of 1988, which requires employers with federal government contracts to maintain a drug-free workplace.

Employment Laws

(2) Permissible ways and situations in which to test employees are still not clearly defined.

EXAMPLE: A court is more likely to approve random drug testing for employees of an electrical utility company working at a nuclear plant than accounting personnel at the home office.

c. *Privilege against defamation:* Many terminated employees have begun to win lawsuits against former employers who, after termination, make untrue statements about their employment, integrity, or person. As a result, many employers are limiting their exposure to lawsuits by what they will say about a former employee, good or bad.

d. *Intrusions into personal privacy:* Employers are prohibited from unreasonable intrusions into the personal privacy of employees.

EXAMPLE: A retail chain store manager was found to have violated an employee's right of personal privacy when he severed the employee's personal lock on a store locker while looking for possible stolen store inventory. (Because the employee was allowed to apply her own lock, there was a higher expectation of privacy.)

Employment Laws   337

Chapter 13: Review Questions

PART A: Multiple-Choice Questions

DIRECTIONS: Select the best answer from the four alternatives. Write your answer in the blank to the left of the number.

_____ 1. Skyler Corporation has been charged with sex discrimination. Which defense could be recognized?

   a. Lifting of heavier weights is involved in the designated men's positions.
   b. Men and women are paid the same piecemeal rate.
   c. The employees are represented by a union.
   d. Women are excluded because the work involved is extremely dangerous.

_____ 2. John was injured while working for Acme Manufacturing because he failed to use a machine's safety mechanism. John's claim for workers' compensation will be

   a. denied if John was negligent.
   b. denied if John was grossly negligent.
   c. reduced by the amount of damages attributable to John's own fault.
   d. paid in full.

_____ 3. Under the Fair Labor Standards Act, the following is required:

   a. double time on Sundays or holidays if hours worked for week exceed 40.
   b. minimum wage.
   c. pay for hours worked in excess of eight hours for any day must be time and a half.
   d. children under the age of 16 can only work for their parent(s).

_____ 4. Which of the following statements about Social Security is correct?

   a. A self-employed individual is exempt from social security coverage.
   b. An employer must make contributions for each employee.
   c. Social security coverage is optional.
   d. An employer may decide whether to make contributions for each employee.

5. Calvin was laid off by Atlas Corporation. Calvin might be denied unemployment compensation

   a. if he had not worked enough weeks prior to being laid off.
   b. if he is wealthy and does not need it.
   c. if the employer was forced to lay off Calvin because of the economy.
   d. if he is an hourly employee.

6. ABC Corporation would have to recognize Union A if

   a. Union A had recognition cards from 60 percent of the ABC employees.
   b. in an election 100 workers voted for the union, 95 voted for no union, and 7 abstained from voting.
   c. an employer strongly urged employees to vote against the union.
   d. Union A represented ABC's major competitor.

7. The federal agency that directly oversees private employer-union relationships is

   a. the Equal Employment Opportunity Commission.
   b. the National Labor Relations Board.
   c. the Occupational Safety and Health Act.
   d. the Department of Labor.

8. Union A is trying to organize the employees of Huskie Corporation. In a speech to the Huskie employees, the corporation president may

   a. state the corporation wishes no union.
   b. tell employees that the usual Christmas bonus will be suspended pending the election.
   c. poll the employees as to their preference.
   d. threaten retaliation if the union should win.

9. The first comprehensive labor act was

   a. the Equal Pay Act.
   b. the Landrum-Griffin Act.
   c. the Taft-Hartley Act.
   d. the Wagner Act.

Employment Laws

_____ 10. Which of the following is totally a matter of state law?

   a. Workplace safety rules
   b. Unemployment compensation
   c. Workers' compensation
   d. Child-labor laws

_____ 11. Which of the following is not a recognized BFOQ?

   a. Religion
   b. Sex
   c. National origin
   d. Race

_____ 12. Which statement concerning the employment at-will doctrine is incorrect?

   a. The doctrine is being challenged in many courts today.
   b. The doctrine is not applicable to persons subject to a collective bargaining agreement.
   c. The doctrine prohibits removal of an employee except for cause.
   d. The doctrine has especially been challenged in regard to public policy matters.

PART B: Matching Sets

Matching Set 1

Match each fact statement (13-16) with the appropriate statement as to BFOQs (A-B). Write the letter of your answer in the blank to the left of the number.

STATEMENTS AS TO BFOQs

A. The court would likely find illegal discrimination.
B. The court would likely not find illegal discrimination.

FACT STATEMENTS

_____ 13. Company refuses to consider women applicants because considerable heavy lifting is involved.

_____ 14. Casino rejects woman applicant because management wishes to hire man for men's restroom attendant.

_____ 15. Airline requires pilot to retire or take a nonflying position upon reaching the age of 65.

_____ 16. Full-time work applicant is refused because the applicant would be unable to work Saturday mornings because of religious beliefs and practices.

Employment Laws

Matching Set 2

Match each fact statement (17-20) with the appropriate statements as to discrimination (A-B). Assume the applicable employer has significant contracts with the federal government. Write the letter of your answer in the blank to the left of the number.

STATEMENTS AS TO DISCRIMINATION

A. The court would likely find illegal discrimination.
B. The court would likely not find illegal discrimination.

FACT STATEMENTS

_____ 17. Applicant does not have a high school diploma as required for all maintenance employees.

_____ 18. Applicant has symptomatic HIV infection (AIDS) but is otherwise qualified.

_____ 19. Manager of a shoe store is forced to retire at the age of 70.

_____ 20. Aerobics instructor is forced to take maternity leave from classes at six-month point of pregnancy against her wishes.

PART C: Case Problems

DIRECTIONS: For each of the questions relating to the following case problem, select the best answer from the four alternatives. Write the letter of your answer in the blank to the left of the number.

Case 1
Revel, Inc. employs 20 persons in the production of sport watches. The plant is unionized.

_____ 21. Revel has had some serious employee theft problems that they wish to deter. Revel seeks your counsel. Which of the following ideas would probably be legal?

    a. Begin random testing for drugs.
    b. Use random lie detector tests.
    c. Fire all of the union employees and hire a new workforce.
    d. Search outer garments of workers as they exit the plant.

_____ 22. Revel changed the working schedules of five employees from eight hours a day/five days a week to ten hours a day/four days a week. These workers

    a. may be eligible for workers' compensation.
    b. would be eligible for time-and-a-half pay for hours worked above eight hours each day.
    c. would deserve a pay adjustment under the Equal Pay Act.
    d. would have no claim under the Fair Labor Standards Act.

_____ 23. Revel has a right-to-work work force. One employee, not a member of the union, was discharged for a third violation of drinking on the job. The discharge was consistent with Revel policies and past actions. Which of the following statements is correct?

    a. The employee has no right to union assistance.
    b. If the employee is a minority covered by Title VII, then the employer will probably lose.
    c. The employee will probably be eligible for unemployment compensation.
    d. The discharge would probably not violate the NLRA.

Chapter 13: Solutions

PART A: Multiple-Choice Questions

	Answer	**Refer to Chapter Section**
1.	(b)	[C-2-a] A bona fide piecemeal plan is a legal defense under the Equal Pay Act even if it generally results in higher net pay for men.
2.	(d)	[B-3-b] An employee recovers under *workers' compensation* for all injuries suffered during work except intentional injuries. The employee either recovers the full permissible amount or none.
3.	(b)	[A-1-b and A-1-d] The Fair Labor Standards Act provides for a minimum wage to be paid employees except for some specific exemptions.
4.	(b)	[A-3-c] The amount deducted for FICA for an employee must be supplemented by an additional amount contributed by the employer.
5.	(a)	[A-2-c] To recover unemployment compensation, an employee must show substantial past employment and involuntary severance.
6.	(b)	[D-5-b] An employer must recognize a union when the union gets the majority of votes in a union-choice election.
7.	(b)	[D-1] The National Labor Relations Board is the agency with the responsibility of overseeing private employer-union relationships.
8.	(a)	[D-3-a] Answer (a) is correct so long as no threats or inducement accompany the free speech.
9.	(d)	[D-2] The Wagner Act (1935) created the National Labor Relations Board.
10.	(c)	[B] Workers' compensation is the correct answer. All other choices are matters of both state and federal concern and involvement.
11.	(d)	[C-1-c(2)] Race can never be a *bona fide occupational qualification* (a justification for employment discrimination). The other choices may be BFOQs where warranted by particular facts. In no case, however, is the BFOQ defense permissible solely because of customer preferences.
12.	(c)	[E-1-a] The employment at-will doctrine permitted just the reverse: termination without any cause (or even bad cause).

PART B: Matching Sets

Matching Set 1

13. (A) [C-1-b(3)] An employer must not presume that all women would be unable to do the lifting involved.

14. (B) [C-1-c] Attendants in restrooms being of the same sex would be a reasonable business necessity/BFOQ.

15. (B) [C-3-b(1)] The BFOQ would probably be permitted because medical research indicates aging is characterized by the falling off of critical reaction abilities. An older pilot could pose a potential threat to many innocent passengers.

16. (A) [C-1-b(4)] An employer is expected to make reasonable accommodations for a full-time employee's religious beliefs and practices.

Matching Set 2

17. (A) [C-1-b(2)] It is doubtful that an employer could show the relevancy of a high school degree to the skills required for a maintenance position. (Courts have rejected the idea that the degree shows greater maturity or commitment.)

18. (A) [C-4-c(2)] This is a change in the law which began in 1989.

19. (B) [C-3-b(2)] A shoe store manager would be considered a bona fide executive rather than being in a position requiring critical physical skills.

20. (A) [C-1-b(3)] Employers are not to prejudge an employee's abilities or superimpose their own moral codes concerning a woman's ability to perform. If she can still perform as an instructor, then she ought to be able to work.

PART C: Case Problems

21. (d) [E-3-d] Given the problems of theft in the plant, the search of outer garments would probably not be considered to be an unreasonable intrusion into the personal privacy of the workers.

22. (d) [A-1-c] So long as the employees are not working more than 40 hours a week, they have no right to overtime.

23. (d) [D-7] A discharge of an employee for cause would not result in a violation of the NLRA.

Glossary

ACCEPTANCE. A clear expression by the offeree of agreement to the terms of the offer. (3)[1]

ADMINISTRATIVE LAW JUDGE. An official who hears cases within an administrative agency. (12)

ADVERSE POSSESSION. The taking of real property belonging to another by notorious, adverse, open, hostile, or continuous possession for a period of years, often ten to twenty years. (7)

AFFIDAVIT OF SERVICE. A sworn statement by one who has served a legal notice specifying how and when the service was accomplished. (2)

AFFIRMATION. A ruling by an appellate court upholding the lower court's judgment. (2)

AGE DISCRIMINATION IN EMPLOYMENT ACT (ADEA). The law prohibiting employment discrimination on the basis of age for persons over the age of 70 and employers with 19 or more employees. (13)

AGENCY. A relationship in which one party acts for and on behalf of another party. (10)

AGENT. One who has authority to act for and on behalf of another party (the principal). (10)

ANSWER. A document filed in court by the defendant in response to the complaint. (2)

APPARENT AUTHORITY. Authority that a third party reasonably believes an agent possesses based upon circumstances which the principal has allowed to exist, even though the agent in fact does not have the express or implied authority. (10)

APPELLANT. One who brings an appeal. (2)

APPELLEE. One who defends the lower court's judgment against an appeal (the winning party at the trial). (2)

ARTICLE 9. The article of the Uniform Commercial Code (UCC) dealing with secured transactions. (8)

ARTICLES OF INCORPORATION. The legal framework in which a corporation operates. It is filed with the state at the time of incorporation. (11)

ASSAULT. An act or threat that causes another person to reasonably believe that he/she is in immediate danger of suffering a battery. (2)

ASSIGNEE. One to whom an assignment is made. (3)

ASSIGNMENT. A transfer of a contractual right to one who is not a party to the original contract. (3)

ASSIGNOR. One who makes an assignment. (3)

ATTACHMENT. The process of securing a security interest in collateral against the debtor. Attachment requires the giving of value by the secured party, a legal interest in the collateral by the debtor, and a security agreement unless property is pledged. (8)

AUTHORITY. The power granted to an agent by a principal to enter into contracts. (10)

AUTHORIZED SHARES. The number of shares established in the articles of incorporation. (11)

BAIT AND SWITCH. The advertising ploy whereby the advertiser lures buyers into the store on the pretense of wishing to sell one item, whereas his/her objective is to have the consumer purchase another, often more costly, product. (12)

BANKRUPTCY. A procedure governed by federal law which provides a means of obtaining relief for debtors and for the uniform and fair treatment of creditors. (2, 8)

BANKRUPTCY PETITION. A document filed in the bankruptcy court to commence a bankruptcy proceeding. (2, 8)

BATTERY. An intentional and unjustified contact with another person which is either harmful or offensive. (2)

BATTLE OF FORMS. A typical situation in business wherein agreement has been reached by the parties through the use of printed forms with the terms on buyer's forms and seller's forms not being identical. The UCC

---
[1] The number in parentheses after each entry indicates the chapter number in the text.

rule between merchants states that additional terms in the offeree's acceptance will be binding unless the offer precluded such additions, the terms would materially alter the offer, or the offeror objects to the additional terms within a reasonable amount of time. (4)

BEARER. One who is in possession of a negotiable instrument. (5)

BENCH TRIAL. A trial before a judge without a jury. (2)

BENEFICIARY. The party who is entitled to collect from the insurer in the event of an insured loss. (9)

BILATERAL CONTRACT. A contract in which the parties make a bargained for exchange of promises. (3)

BONA FIDE OCCUPATIONAL QUALIFICATION (BFOQ). In limited situations, an employer is permitted to discriminate on the basis of sex, religion, or national origin if any of these characteristics are required as occupational qualifications. (13)

BREACH OF CONTRACT. A failure by a party to a contract to perform the duties imposed by the terms of the agreement. (3)

BULK TRANSFER. Any transfer not in the ordinary course of business of a major portion of the assets, materials, or inventory of an enterprise. (4)

BYLAWS. Regulations of the corporation that govern internal management and day-to-day operational structure. (11)

CASHIER'S CHECK. A check drawn by a bank on itself. (5)

CEASE AND DESIST ORDER. An administrative agency's demand that the defendant stop a certain action and not resume it (similar to a court's injunction). (12)

CERTIFICATE OF DEPOSIT. An instrument in which a bank acknowledges the receipt of money and its obligation to repay the money on a certain date. (5)

CHATTEL MORTGAGE. The legal document used when the collateral securing a loan is personal property, such as in the purchase of a car financed through a lender. (6)

CIVIL LAW. Law pertaining to private as opposed to public rights. (1)

CLOSING ARGUMENT. An address delivered to the judge or jury by a lawyer representing a party to the suit. It is delivered after all evidence has been presented. (2)

COMMON LAW. A vast body of law, consisting of decided case law, which includes the case law and custom of England prior to the American Revolution to the extent that it has not been expressly superseded or overruled by cases or laws of the United States. Common law includes all published opinions of courts in the United States. (1)

A vast body of recorded cases that have been decided by courts (past decisions). (3)

COMMON STOCK. Stock that represents ownership in a corporation. Each share of stock may earn a dividend only after all corporate obligations, including those to owners of preferred stock, are satisfied. (11)

COMPENSATORY DAMAGES. Damages which consist of the amount of money required to compensate the plaintiff for his/her loss. (2)

COMPLAINT. A document filed in court by the plaintiff in which the plaintiff sets forth an account of the facts and requests a certain remedy. (In some contexts, such a document may be designated as a petition.) (2)

CONFLICT OF INTEREST. A conflict between personal interest and the official responsibilities of a person in a position of trust, such as an agent. (10)

CONSENT DECREE. An agreement whereby the defendant admits no guilt but agrees to pay damages, cease an action, and/or other remedial action. (12)

CONSIDERATION. The bargained-for exchange of something of value; an essential element of an enforceable contract. (3)

CONSTITUTIONAL LAW. Law derived from the United States Constitution and the Bill of Rights. (1)

CONSUMER PURPOSE (under Truth in Lending Act). The borrowing of money for personal, family, or household purposes. (8)

CONTEMPT OF COURT. A willful disobeyance of a court order. (2)

CONTRACT. A legally enforceable agreement. (3)

CONTRACTUAL CAPACITY. The ability to understand the subject matter and consequences of an agreement; only adults may possess this kind of capacity. (3)

CONVERTIBLE STOCK. Stock that can be exchanged for shares of another class (such as preferred to common) at the option of the holder of the stock. (11)

COPYRIGHT. Legal protection available to the author of a literary work. A copyright gives the author the exclusive right to use the work subject to certain legally recognized exceptions. (6)

COUNTERCLAIM. A document filed by a defendant asserting a claim and seeking a remedy from the plaintiff. A defendant who files a counterclaim is known also as a counterplaintiff, and the plaintiff is known also as a counterdefendant. (2)

COVER. Discretionary right of the buyer to secure substitute goods upon the seller's failure to perform. (4)

CRIMINAL LAW. Law which defines offenses against the government (representing all of society) and provides penal sanctions. (1)

Glossary

CROSS EXAMINATION. Questioning of a witness who was called to testify by the opposing party to the suit. (2)

CURE. Seller's right to remedy nonconforming delivery where time yet remains for contract performance or seller reasonably believed buyer would accept nonconforming delivery and buyer did not. (4)

DEFENDANT. One against whom a complaint is filed. (2)

DELEGATION. A transfer of one's contractual duties to another party. (3)

DEPONENT. One who is questioned at a deposition. (2)

DEPOSITION. A discovery device which consists of the taking of sworn testimony outside of court prior to the trial. (2)

DIRECT EXAMINATION. Questioning of a witness who was called to testify by the party doing the questioning. (2)

DISAFFIRMANCE. An expression by a person lacking contractual capacity of an intent not to be bound by the terms of an agreement. (3)

DISCLAIMER. A seller's statement that the sale of goods is without warranty(ies). (4)

DISCLOSED PRINCIPAL. A principal whose identity is known to the third party with whom the principal's agent deals. (10)

DISCOVERY. A process through which parties to a suit gather information from each other. (2)

DISSOLUTION. The change in the relationship of the partners caused by any partner ceasing to be associated with carrying on the business. (11)

DIVESTITURE. A court order that a corporation divest (sell) some of its particular operations and/or assets. (12)

DOMESTIC CORPORATION. A corporation doing business in the state in which it is incorporated. (11)

DRAFT. A negotiable instrument which contains an unconditional order directing another to pay a certain sum of money. (5)

DRAWEE. A party who is ordered by the terms of a draft to pay a certain sum of money. (5)

DRAWER. One who issues a check or other draft. (5)

DURESS. The use of a wrongful threat that causes a person to enter into an agreement which the person would otherwise have rejected. (3)

EASEMENT. The right of a nonowner to use a piece of land in a specific way (affirmative) or to prevent the owner from using his or her own land in a specific way (negative). (7)

EMERGENCY AUTHORITY. A type of implied authority that exists during a sudden, unexpected happening or unforeseen combination of circumstances that requires immediate action. (10)

EMPLOYEE. One who works for another and is subject to the other person's right to control his or her physical conduct. An agent may be, but need not be, an employee. (10)

EMPLOYEE RETIREMENT INCOME SECURITY ACT (ERISA). A federal pension law; an employer is not required to have a pension plan for employees, but ERISA applies if the employer does have a pension plan for employees. (13)

EQUAL CREDIT OPPORTUNITY ACT. Federal act, administered by the Federal Trade Commission, designed to promote equal opportunity in the securing of credit. (8)

EQUAL EMPLOYMENT OPPORTUNITY COMMISSION (EEOC). The administrative agency that oversees the enforcement of Title VII and other employment discrimination laws. (13)

EQUAL PAY FOR EQUAL WORK ACT. An amendment to the Fair Labor Standards Act that requires equal pay for women who are performing work substantially equal to that of men; also known as the Equal Pay Act. (13)

ESTOPPEL. A party to a lawsuit will be precluded (stopped) from raising a defense. (11)

EXECUTIVE BRANCH. The President or governor and the administrative agencies thereunder (the bureaucracy). (12)

EXECUTIVE ORDER. A law issued by the President of the United States. (1)

EXEMPT PROPERTY. Property that may be kept by a debtor when property is taken away from a debtor by a court order such as in judgment debt or bankruptcy. (2)

EXPRESS AUTHORITY. Authority granted by the principal in words, whether they be written or oral. (10)

EXPRESS CONTRACT. A contract in which the agreement is put into words, either written or oral. (3)

FAIR CREDIT BILLING ACT. Federal act, administered by the Federal Trade Commission, which provides consumer protection against incorrect and/or unfair billing practices. (8)

FAIR DEBT PRACTICES ACT. Federal act, administered by the Federal Trade Commission, which regulates the manner in which creditors can attempt to collect consumer debts. (8)

FAIR USE. Legally recognized exceptions to copyright protection that allow those other than the author to use the copyrighted work for certain limited purposes. (6)

FEDERAL INSURANCE CONTRIBUTION ACT (FICA). The federal legislation that created the social security system. (13)

FEDERAL TRADE COMMISSION (FTC). A federal administrative agency whose primary responsibility is to keep business competition fair. (8) An administrative agency whose primary responsibility is to keep business competition fair, free, and open. (12)

FELONY. A crime punishable by one year or more of incarceration. (1)

FIDUCIARY DUTY. A duty of trust, loyalty, and full disclosure owed by one person to another. (11)

FINANCING STATEMENT. A document summarizing a security agreement which is filed in a designated place of public records, generally a courthouse. (8)

FIRM OFFER. A written offer by a merchant stating that the offer will be held open for a period of time, not to exceed three months. (4)

FIXTURES. Personal property so attached to real property as to become a part thereof, for example, paneling in a home; hot water heater. (6, 7)

FORECLOSURE. The act of the mortgagee (lender) in forcing the sale of property secured to a loan as a result of default by the mortgagor (borrower/owner of property). (7)

FOREIGN CORPORATION. A corporation doing business in a state other than the one in which it is incorporated. (11)

FORMAL CONTRACT. One that complies with a specific form required by law for contracts of that particular type. (3)

FRAUD. A misstatement or misrepresentation of a material fact made with knowledge of its falsity. (10)

FREE ON BOARD (FOB). Delivery term which designates the place the seller must deliver the goods at seller's expense, for example, FOB Chicago; the seller pays for shipping and has the risk of loss to the place named as the destination. (4)

GARNISHMENT. A legal means whereby a creditor may obtain a debtor's property which is held by a third party (such as an employer). (2)

GENERAL AGENT. One who is authorized to represent a principal in a number of transactions over a period of time. (10)

GENERAL COUNSEL. The person within an administrative agency who oversees agency enforcement prosecution. (12)

GOOD FAITH. Acting in good faith; defined as being "honesty in fact" and observing reasonable commercial standards. (4)

GOODS. All things which are movable at the time of identification to the contract for sale (in essence, tangible personal property other than money). (4)

GRANTEE. One to whom property is conveyed. (7)

GRANTOR. One who conveys property. (7)

GRATUITOUS AGENT. One who agrees to represent a principal without being compensated for services. (10)

GRATUITOUS ASSIGNMENT. An assignment made without consideration. (3)

HOLDER. One who possesses an instrument which is issued or indorsed to him/her or is payable to the bearer. (5)

HOLDER IN DUE COURSE. A holder who has given value for an instrument and has taken it in good faith without knowledge of any defect. (5)

ILLUSORY PROMISE. A promise that does not impose a legally enforceable obligation upon the promisor. (3)

IMPLIED AUTHORITY. Authority to do those things that are reasonably necessary to the exercise of express authority and to the achievement of the objectives of the agency. (10)

IMPLIED CONTRACT. One in which the parties' agreement is expressed by their conduct rather than by their words. (3)

INDEPENDENT CONTRACTOR. One who is retained to achieve a desired result and who is given substantial freedom in deciding the manner to be used to accomplish the objective. An agent may be, but need not be, an independent contractor. (10)

INDORSEE. One who receives an indorsed instrument. (Note: The word *endorse* is commonly used in business. The word *indorse* is used in the UCC.) (5)

INDORSEMENT WITHOUT RECOURSE. One in which the indorser disclaims liability in the event the maker or drawer fails to pay. (5)

INDORSER. A payee who transfers an instrument by signing it and delivering it to an indorsee. (5)

INFRINGEMENT. Illegal use of patented or copyrighted work. (6)

INJUNCTION. A court order directing a party to do or to refrain from doing a particular act. (2)

INSTRUCTIONS. An explanation by the judge to the jury directing the jury as to the law which must be applied in deciding the case. (2)

INSURABLE INTEREST. A legally recognized interest in the life of another person or in property. To be insurable, the interest must be such that a loss is experienced in the event the insured dies or the insured property is destroyed. (9)

INSURED. One who purchases insurance or one whose

life is insured. (9)

INSURER. The party who provides insurance. (9)

INTERROGATORIES. A discovery device which consists of written questions which must be answered in writing and under oath. (2)

INTERSTATE COMMERCE. Sales, purchases, or transit (commerce) among states. (12)

INTRASTATE COMMERCE. Sales, purchases, or transit (commerce) within a state. (12)

ISSUED STOCK. Authorized stock actually sold by the corporation. (11)

ISSUER. A seller of new securities. (12)

JOINT AND SEVERAL LIABILITY. In partnership law, a party suing the partnership on a tort claim may include any number of partners in the suit; responsibility either as a group or individually. (11)

JOINT LIABILITY. In partnership law, a party suing the partnership on a contract claim must sue all partners individually if any partner(s) is (are) included in the suit; responsibility as a group. (11)

JOINT TENANCY. Co-ownership of property whereby a deceased party's interest goes to the surviving party(ies). (7)

JUDGMENT. The official decision of a court. (2)

JURISDICTION. The power of a particular court to decide a case. (2)

LANDRUM-GRIFFIN ACT. Federal legislation that established rights of individuals with union and union internal affairs. (13)

LIBEL. A written statement which is false and which injures another party's reputation. (2)

LIMITED PARTNER. The partner is treated as an investor only and may not engage in active day-to-day management of the business or lend his/her name to the partnership name. A limited partner is potentially liable on partnership debts only to the extent of capital contribution. (11)

LIQUIDATE. To settle debts by distributing the debtor's assets. Liquidation usually involves selling property to obtain cash for the purpose of paying creditors. (2) To settle debts by distributing the debtor's assets. Liquidation usually involves selling property to obtain cash for the purpose of paying creditors. (8)

LITERARY WORKS. Works such as books, magazines, newspapers, plays, musical compositions, artwork, photographs, motion pictures, recordings, computer programs, data bases, and other verbal or numerical symbols that can be copyrighted by the author. (6)

MAGNUSON-MOSS WARRANTY ACT. An act passed by Congress to provide federal modification of the state UCC warranty rules as applied to consumer goods. (4)

MAKER. One who signs a promissory note. (5)

MERCHANT. A person who deals in the kind of goods being sold or who holds himself out as possessing expertise as to the good(s) involved or who hires an agent who has expertise with regard to the good(s) involved. (4)

MISDEMEANOR. A crime punishable by up to one year of incarceration. (1)

MORTGAGE. The legal document used when collateral securing a loan is real or personal property. (7)

MORTGAGEE. The lender; party to whom the mortgage is given. (7, 8)

MORTGAGOR. The borrower; party putting up property to secure a loan. (7) The party giving a mortgage to secure the borrowing of money, the borrower. (8)

MOTION. A formal request for a court order. (2)

NATIONAL LABOR RELATIONS ACT (NLRA). The federal act that deals with private employer-union relations. (13)

NATIONAL LABOR RELATIONS BOARD (NLRB). The administrative agency established by the National Labor Relations Act that oversees and monitors union-management relations in the private sector. (13)

NEGLIGENCE. The failure to exercise reasonable care in a situation where a law recognizes a duty of care. (2) Liability to the manufacturer and/or seller due to the failure to exercise reasonable care. (4)

NEGLIGENT CONDUCT. Careless behavior that results in injury to another person or organization. (10)

NEGOTIABLE INSTRUMENT. A written document containing a signed, unconditional promise or order to pay a certain sum of money at a specified time or upon demand to the order of a named party or to the bearer. (5)

NEGOTIATION. The transfer of an instrument in such form that the transferee becomes a holder. (5)

NOMINAL DAMAGES. Damages awarded when the plaintiff has established that his/her rights were violated but has failed to prove any loss. Nominal damages typically consist of one dollar. (2)

NOVATION. An agreement by a party to a contract to release the other party from its contractual obligation and to accept another party's promise to perform those duties. (3) The release of a party to a contract in consideration of the assumed liability of another, that is, the substitution of a new contract for an old contract. (7)

OCCUPATIONAL SAFETY AND HEALTH ACT (OSHA). Federal law that provides for the establishment of health and safety standards for the workplace. (13)

OFFER. A communication of an intent to be bound to the terms of a specific proposed contract. The communication invites acceptance on the part of the intended recipient. (3)

OFFEREE. One to whom an offer is made. (3)

OFFEROR. One who makes an offer. (3)

OPEN TERMS. Terms that need not be expressly stated. (4)

OUTSTANDING STOCK. Stock sold by the corporation and not reacquired. (11)

PARTIALLY DISCLOSED PRINCIPAL. A principal whose existence is known but whose identity is unknown to the third party with whom the principal's agent deals. (10)

PARTNERSHIP. An association of two or more persons to carry on a business for profit as co-owners. (11)

PATENT. Legal protection available to the inventor of a machine, process, product, chemical, a new variety of nonpollinating plant life, or other new useful invention. A patent gives the inventor the right to prevent others from using the patented invention in the United States and its territories and possessions. (6)

PATENT AND TRADEMARK OFFICE. Federal agency in U.S. Department of Commerce that administers patent law. (6)

PAYEE. The party to whom a check or draft is made payable. (5)

PER SE VIOLATION RULE. A rule of antitrust conduct stating that some business arrangements are per se violations of antitrust laws without specific proof of their having hurt competition; the harm is presumed. (*Per se* means "inherently.") (12)

PERFECTION. The process by which the insured party gains protection against third parties. (8)

PERSONAL PROPERTY. Everything subject to ownership which is not real property. (6) Property owned other than real property. (7)

PLAINTIFF. One who files a complaint. (2)

POLICY. The written contract of insurance. (9)

POWER OF ATTORNEY. A document that formally authorizes one person to act on behalf of another person as to matters stated in the document. (10)

PRECEDENT. A previously decided case. (1)

PREEMPTIVE RIGHTS. The right of a shareholder to retain his/her percentage of corporate ownership by being able to purchase that percentage of a new stock issue. (11)

PREFERRED STOCK. Stock that represents ownership in a corporation entitling the stockholder to certain advantages not available to owners of common stock. (11)

PREMIUM. The payment to which the insurer is entitled in return for providing insurance. (9)

PRETRIAL CONFERENCE. A meeting held before the trial between a judge and the lawyers who represent the parties to the suit. (2)

PRICE DISCRIMINATION. A seller's sale of identical goods at different prices to different buyers without legal justification. (Robinson-Patman Act) (12)

PRICE FIXING. The agreement by one party with one or more others as to the setting of a price of a good or type of good. (Sherman Act) (12)

PRINCIPAL. One who acts through an agent. (10)

PROCEDURAL LAW. Law which specifies rules governing how rights are to be enforced. (1)

PRODUCTS LIABILITY. The term used to describe the potential liability of any business involved in the manufacture, distribution, and/or sale of a product (good). (4)

PROMISSORY NOTE. A negotiable instrument which contains a promise by the maker to pay a certain sum of money to another party at a specified time or on demand. (5)

PROMOTER. The person(s) who organizes (creates) a new corporation and solicits stock subscriptions. (11)

PROMULGATE. A term describing the act of an administrative agency in creating a regulation. (1)

PROSPECTUS. A summarized version of the registration statement provided investors before purchase of securities. (12)

PROXY. Written authorization by a shareholder to another person granting the power to vote the shareholder's stock. (11)

PUNITIVE DAMAGES. Damages which are designed to punish the defendant for wrongful conduct that was willful or outrageous. (2)

QUASI CONTRACT. A legally enforceable obligation that does not stem from the agreement between the parties, but rather from the court's interest in preventing an injustice. (3)

QUITCLAIM DEED. Grantor (the party conveying the property) transfers entire interest, if any, without any warranty of title. (7)

RATIFICATION. An expression of an intent to be bound by the terms of an agreement that was entered into at a time when the party was lacking in contractual capacity. Ratification can only occur after capacity is attained. (3)

REAFFIRMATION AGREEMENT. An agreement whereby a debtor may agree to pay debts which would otherwise be discharged. (2)

REAL ESTATE MORTGAGE. The giving of a certain type of security interest in land owned or being purchased by the mortgagor. (7)

REAL PROPERTY. Land and permanent attachments thereto such as crops, buildings, and fixtures. (6, 7)

REDEEMABLE STOCK. Stock that can be reacquired at the option of the corporation (generally preferred stock). (11)

REDEMPTION. The mortgagor's statutory right to pay overdue payments and penalties and be restored to predefault status. (7)

REGISTRATION STATEMENT. A statement filed by the issuer with the Securities and Exchange Commission to gain approval of the sale of new securities. (12)

REGULATION. A law promulgated by an administrative agency. (1)

RESTITUTION. A remedy for a breach of contract that involves the return of things received under the contract in an effort to put the parties in the position they were in before the contract. (3)

RESTRICTIVE INDORSEMENT. One which requires the indorsee to accept the instrument subject to certain specified conditions. (5)

REVERSE. A ruling by a court to which an appeal was taken, setting aside the lower court's judgment. (2)

REVOCATION. The withdrawal of an offer by the offeror. (3)

RIGHT TO WORK. One of the provisions of the National Labor Relations Act that permits states to decide whether union shops may exist and whether an employee can be forced to join a union as a condition of continued employment. (13)

RISK OF LOSS. The allocation of loss for damages and/or destruction used to designate which contracting party should bear the financial loss if damage and/or destruction should occur prior to complete performance of the sales contract. (4)

RULE OF REASON. A rule of antitrust conduct stating that only unreasonable restraints of trade shall be considered illegal. (12)

SECOND MORTGAGE. Any mortgage secured after the original (or first) mortgage. (7)

SECURED CREDITOR. One who extended credit to the debtor in return for a legally recognized interest in certain property of the debtor. (2) One who extends credit to another where the debtor's promise to repay is tied to legally recognized property of the debtor. (8)

SECURED TRANSACTIONS. Article 9 of the UCC which deals with security interests in personal property. (8)

SECURITY. The evidence of ownership in a business enterprise such as a stock certificate. (12)

SECURITY AGREEMENT. An agreement whereby the debtor gives to the creditor an interest in personal property to secure a loan. Unless the creditor retains the collateral, the security agreement must be in writing. (8)

SECURITY INTEREST. A legally recognized interest of a creditor in certain property of the debtor. (2, 8) The giving of a legal interest (lien) in one's property to another to secure a loan. (7)

SERVICE BY PUBLICATION. A type of service which is accomplished by publishing a notice in a newspaper of general circulation in the area of the defendant's residence. This type of service is permitted only in certain types of cases when the defendant cannot be located. (2)

SIGHT DRAFT. A draft which is payable when presented for payment by the holder. (5)

SIMPLE CONTRACT. A contract that does not come within the narrow category of formal contracts. (3)

16b INSIDER. Officer, director, or shareholder of 10 percent ownership shares. (12)

SLANDER. An oral statement which is false and which injures another party's reputation. (2)

SPECIAL AGENT. One who is authorized by a principal to perform a single task or to achieve a narrow goal on behalf of the principal. (10)

SPECIAL INDORSEMENT. One which names the party to whom the indorser makes the instrument payable. (5)

STARE DECISIS. The doctrine that precedent should be followed. (1)

STATUTE. A law passed by a legislative body. (3)

STATUTORY LAW. Law enacted by legislative bodies. (1)

STAY. A court order suspending all other court actions from proceeding any further. (2)

STIPULATION. An agreement between the parties that certain facts exist and should be presented as evidence in the case (usually in the form of a written statement). (2)

STRICT LIABILITY. A legal doctrine that requires one engaged in a highly dangerous activity to compensate those injured as a result of the activity even in the absence of any negligence. One who sells a product in a defective, unreasonably dangerous condition is liable for physical harm caused to the consumer or user of the product if the seller is in the business of selling such a product and the product is expected to and does reach the consumer or user without substantial change in the condition in which it is sold. (1) Liability to a manufacturer and/or seller of a product because of its inherently dangerous nature. (4)

SUBPOENA. A court order directing a person to appear at a certain time and place. (2)

SUBPOENA DUCES TECUM. A subpoena which requires the person to whom it is directed to produce certain documents at the required time and place. (2)

SUBSTANTIVE LAW. Law which defines rights and duties. (1)

SUMMONS. A document which notifies the defendant that a complaint has been filed against him/her and that there is a certain time period within which to respond to the complaint. (2)

TAFT-HARTLEY ACT. Federal legislation that established free-speech rights for employees and identified union unfair labor practices. (13)

10b-5 INSIDER. Anyone using proprietary (inside, nonpublic) information to make an investment decision. (12)

TENANCY IN COMMON. Co-ownership of property whereby a deceased party's interest passes according to the will and/or inheritance laws. (7)

THIRD PARTY. One who deals with an agent who is representing a principal. (10)

TIME DRAFT. A draft which is payable in the future. (5)

TITLE VII—CIVIL RIGHTS ACT OF 1964. The law that prohibits employment discrimination on the basis of race, color, religion, sex, or national origin. (13)

TORT. A wrongful act committed against another person or that person's property. A tort is civil in nature rather than criminal. A breach of contract is not a tort. (2)

TORT LAW. The law of civil wrongs including intentional acts, negligence, and strict liability. (1)

TRADE ACCEPTANCE. A type of draft commonly used in connection with the sale of goods in which the seller is both the drawer and the payee and the buyer is the drawee. (5)

TRADING PARTNERSHIP. A partnership engaged in the buying and/or selling of goods. (11)

TREASURY STOCK. Stock sold by the corporation but subsequently reacquired. (11)

TREBLE DAMAGES. Triple the amount of actual damages given in some lawsuits to strongly discourage certain kinds of wrongful actions. A statute must authorize treble damages; most antitrust statutes do just that. (12)

TRESPASS. An act of wrongfully entering another person's property, real or personal. (2)

TRUSTEE. A person appointed by the court in a bankruptcy case who has the duty of managing the bankrupt party's property. (2, 8)

TRUTH IN LENDING ACT (TILA). A federal act, administered by the Federal Trade Commission, designed to provide consumers with information about the costs of borrowing money prior to the actual commitment to borrow. (8)

UNDISCLOSED PRINCIPAL. A principal whose existence is unknown to the third party with whom the principal's agent deals. (10)

UNEMPLOYMENT INSURANCE. Payments made to employees because of involuntary severance from work; to qualify, the employee must have worked a minimum number of weeks and be ready, able, and willing to take equivalent new employment. (13)

UNFAIR LABOR PRACTICES. Management and union practices that are deemed to be unfair and illegal as set forth in the National Labor Relations Act. (13)

UNIFORM COMMERCIAL CODE (UCC). A body of law that governs many commercial transactions; it has been adopted in every state. (Louisiana has adopted major parts of the UCC, but not all of it.) (3)

UNILATERAL CONTRACT. A contract in which the offer is accepted by performance of the requested act. Only one promise is involved. (3)

VERDICT. The decision of a jury. (2)

VOID CONTRACT. An attempt at forming a contract which failed due to the absence of an essential element. (3)

VOIDABLE CONTRACT. A contract that may be set aside at the option of one of the parties. (3)

VOIR DIRE. The process by which impartial jurors are selected from among those gathered for jury duty. (2)

WAGNER ACT. The first comprehensive labor act to regulate private employment; this act provides protection for employees to engage in concerted union activity. (13)

WARRANTY. Any affirmation of fact (expressed or implied) by the seller to the buyer which becomes a part of the sales contract. (4)

WARRANTY DEED. In essence, a warranty by the grantor that the property is transferred free from all unknown defects or claims.

WORKERS' COMPENSATION. Laws passed in most states to pay money to employees who are injured on the job, even though the employee failed to follow directions and/or was negligent as long as there was no intentional infliction of injury. (13)

WRIT OF MANDAMUS. A court order directed to a public official commanding that official to perform a certain act. (2)